Autobiography
Exile's Odyssey

MIRCEA ELIADE
after leaving Romania, 1940

MIRCEA ELIADE

Autobiography

Volume II: 1937–1960
Exile's Odyssey

TRANSLATED FROM THE ROMANIAN BY

Mac Linscott Ricketts

THE UNIVERSITY OF CHICAGO PRESS

Chicago and London

The University of Chicago Press, Chicago 60637
The University of Chicago Press, Ltd., London

97 96 95 94 93 92 91 90 89 88   5 4 3 2 1

Design courtesy of Jim Mennick

Library of Congress Cataloging-in-Publication Data

Eliade, Mircea, 1907–
    1937–1960, exile's odyssey.

    (Autobiography / Mircea Eliade; v. 2)
    Includes index.
    1. Eliade, Mircea, 1907–   . 2. Religion historians
—United States—Biography. I. Title. II. Series:
Eliade, Mircea, 1907–   . Autobiography; v. 2.
BL43.E4A315 vol. 2   291'.092'4 s   88-4743
ISBN 0-226-20411-1   [291'.092'4] [B]

Contents

A group of photographs follows p. 122

Translator's Preface

ON DECEMBER 10, 1984, as he began to compose chapter 23 of his memoirs, Mircea Eliade asked himself: "Will I succeed in writing the *Autobiography* up to the point of last night's celebration?" The celebration in question was the ceremony given in his honor at the seventy-fifth anniversary meeting of the American Academy of Religion held in Chicago, an occasion Eliade describes with modest brevity in the second paragraph of the chapter. He had decided to write the last section of his autobiography, on the "Chicago years" (from late 1956 on), in the form of a "flashback" from that culminating event of the night of December 9, 1984. (He had used this "flashback" style also in writing about his sojourn in India and his last three years in Romania.) But would he be able to complete the task? He was all too aware of the physical debilities that hampered his working: above all, the rheumatoid arthritis in his hands, against which he had been waging an unceasing warfare since 1960 and which made the writing of every sentence an excruciating ordeal. Moreover, he had other essential works in progress: the editing of the massive *Encyclopedia of Religion* and the completion of the final (fourth) volume of his *History of Religious Ideas*. For several years, these two projects had been his chief "scientific" concerns. But the project dearest to his heart, the one to which he longed to give himself wholly (as he told me in more than one conversation in these years), was his *Autobiography*. At one point he did not believe he would need to write more than three or four chapters to cover his time at the University of Chicago; but to judge from the last chapter he finished (chapter 24, which deals with less than two years' activities), he would have been hard put to compress his rich and varied activities of that quarter-century-plus into less than seven or eight chapters.

Fortunately, for many of those Chicago years—up through 1978—as well as for his years in Paris, we have his published journal extracts, even though the major part of this material awaits publication in English.[1] However, comparison of the *Journal* fragments with the *Autobiography* where they overlap (1945–60) reveals that the two are complementary and neither is sufficient in itself to encompass all of Eliade's activities and thoughts. It is, then, a matter of deep regret that he was unable to complete his memoirs up to the targeted conclusion, his night of honor at the American Academy of Religions meeting.[2]

Mircea Eliade died on the morning of April 22, 1986, at the Bernard Mitchell Hospital of the University of Chicago. He had been stricken eight days earlier with a cerebral blood clot at his apartment, as he sat reading a new book by his friend from youth and compatriot, Emil Cioran. His physical condition had been deteriorating for several years, but his mind had lost none of its keenness and vigor.[3] He had suffered a severe blow to his morale, however, on December 18, 1985, when his office in Meadville-Lombard School of Religion caught fire and was gutted.[4] (A note concerning the fire is appended to the last chapter of this volume.) Papers on his desk were destroyed (mainly material for his *History*, files of correspondence, and perhaps some autobiographical pages). The contents of the drawers, including notebooks of his *Journal*, survived relatively untouched. Most of his precious books were damaged by smoke and water, and he was unable to

1. In French: *Fragments d'un Journal* (Paris: Gallimard, vol. I [1945–69], 1973; vol. II [1970–78], 1981; in English: *No Souvenirs: Journal, 1957–1969* (New York: Harper and Row, 1977). The entire *Journal*, written in Romanian in many notebooks, is deposited with the Mircea Eliade Special Collection at the Regenstein Library of the University of Chicago. I have been able to consult the Romanian text of most of the published fragments.

2. But this was by no means Eliade's last great honor. In May of 1985 the University of Chicago established an endowed chair in his name (see below).

3. It was discovered at the hospital that he was suffering also from lung cancer.

4. The fire appears to have started on the desk, perhaps from pipe ashes in the ashtray. It was discovered about two hours after he had left the room for the night.

use them again. He never recovered from the shock of this disaster. Had it not occurred, he probably would have succeeded in writing at least one additional chapter for the *Autobiography*.

In accordance with his wishes, his body was cremated on the day following his death (while David Tracy of the university's Divinity School read prayers). On April 28 a memorial service, attended by more than a thousand people from throughout the country and abroad, was held for him at the Rockefeller Chapel on the university campus. Readings from his works were given by Ioan Culianu (from *Noaptea de Sânziene*—the Romanian original of *The Forbidden Forest*), Saul Bellow (from the *Autobiography*, I), Paul Ricoeur (from *Le Mythe de l'éternel retour*), and Wendy D. O'Flaherty (from *Yoga: Immortality and Freedom*). His former colleague and dear friend, Charles H. Long, delivered a moving eulogy. Somewhat later, his ashes were interred in Oakwood Cemetery, not far from the university.

This second volume of Eliade's *Autobiography* continues the narrative of his life from the point where the first ended—the summer of 1937—but the first two chapters (15 and 16) and a part of the third are written retrospectively from the time of the London Blitz of September 1940. (Indeed, there is considerable moving back and forth in time in these chapters, somewhat as in the first part of *The Forbidden Forest*.) Eliade had already written an account of his last years in Romania (up to his departure for England in April 1940) as early as March 1973.[5] A part of this account, however, seems to have remained in manuscript form only, because in late 1978, when he was making the decision as to what he would include in volume 1 of the *Autobiography*, he wrote in his journal:

The text [of the *Autobiography*] already typed carries the story down to the autumn of 1938. For a long time I planned to conclude the first volume in the spring of 1940 with my departure for London. I believe, however, that I'll have to write another two chapters, telling all I experienced and all that happened to me from April 1940 till September 1945 when I arrived in Paris. Only *then*, in the fall of 1945, does the rupture take place and the new life begin. . . . [6]

5. See *Journal*, March 10, 1973; cf. March 9, 1978 (Romanian text only for latter).
6. Translated directly from the Romanian typescript. Cf. *Fragments*, II, pp. 393–94.

Ultimately, however, he decided to end the first volume with the early summer of 1937, when, at age thirty, he emerged victorious from an attack in which he was accused of writing "pornography" (see chapter 14 in the previous volume). By ending the story here, he was able to avoid having to write two or more additional chapters for which he did not then have the leisure, and also to postpone publishing the account of his last years in Romania which, as this volume reveals, were times of painful hardships and sorrows for him and his fellow countrymen.

For the first time, in this volume of his *Autobiography*, Eliade writes openly and in detail about what has been the most obscure era of his life: 1938–45. He reveals the circumstances that led to his being interned—rather like Ștefan Viziru in *The Forbidden Forest*—in a Romanian concentration camp for refusing to denounce the Legion of the Archangel Michael (the "Iron Guard") with which his colleague Nae Ionescu and other close friends were associated. He relates the strange series of events that resulted in his release, and he discloses the difficulties under which he labored afterward when he was unable to secure any regular employment. We learn for the first time how Eliade came to enter diplomatic service in 1940 as cultural attaché, and what services he rendered in that capacity during the war years. We read the moving account of the devastating personal tragedy he suffered in 1944: the death of his first wife—a tragedy that followed by only a few months the fall of Romania to the Soviets. We can only try to imagine how difficult these chapters were for him to write.

In subsequent chapters Eliade relates the story of his slow and laborious rise from the obscurity and penury of a stateless refugee in Paris following World War II to the status of an internationally known historian of religions. He tells us how he wrote such masterworks as *Patterns in Comparative Religion, Cosmos and History, Shamanism, Yoga,* and *The Forbidden Forest.* Touchingly he narrates the tale of his courtship of his second wife, Christinel, and how, several years later, they discovered America together. Balancing candor with discretion and pathos with humor, Eliade tells his own story with the skill of a gifted writer and the interpretive insight of a true hermeneuticist. One reviewer of the first volume thought he had demolished Eliade's autobiographical effort by calling it a piece of "creative hermeneutics" and "sacred fiction": a work that ascribes meanings to events "even when they aren't there." I believe that Eliade would not have objected to these characterizations, nor would he have considered them to be destructive criticism. It was one of his life's purposes to point to the sacred sense that is camouflaged in the profane; why should he not also try to show us the hidden meaning and the hand of destiny in the events of his own life?

After assuming the chair of the History of Religions Department of the University of Chicago Divinity School in 1957, Eliade and his colleagues Joseph M. Kitagawa and Charles H. Long soon made of the Divinity School a unique and internationally renowned center for the study of the history of religions. (In later years he would have other distinguished colleagues: Frank Reynolds, Jonathan Z. Smith, Wendy D. O'Flaherty, and others). Named Sewell S. Avery Distinguished Service Professor in 1962, Eliade continued teaching in the Divinity School (and the Committee on Social Thought) until 1983, retiring then at age seventy-six after more than a quarter of a century as a faculty member. In honor of his singularly distinguished career at Chicago, the trustees of the university in May 1985 took the unprecedented step of establishing an endowed chair in his name. This was an entirely appropriate action, inasmuch as Mircea Eliade loved the university, preferring to remain there despite numerous lucrative and enticing offers from other prestigious institutions.[7] As he reportedly told Jerald C. Brauer, dean of the Federated Faculty, after having received an especially attractive offer in 1965:

> Is there any reason why I should leave? I came here to establish the discipline of the History of Religions, and we are well on the way. I have my journal, I have my students, I have my colleagues, I have the University, and we have our friends here in Chicago. Why should I leave?[8]

Eliade enjoyed a situation at the Divinity School that was, from his point of view, nearly ideal. He taught, ordinarily, only during two quarters per year, autumn and winter, being required in the spring

7. Among institutions extending professorships to him were Harvard and Princeton (cf. *Journal*, May 1, 1963) and New York State (an Albert Schweitzer professorship); see Jerald C. Brauer, "Mircea Eliade and the Divinity School," in *Criterion* 24, 3 (Autumn 1985):25–26.
8. Brauer, "Mircea Eliade," p. 26.

quarter merely to be available for advising advanced students. In 1962–63 he taught only in the Committee on Social Thought. He did not teach in the fall of 1971 due to a recent illness, nor in the fall of 1976 because of the illness of his sister-in-law in Paris. After 1976, having reached the age of seventy, he conducted only one class per quarter, a seminar, always directed jointly with another member of the faculty. During several teaching quarters he was allowed to be absent from the campus for up to four weeks, and thus he did not always meet his classes as scheduled. Yet he was devoted to his students and readily made himself available to them as needed. During the quarters he held classes (until 1977), he taught a lecture course and a seminar each quarter, always on new topics, as had been his custom at the University of Bucharest.

In the winter and autumn quarters of 1964 he conducted joint seminars with Paul Tillich, the celebrated theologian who spent his last years at Chicago. In 1968, 1973, and 1983 Eliade and Paul Ricoeur cooperated in three outstanding joint seminars.

Only rarely did Eliade accept invitations to lecture or be in residence at other schools. Institutions for which he made exceptions were the University of Mexico (1965), Princeton (1965), the University of California at Santa Barbara as Fellow of the Hutchins Institute (1968 and 1969), Albion College (1971; this was planned as a full quarter's residency, but Eliade suffered a pericardiac attack and spent most of the time in a hospital), the University of North Carolina at Chapel Hill (1978), and the University of Colorado at Boulder (1982). He was a Fellow of the Center for Advanced Studies, Wesleyan University, in 1966, together with Michael Polyani and Patrick Moynihan—now United States senator from New York. More frequently he consented to visit a campus for one to three days, presenting one or two lectures or conducting a class or seminar. Harvard, Princeton, the University of Rochester, Loyola (Chicago), Wesleyan, Boston, the University of Iowa, Milwaukee, the University of Washington, Dartmouth, and George Washington were among the American universities privileged to have had Eliade lecture at least once on their campuses.

He participated, of course, in professional organizations, feeling a sense of duty to do all he could to promote the cause of the discipline. He was president of the American Society for the Study of Religions (1963–67). In 1972 and 1975 he addressed the American Academy of Religion when it met in Chicago. He was a prominent participant in the International Congresses for the History of Religions (Marburg, 1960; Helsinki, 1973, etc.). However, it pleased him as much or more to be invited to address audiences of persons other than historians of religions. Among such groups were the Eranos Conferences (the last one he addressed was in 1963), Catholic monastic communities in Wisconsin and France, artists and critics in Washington, D.C., in 1963,[9] a conference of philosophers in Geneva (1966), the Center for Democratic Institutions (1972), and a society of Freudian psychologists in Philadelphia (1974). Indeed, his audiences at university lectures typically included faculty and students from many departments and disciplines—a fact which continually gratified him, because he was always seeking to reach the broader, cultured public with his "message."

The pattern of living and working in Chicago for the academic year and going to Europe for the summer (usually June through September) that the Eliades established during their first years in America was followed for nearly all the years afterward. However, in 1964 they spent the entire summer in Chicago, and again in 1971 (after the pericardiac attack in the spring), and they returned from Paris for the month of August in 1972 when Eliade was participating in the Center for Democratic Institutions in Santa Barbara. They made a special trip to Paris in January of 1975 to celebrate their twenty-fifth wedding anniversary, and they remained in Paris during the fall quarter of 1976 because of the grave illness of Christinel's sister, Sibylle. The European summers were spent partly in Paris, where they purchased an apartment in the Montmartre sector, and partly in other places: Provence, Holland, Switzerland, various locales in Italy, and, beginning in 1974, Puerto de Andraitx on Majorca—a place to which they returned for a month each summer for many years. They began going to visit friends in Palm Beach, Florida, each winter for Christmas in 1973, and they often visited with Christinel's other sister, Lisette, in New York at New Year's. This routine was broken by occasional trips to other countries, usually in connection with conferences (for example, Sweden and Norway, 1970; Finland, 1973; Stockholm, 1978). There were two major "tourist" type vacation trips in these years not

9. See Eliade, *Symbolism, the Sacred, and the Arts* (New York: Crossroads, 1985), pp. 86–92.

covered in the *Autobiography*, for which Eliade (of course!) wrote extensive travel journals: to Egypt in September 1976 and to the Yucatan and Guatemala in the winter of 1978–79.[10] Interestingly enough, Mircea Eliade never revisited India. The Eliades, likewise, never visited Australia, the South Seas, or black Africa.

Neither did Eliade ever return to his beloved Romania. Prior to 1967 he would not have been welcomed. When he was mentioned at all in print in his homeland during the first two decades after the Communist government took power there, Eliade was denounced as an "obscurantist," "mystic," and "Fascist" for having written on religion and having been associated with the despised Nae Ionescu. His writings were banned, and in 1959 five intellectuals (one of them his old friend Constantin Noica, a leading Romanian philosopher) were sentenced to long prison terms for having read and praised *Forêt interdite* (*The Forbidden Forest*), a copy of which had somehow reached their hands. (They were released in 1964 and subsequently "rehabilitated.") In the autumn of 1967, however, the political climate had moderated sufficiently to allow articles about Eliade and selections from his writings to be published in certain Bucharestian literary reviews. Also, it became possible for Eliade to talk by telephone with his mother and sister in Romania, whom he had not seen since 1942 and with whom even correspondence had been difficult since the War. (Later, his sister and others would be allowed to travel to Paris, but Eliade never saw his mother again. She died at age ninety in 1974.)[11]

Had Eliade been permitted to finish his *Autobiography* as planned, he would, very likely, have had much to say about his relations with Romania during the time subsequent to 1967. For about three years many articles about Eliade appeared there, concerned mainly with his literary works, older and more recent, for which everyone now had words of praise. Two large books that reprinted some of his novels and novellas were published by one of the state-controlled publishing houses in 1969. Romanian visitors to Eliade in Paris and Chicago urged him to return for a visit, saying, "Something has changed!" But Eliade refused to go back. Then, suddenly, in 1970 his name vanished from the reviews, and only a handful of articles about him appeared

10. See *Fragments*, II, pp. 284–301, 402–32.
11. See *Journal* for August 24, 1974.

over the next six or seven years. Not until after the Sorbonne had conferred on him an honorary doctorate in early 1976 did Eliade once again become widely mentioned in the Romanian press. Now he was visited by persons sent from the government and begged to return and accept honorary membership in the Romanian Academy. He refused, for the same reason he had refused to visit the country earlier: he knew that for him to do so would constitute a compromise of principles, in that it would suggest that he had in some sense accepted the Communist dictatorship as legitimate—and this he adamantly refused to do. Too many of his friends had suffered and even died in Romanian Communist prisons for him ever to be reconciled with the government.

Nevertheless, several of Eliade's books were published in Romanian translations—usually after long delays and with slight but significant modifications in the texts: *Myth and Reality* (1979), *From Zalmoxis to Ghengis Khan* (1980), *A History of Religious Ideas*, vol. I (1981) and vol. II (1986). In addition, a large collection of his novellas appeared in 1981, and three books about him have been allowed to appear in recent years. Some of Eliade's friends in Romania cherish fond hopes of publishing a "complete works" edition some day, but to date their efforts have yielded no concrete results.

Eliade had published most of the books on which his international reputation as a historian of religions rests prior to 1960 and even prior to his coming to the United States: *Patterns in Comparative Religion*, *Cosmos and History*, *The Sacred and the Profane*, *Yoga*, and *Shamanism*. During his Chicago years English editions of volumes previously available only in French quickly appeared; then came several collections of studies and lectures: *Myths, Dreams, and Mysteries* (1960), *Images and Symbols* (1961), *Mephistopheles and the Androgyne* (1965). *The Quest* (1969) contains some of Eliade's most important methodological studies; *From Zalmoxis to Ghengis Khan* (1972) is an underrated collection of studies in Romanian folk traditions. The thin volume *Occultism, Witchcraft, and Cultural Fashions* contains significant texts on topics not treated elsewhere. *Myth and Reality* (1963), Eliade's best book on myth, was written in the early sixties in Chicago. Forced to abandon the project of a general volume on primitive religions, he nevertheless completed an admirable monograph on one primitive group, published as *Australian Religions* (1973), and a study of "South American High Gods" (published in the journal *History of Religions* in 1969 and 1971).

Soon after beginning to teach at Chicago, Eliade realized that students had no ready access to the myth-texts and scriptures they needed to read for his courses, so he began forming an anthology of choice specimens, eventually published as *From Primitives to Zen* (1967). The task proved to be very time-consuming, and before it was done he regretted that he had ever begun it: he felt the time he had lost on it might better have been spent in research and original writing.

About 1971–72 Eliade launched his last and perhaps most ambitious personal project—one that only he among contemporary scholars could have dared: a universal, chronological history of religious beliefs and ideas. Originally conceived as a two-volume work, it was later projected for three volumes, and eventually the third volume was divided into two, only one of which Eliade lived to finish. Written with precision and economy, and informed by the latest scholarship as well as Eliade's penetrating insights, the work breaks off at the end of the first part of volume 3, with alchemy and occultism in the West at about 1700 and with Tibetan religion in Asia. The final book, as he planned it, was to have been written mainly by his students, with only one or two chapters by himself.[12] Once he began work on it, he devoted most of his time and energy to the *History*. Even when on vacation, he would find time to consult the files of material for the chapter over which he was currently toiling. Although uncompleted, the work is a classic, a synthesis that represents the distillation of a half-century of research in the religious history of humankind by one of the keenest minds of our century.

Two other living monuments to Eliade's memory are his scholarly journal, *History of Religions*, founded (with two colleagues) in 1961, and the sixteen-volume *Encyclopedia of Religion*, published by Macmillan in 1987, of which Eliade was the editor-in-chief from 1980 until his death (when it was virtually ready to go to press).

Another side of Mircea Eliade, one still too little known to English-speaking readers, is his literary creativity. Whereas his works in the

---

12. Ioan Culianu, Romanian-born historian of religions teaching at Groningen, is preparing the final part for publication.

history of religions were written ordinarily in French (occasionally in English), Eliade continued until the last years of his life to compose fiction—mostly novellas and short stories—in his native Romanian. The lack of success in France of the French translations of *Maitreyi* and *The Forbidden Forest* in the fifties discouraged him from trying to promote himself in the French literary world. Consequently, as he writes in his journal for July 20, 1974: "my literary activity was reduced for a long time to writing 'fantastic' novellas and short stories for myself, Christinel, and a few Romanian friends." After coming to Chicago, Eliade wrote some fifteen short fictional works and one play, most of which have not yet appeared in English. Many of them are in the fantastic mode or else contain "mysteries" in which the supernatural (= the sacred) is both concealed and revealed. Critics familiar with his whole *oeuvre* judge these last literary pieces to be among some of the best he ever wrote.[13] In the seventies and eighties, European readers "discovered" Eliade, and a goodly number of his fictional writings were published in French, German, Italian, and other translations (as well as in Japanese in Asia). These were widely reviewed in the presses of these nations, and in 1978 Eliade was a prominent candidate for the Nobel Prize in literature. The Italians, especially, have honored Eliade for his literary achievements: in 1984 he received the Dante Alighieri Prize in June and the Elba-Brignetti Prize in September—the latter for the new Italian translation of his 1938 novel, *Nuntă în Cer*! In 1986, after his death, the Istituto superiore per l'aggiornamento culturale of Florence changed its name to the Eliade Institute.

13. The following literary works of Eliade written in the "Chicago years" are available in English translation:
   The Old Man and the Bureaucrats, trans. Mary Park Stevenson. Notre Dame and London: Notre Dame University Press, 1979.
   "Les trois grâces," trans. Mac Linscott Ricketts, and "With the Gypsy Girls," trans. William Ames Coates, in Eliade, *Tales of the Sacred and the Supernatural*. Philadelphia: Westminster Press, 1981.
   "Good-bye!" trans. Mac Linscott Ricketts, in Norman Girardot and Mac Linscott Ricketts, eds., *Imagination and Meaning: The Scholarly and Literary Worlds of Mircea Eliade*. New York: Seabury, 1982 (now distributed by Harper and Row), pp. 162–78.
   "The Endless Column," trans. Mary Park Stevenson, in *Dialectics and Humanism*, 1983.
   "The Cape," "Youth without Youth," and "Nineteen Roses," trans. Mac Linscott Ricketts, in Eliade, *Three Fantastic Novellas*. Columbus: Ohio State University Press, 1988 (edited by Matei Calinescu).

Mircea Eliade received many honors in the last quarter-century of his life. He was awarded numerous honorary doctorates by American universities, beginning with Yale in 1966 and ending with George Washington University in 1985. The doctorate in which he took greatest pride and satisfaction, however, because he looked upon it as also an honor for his nation, was the *doctor honoris causa* bestowed by the Sorbonne in February 1976. His only fellow countryman to have been so honored before was Nicolae Iorga, the great Romanian historian, one of his boyhood heroes. The previous year he had been made a member of the Belgian Royal Academy of French Language and Literature, and in 1978 he received the French Legion of Honor. Austria made him a member of its Academy of Science (1973) and England a corresponding member of the British Royal Academy. Two South American universities granted him distinguished titles: Universidad Nacional de la Plata (Argentina) and Universidad del Salvador (Buenos Aires).

In chapter 24 below, Eliade mentions the first master's thesis to be written on his thought (by Richard Welbon, who later took a doctorate under Eliade). Subsequently, dozens of doctoral dissertations were composed on various aspects of Eliade's work by students at many universities in the United States, Canada, France, Italy, and elsewhere. Several of these were published, including those by D. Allen, G. Dudley, J. Saliba, and I. Culianu.[14] Other books have been written about him or in honor of him. A major anthology of his less accessible works, both scientific and literary, together with articles about him, appeared in 1978 in the French series Cahiers de l'Herne (no. 33), edited by C. Tacou. A smaller collection in English, edited by Norman Girardot and myself under the title *Imagination and Meaning*, was published in 1982. Two other important anthologies in English appeared in 1985, edited by disciples.[15]

For Eliade's sixtieth birthday the University of Chicago Press issued a *Festschrift*, important especially for the studies of Eliade's literary works it includes.[16] A German historian of religions, Hans Peter Duerr,

14. See Douglas Allen and Dennis Doeing, *Mircea Eliade: An Annotated Bibliography* (New York and London: Garland Publishing, 1980), pp. 97–105.
15. Eliade, *Symbolism, the Sacred, and the Arts*, ed. by Diane Apostolos-Cappadona (New York: Crossroads, 1985); and David Carrasco and Jane Swanberg, eds., *Waiting for the Dawn* (Boulder and London: Westview Press, 1985).
16. Joseph Kitagawa and Charles H. Long, eds., *Myths and Symbols: Studies in Honor of Mircea Eliade* (Chicago: University of Chicago Press, 1969).

edited a three-volume *Festschrift* in honor of Eliade on his seventy-fifth birthday (1982), selections from which are scheduled to be published also in English.[17]

These books, only some of those published about Eliade or in his honor, testify to the fame and prestige he attained largely after his coming to America. In this connection, there have been conferences or symposia devoted to him, of which two, held in the United States, should be mentioned here also: one at the University of California at Santa Barbara in 1974, and one at Notre Dame University in 1978. At the latter conference, the first performance was given of Eliade's 1970 play, *The Endless Column* (written in Romanian).[18] Noteworthy also, was a three-day conference on Eliade (which he attended), organized in the fall of 1982 by the University of Colorado at Boulder.

Those who knew and admired Eliade regret that his untimely death prevented him from completing his *Autobiography*. From his published journal extracts and from the first volume of his memoirs, his readers had learned to know him personally, in a way they could not through his more impersonally written works in the history of religions. There are many things we wish he might have commented on, had he written the other chapters. It is unfortunate he wrote no commentary on the proceedings at the Marburg Congress for the History of Religions (September 1960) at which some important decisions were taken. One wishes he had given his impressions of Tillich gained from their joint seminars. I believe he would have had much to say about the "Death of God" movement of the sixties, to which his name was inappropriately linked in the press due to Altizer's book about him.[19] I had hoped to read in the *Autobiography* Eliade's reactions to his reunion with Sorana Ṭopa in Paris in 1970 and especially to the meeting with Maitreyi who, suddenly and without any warning, barged into his Meadville office one spring day in 1973![20] It is unfortunate, too, that Eliade did not live to write commentaries and explanations for his novellas—though, perhaps, it is better that they be left to

17. Hans Peter Duerr, ed., *Alcheringa, oder die beginnende Zeit* (Frankfurt am Main: Qumran, 1983); *Die Mitte der Welt* (Frankfurt am Main: Suhrkamp, 1984); *Sehnsucht nach dem Ursprung* (Frankfurt am Main: Syndikat, 1984).
18. See note 13 above.
19. Thomas J. J. Altizer, *Mircea Eliade and the Dialectic of the Sacred* (Philadelphia: Westminster Press, 1963).
20. See *Journal* for August 29, 1970 (Sorana) and April 13 and 26, 1973 (Maitreyi).

speak for themselves. His admirers and disciples will always regret, too, that he never wrote his long-promised book on *Mythologies of Death* or the volume *Homo Religiosus*, in which he said he would "expound all I believe and all I've understood after fifty years of research and reflection."[21] And finally, we regret that he left unanswered those questions asked by his Parisian interviewer, Rocquet, in 1977, questions he deferred to a later time—above all, the ultimate question, about God.[22]

At the end of chapter 24, the last of the *Autobiography* Eliade was to write, he speaks of *destiny*. This is no mere metaphor for him; Eliade believed in destiny, or, as he also called it, *māyā*. Asked by a reporter in an interview for a magazine only weeks before he was stricken, "Do you believe in destiny?"—he replied:

> Yes, in the sense that I think there is something that cannot be explained—I can't call it Providence—but certainly there is something that cannot be explained. . . . [In my own life] it has worked in such a way as not to keep me a prisoner of a career at the University of Bucharest, which would have ended after the Russian occupation of Romania. Destiny arranged that I be in London, and then in Portugal during World War Two, and then in Paris, keeping me free all the time to do what I wanted to do. I didn't accept a position in a European university because I knew that to be a professor there you are bound. But I accepted a position in an American university because, at least in my case, they gave me the freedom to do what I wanted to do.[23]

But in April 1986, at age seventy-nine, destiny overtook Mircea Eliade, and his pen was laid down forever.[24] Although regretting that he was unable to complete his autobiography as planned, we can be thankful

21. *Journal*, March 9, 1977 (from the Romanian typescript).
22. See Eliade, *Ordeal by Labyrinth, Conversations with Claude-Henri Rocquet* (Chicago: University of Chicago Press, 1982), pp. 132, 147, 186, 188–89. E.g.: "The question of divinity, central as it is, is one I would not wish to let myself speak of lightly. But I do hope to tackle it one day, in a completely personal and coherent way, in writing" (p. 188).
23. Delia O'Hara, "*Chicago* Interview: Mircea Eliade," *Chicago*, June 1986, p. 151.
24. To be sure, many works from his colossal *oeuvre* have never been published, and many of those published in Romanian or French still await publication in English.

that we have at least these ten additional chapters from the odyssey of Eliade, who once said that "every exile is a Ulysses traveling toward Ithaca . . . toward the center."[25]

Mac Linscott Ricketts

Acknowledgment
I wish to express here my deep gratitude for the assistance given me in this work by Christinel Eliade, who read the entire manuscript with loving care and offered numerous suggestions for corrections and improvements in the translation.

25. *No Souvenirs,* p. 84.

15. Destiny Shows Its Teeth

WHEN, on the night of September 9, 1940, we descended into the London air-raid shelter from the fifth floor of the building where one of my colleagues from the Romanian Legation lived, I remembered suddenly—instantaneously, as though they consisted of a single episode, without interruptions—a great many things that had happened to me in the past three years. The sensation was so strange that I said to myself that, very probably, I would not come out of that shelter alive. I don't know if I was afraid or not. But seeing several children there, I had difficulty resisting the temptation to go over and urge their parents to leave with them as quickly as possible, *while there was still time*, to hide in the first basement or shelter they could find, because *this* shelter would be destroyed.

A few minutes later, in order to be left in peace, I pretended to have a terrible migraine, and, removing my glasses, I pressed my palms against eyes and returned to the interior film which I had tried in vain to stop. September 9, 1940. London had been bombed before, but never like this.[1] I had ceased spending my afternoons at the British Museum. By now I had bought enough books so that I could work at home—although, in the tiny apartment I had rented close to the legation, there was no table sturdy and large enough for me to be able

---

1. I have related these events in detail in *Noaptea de Sânziene* (*The Forbidden Forest*), and I do not repeat them here.

to spread out my manuscripts and files of notes. I had promised to buy myself a desk, but I kept putting it off, waiting to see what would "develop"; that is, to see if the auxiliary services of the Legation would be evacuated from London.

I was cultural attaché, and thus I belonged to the auxiliary services, as did the members of the economic and military commissions, which were reduced to inactivity after Pétain's signing of the armistice. The post of cultural attaché seemed a sinecure anyway. I remember that in April, a few days before leaving Romania, when I presented myself to a secretary of the British Legation in Bucharest (my first "official" visit), the young man, very polite but also very droll, expressed surprise on hearing the term "cultural."

"I don't believe you'll be able to carry out your duties," he said to me, smiling. "Great Britain is at war. Even the poets and philosophers have been mobilized."

I tried to explain to him that the cultural presence of England in Romania, as in the rest of Central Europe, is more than something "useful"; perhaps it constitutes a political activity also. I don't believe I convinced him, but a short while later all the legations and embassies of the major nations doubled their press services by adding cultural positions and missions. Moreover, I quickly realized that press attachés and counselors, whose attention was preempted by military and political events, did not have the time necessary for the development and consolidation of cultural relations: for instance, lecture tours or artistic performances, exhibitions, the translation of "useful" books (i.e., not propaganda exclusively), and so on. Together with Matyla Ghica, a former diplomat who at that time was cultural counselor at London, I participated in meetings of the PEN Club, I met a great many writers, savants, and historians, I obtained the translation rights for several books, and I found publishers for an anthology of modern Romanian prose and a history of the Romanian people. Only a part of this program could be completed because, on February 10, 1941, England broke diplomatic relations with Romania.

The interior film began spinning faster. I saw England again on the afternoon of April 15, when I arrived. It was not, of course, the same London I had known in the summer of 1936. The sky was filled with elongated balloons which quivered slightly, floating at various altitudes. Not one airplane of the Stuka type had been able to get through them. We spent the night in a room at the Rembrandt Hotel.

The following day I presented myself to our minister, V. V. Tilea. I met also the press counselor, Diamanescu; the secretary of the legation, Ion Vardala; and the commercial attaché, Dimitrie Danielopol. From the first night I adjusted to the blackout; I had already had a taste of it from our stopover at Paris. On the third day I started my work: preparing a bulletin based on British periodicals and especially the various newsletters that had recently appeared. I summarized important articles and translated significant passages, trying to render the mood of the British "intelligentsia." I was perhaps naive, but it seemed to me that such information, conveyed in good time to the homeland, could contribute to the understanding of the real situation in England. My bulletins, as well as those of the press service, were transmitted weekly, via diplomatic pouch, to Paris, and from thence to Bucharest. Obviously, after the fall of France, the bulletins reached their destination only rarely.

A surprise and great joy to me was the arrival at the beginning of May of the economic mission, headed by Mircea Vulcănescu. (Mircea was one of the first persons to whom I had spoken, at the beginning of the war, about my desire to go to the United States, with the hope of finding there a teaching position in the history of religions.) We lunched and dined together frequently. As was to be expected, we discussed in particular the military situation, especially after the launching of the German offensive on May 10. For a long while, Mircea remained optimistic. The lightning advance of the German divisions did not discourage him; he expected a decisive battle at the gates of Paris. He kept reminding us of the autumn of 1914, of the Battle of the Marne. I don't know what results the economic mission obtained, but shortly after the occupation of Paris the members of the commission were recalled home. At our last meeting, Mircea told me privately that he did not believe in a German victory.

"It's possible only if they invade England *now*, in a few days or, at the most, a week. But I don't believe Hitler will do it."

After Mircea left, I felt more alone, although I had become closer with two of my colleagues, Ion Vardala and Dimitrie Danielopol. Since the work at the legation left me with plenty of free time, I worked furiously at the British Museum, putting the finishing touches to several chapters of *La Mandragore* (The Mandrake) and gathering material for *Le chamanisme* (Shamanism). Of the summer which had just ended, I remembered very little on that night of September 9,

1940. I passed rapidly (seemingly driven from behind by a harsh, unfamiliar spirit) over the tragic events of June 26 (the loss of Bessarabia) and August 30 (the Vienna Diktat, which had ceded to Hungary a part of Transylvania). I remembered the few days (April 12–15) spent at Paris, where I had renewed acquaintances with Emil Cioran, Eugène Ionesco, and my former student Mihail Şora. Worried, I wondered about their fate. But I was plunging more and more deeply into the past.

Isn't this how it is on the threshold of death? I asked myself, listening to the bombs exploding, seemingly closer and closer. Destiny had begun to "show its teeth," as Nae Ionescu had put it once (in connection with what personage or event I no longer recall). I remembered with a perturbing precision how, when with three other friends I was carrying Nae Ionescu's coffin to the grave, I had stumbled and, with a great effort, had supported myself on one knee until someone had helped me to rise. I knew the popular superstition that the one who slips while bearing a dead man to his grave is fated to die in the course of the same year. When I told Mother what had happened, she tried to calm me, citing examples from the history of our family which refuted, sometimes in a humorous way, the folk superstition.

It is true, I hadn't given another thought to that "sign," although I had thought often about the last months of Nae Ionescu's life and, especially, about his death. On the morning of March 15, 1940, the telephone had rung. Nina, as usual, had answered it. Then she started toward me.

"The Professor's dead!" she told me, looking very pale.

I had seen him a few days previous, at his villa at Băneasa. He was lying in bed, covered with a blanket. He gazed at me a long while, trying to smile. Not a word was spoken. Then the doctor took me by the arm and we tiptoed out of the room. The Professor had asked to see us again—us\ his closest friends, pupils, and coworkers; it was as though he wanted to bid each of us farewell individually.

It was due to Nae Ionescu's death that I found myself now in London. I had spoken long before with Professor Alexandru Rosetti, as well as with Mircea Vulcănescu, about my desire to go to the United States. When his colleague and friend, C. C. Giurescu, was named minister of propaganda in what has been called the "last free government of King Carol," Professor Rosetti asked him to send me as cultural attaché to England. He called me into his office at the Royal Foundations and said:

"Now that Nae Ionescu has died, there's nothing to keep you in Romania. As you know, the creation of a chair in Indian studies or the history of religions is out of the question. As for America, don't forget what Coomaraswamy wrote you. On the other hand, you won't be able to live on what you'll earn from translations and writing for reviews. You will be more useful in London, working with V. V. Tilea and Matyla Ghica."

I went to see Professor C. C. Giurescu, who was one of those who had supported me on the occasion of the scandal provoked by the communiqué of the minister of instruction (cf. Chap. 14, vol. I). He assured me that cultural propaganda, carefully thought out, is quite as valuable as an antiaircraft battery. Unfortunately, he added, the post of cultural attaché was not yet officialy confirmed. I would not be given a diplomatic passport but only a more general kind, for those "on service."

I left on April 10, and for the first time in my life I was traveling in first class, in a sleeping car. My family and friends accompanied me to the station. When they asked me how long I'd be gone, I answered, "A year; at most, a year and a half." But Mihail Sebastian declared, "He's leaving for ten years."

Now I wondered, after an especially powerful bomb explosion, if Nae Ionescu's death, which had made possible this unexpected and fortunate change in my life and career, had brought me near to my own end. I wondered if our destinies were not linked together in some mysterious way, the meaning of which I could not decipher. I remembered my first hemoptyses in the prison camp at Miercurea Ciucului, owing to which I was transferred to a sanatorium a few days before Nae's heart attack and his transportation to the military hospital at Braşov. It is true, our destinies seemed linked; but whereas Nae had been felled by a heart attack at age fifty, I had known only the threat of death, and thanks to the very illness that could have killed me I had been saved in time, and soon after reaching thirty-three I had been sent to London on an official mission. Probably, I said to myself, a different kind of end awaits me, one characteristic of the era which scarcely had begun: a "collective death," not only with Nina and a few Romanian colleagues, but in company with several dozen residents of London, the majority of them old people, women, and children. I sensed that the image itself of this immanent "collective death" was trying to reveal to me a secret, but I failed to grasp what it was. For several years, death had been exalted in Romania as the supreme sacrifice on the part of the Legionaries, and killing—individual and collective—had been very much in fashion. On December 30, 1933, a squad of Legionaries had assassinated the prime minister, I. G. Duca; in November of 1938, King Carol and Armand Călinescu had ordered the execution of Codreanu and the Legionaries involved in the plot against Duca. On September 21, 1939, a team of Legionaries killed Armand Călinescu. In reprisal, Carol ordered their execution and those of several hundred other Legionaries, the majority of whom were in prison camps or the jail at Râmnicul Sărat. The corpses were exposed in the squares of all the cities, with the following inscription: "This is the punishment for traitors to the people and country."

But I wondered if the evocation of these political executions would help me to understand the mystery of our collective death: so many scores of people, good and bad (probably more good than bad), condemned to a slow suffocation in the ruins of the air-raid shelter. Of one thing I was sure: from the time I had entered the university and had begun writing for *Cuvântul*, Nae Ionescu had been more than my favorite professor; I considered him my "master," the guide who had been given me to enable me to fulfill my destiny—that is, in the first place, to be a creator in the realm of culture, the only type of creation which I believed had been allowed us by "History." Nae Ionescu, to the contrary, was fascinated by the "mystery of History"; that is why, beginning in 1926, he passionately engaged in journalism; that is, he let himself get embroiled in politics. Directly or indirectly, all of us— his disciples and fellow workers—were united (*solidarizați*) with the professor's political concepts and options. Nae Ionescu's death had affected me profoundly: I had lost my *Maestru*, my guide; spiritually I had been "orphaned." But in a certain sense his death had liberated me from our immediate past: that is, from the ideas, hopes, and decisions of the professor in the last few years, with which, out of devotion, I had made common cause.

Now, on the night of September 9, 1940, the necessity—I might say fatality—of "collective death" in an air-raid shelter in London troubled me by its enigmatic indifference (I dared not call it absurdity). If such a sad finale was awaiting me, it meant that, at a certain moment, I had embarked on a path that did not belong to my destiny. If our destinies were linked together, as it seemed to me they were, then I would have to die *alone*, as Nae had died, being allowed an interval (a few days? a few hours?) to meditate, to pray. The enigma of the collective death

which awaited me prevented me from "collecting" myself, from realizing the fact that at any moment now I would cease to exist.

, , ,

I found myself suddenly transported backward in time three years.
In that summer of 1937 Nina and I had gone to Berlin. We stopped
first at Venice for the Tintoretto exhibition; then we went to Berne,
where Lucian Blaga had been appointed press attaché. He had found
us an inexpensive pension and for a week we took dinner with him
daily. I had met him previously several times, and I knew he liked
what I wrote. He especially liked the variety of my production. On
one of his latest books he wrote the following dedication: "To Mircea
Eliade, from a universal man to a universal man." That summer he
was working on *Geneza metaforei şi sensul culturii* (The Genesis of
Metaphor and the Meaning of Culture). We sat and talked a great
deal—or rather, more precisely, I would ask him questions, wait a
few minutes for an answer, start speaking again and repeat the questions, and, eventually, Lucian Blaga would say a few words—pon-
derous, precise, and yet seemingly under the spell of an archaic
sacrality. After a week of such dialogue I was exhausted and at the
same time intoxicated. As we were leaving, Mrs. Blaga took me aside
and told me confidentially: "Never, since I've known him, have I seen
Lucian in such high spirits—and so talkative!"

A few weeks later in Berlin I wrote "Conversations with Lucian
Blaga" which appeared as a full page in *Vremea*. It constituted part of
a travel diary I had begun in Venice. I had bought a little notebook
which I carried with me in my pocket at all times, in which I was
constantly jotting down all sorts of details: the expression in the
eyes of a child, fleeting associations on hearing the beginning of a
song, an idea related to books I had read or books I was preparing to
write, and other such things. At night, in shabby hotel rooms, at the
pension in Berne, and at the one on Berlinerstrasse, I would go over
these brief notes, scrawled almost in code, and transcribe them, clar-
ifying and elaborating them. In this fashion, I wrote many dozens of
pages—about significant trifles, meetings, landscapes, meditations,
and memories, at Venice, Berne, Ulm, Heidelberg, and other places.
The majority of them appeared in *Vremea* and *Universul literar* in 1937
and 1939. These pages pleased me so much (perhaps partly because
Dinu Noica had said: "I never suspected you were such a good *traveler*; actually, you're the first Romanian traveler!") that I wanted at all

costs to collect them in book form. But along with several other nearly finished books, *Carnet de vacanta* has never appeared. [It is appended to this chapter.]

As soon as we arrived in Berlin, I resumed the schedule of previous years: days at Stadt-Bibliothek, evenings and nights working at home on my book about cosmology. I reworked several texts on Babylonian cosmology which had already appeared in *Vremea,* and I wrote the last chapters (about alchemy), so that by the time I returned, I had the manuscripts finished. *Cosmologie şi alchimie babiloniană* appeared at the end of autumn.[2]

I returned to Romania laden down with notes, documents, and projects. I had almost completed the documentation for *La Mandragore* and I planned to write it in the course of the year. Alexandru Rosetti had asked me for it, for publication by the Royal Foundations, and Paul Guethner in Paris was waiting for it. *Habent sua fata libelli. . . .* I had begun to collect materials for this book at the Imperial Library in Calcutta in 1930–31. I had published two columns on the subject in *Cuvântul* in 1932, and since then, whenever I had the opportunity, I continued to enrich my files. Recently I had requested Ion Muşlea, director of the Archive of Folklore at Cluj, to send me the unpublished documentary material, and that fall I drafted the first chapter, "Le culte de la mandragore en Roumanie." The text was to appear, in the spring of 1939, in *Zalmoxis,* the journal of religious studies I had decided to publish immediately after returning from Berlin. Nae Ionescu, Rosetti, and others encouraged me in this project. General Condeescu promised me a subvention from the Royal Foundations,

2. In this little book are found, *in nuce,* all my interpretations relative to the symbolism of the center of the world; the archetypal models of temples, cities, and dwellings; the Platonic structure of archaic and Oriental thought—interpretations developed later in *The Myth of the Eternal Return (Cosmos and History), Patterns in Comparative Religion,* and *Images and Symbols.* Lucian Blaga, Nae Ionescu, Tudor Vianu, and others read it with enthusiasm. But, of course, it was hard to expect a total adherence of Romanian intellectuals. Camil Petrescu reproached me for squandering my intelligence and culture on such uninteresting problems, instead of studying Husserl, for example, or making a phenomenological analysis of art. Some nationalistic intellectuals deplored my alienation, the fact that I had let myself be absorbed by exotic cultural phenomena instead of studying authentic Romanian creations. Now, to repeat myself, I believe that my efforts to understand the structures of archaic and Oriental thought contributed more genuinely to the decipherment of the values of Romanian folk spirituality than, for instance, the exegesis of Kant or sociological interpretations based on the latest books from Germany, France, or the United States.

and Paul Guethner agreed to publish the journal. Many foreign scholars promised to contribute, and by the winter of 1938 I had already received articles from Ananda Coomaraswamy, R. Pettazzoni, C. Hentze, J. Przyluski, and B. Rowland.

I had decided to bring out *Zalmoxis* in the hope that I would encourage the study of the history of religions in Romania and that I would promote the results of Romanian researchers by publishing them in major languages. There was no chair for the history of religions at the Faculty of Letters and Philosophy (Bucharest), although Vasile Pârvan, Nae Ionescu, and for several years I myself had given courses on the history of religions. I was interested also in "deprovincializing" the study of comparative folklore and ethnology in Romania. I proposed to make Romanian folklorists somehow take seriously the historico-religious value of the materials they were gathering and using: that is, to pass from the philological phase to the hermeneutical moment.[3]

The projects I planned then, in the fall of 1937, were grandiose, but they did not seem to me unrealizable. I proposed to finish *La Mandragore* in a year, in order to begin after that a theoretical book on the structure of myths and symbols. In the past few years I had given courses on these problems. For the fall of 1937 I had announced a special course about religious symbolism in which I would examine in particular aquatic symbolism and that of the cosmic tree. The essence of the lectures appeared later in volume II of *Zalmoxis* and in *Traité d'histoire des religions* (called in English translation *Patterns in Comparative Religion*). Such problems interested a small group of students, whom I knew well from the seminars on *De docta ignorantia* and on Book X of Aristotle's *Metaphysics*. To them I had announced for the year 1938–39 a course on myth. But I was never to teach it.

Imperceptibly, the political atmosphere had changed and threatened to worsen. The popularity of the Legionary movement was continually growing. Some of my friends and colleagues had belonged to

3. I did not suspect then, in the fall of 1937, when I was working on the first volume of *Zalmoxis*, that I would be allowed to publish only three volumes, the last two of them after my departure from Romania. I did not suspect, certainly, that *La Mandragore: Essai sur les origines des légendes*, on which I labored with such enthusiasm, would not have appeared in print even forty years after its writing. In appearance, it was a monograph of comparative folklore; in reality, as the subtitle indicates, I attempted a general theory about the origin and formation of legends. I proposed to present, first, popular beliefs having to do with the mandrake and other "magical" plants, then to examine the legends relative to their birth, and to show their relation to archaic cosmogonic myths.

the Iron Guard for several years. Others seemed to be waiting for the right moment to request admission. Although he did not belong in an official sense, Nae Ionescu was considered the ideologist of the Legionary movement, much to the annoyance of other intellectuals and journalists of the right. A little before the elections of that fall, Iuliu Maniu and Corneliu Codreanu concluded an electoral agreement insuring free elections and allowing them to avoid the usual governmental interference. It is very probable that this agreement sealed the fate of the Legionary movement. This was the prospect not only because the Legion's success at the polls exceeded all expectations, but especially because the government did not obtain its quota of 40 percent of the votes, which would have assured it of a parliamentary majority. Thus, the elections were annulled. The king authorized Octavian Goga to form a government, with Armand Călinescu as interior minister, and a new election was announced for that winter.

In January 1938, after a suspension of four years, *Cuvântul* reappeared. But no longer was it the newspaper I had known and loved in my student years. The recently introduced censorship and especially the presentiment that we were on the verge of decisive events, seemingly had changed the style of the paper. Since Mihail Sebastian and Ion Călugaru no longer contributed (although Sebastian remained as close as ever to Nae Ionescu), I had responsibility for the cultural pages. I wrote two or three short articles weekly and invited several of my former students to contribute.

During the winter, the electoral campaign began again, even more passionately. It was said later that Armand Călinescu, on the basis of information he had received at the Ministry of the Interior, informed King Carol that the results of the elections would be disastrous, that the Legionary movement would garner the largest number of votes. Thus, on February 10, the Goga government was dismissed and a new one was formed under the presidency of Patriarch Miron, but directed in reality by Armand Călinescu. Since the final aim was the destruction of the Legionary movement, there were many of us who wondered where the spark would break out that would ignite the conflict between Carol and Codreanu. The chief of the Iron Guard had chosen the path of nonviolence. In a circular he declared that the government could torture and kill, but the Legionaries would not strike back. Nevertheless, when Nicolae Iorga wrote in his paper, *Neamul românesc*, that in the Legionary restaurants plots were being hatched, Corneliu Codreanu replied to him in another circular, accusing him of being a "spiritually dishonest man." This was the occasion Armand Călinescu had been waiting for. N. Iorga brought charges of slander against Codreanu in court, and in April 1938 Codreanu was arrested, tried, and sentenced to six months' imprisonment. The night before, the Legionary centers were occupied and searched, and the next day all the newspapers published a full page of facsimiles of letters from which it was supposed to be evident that the Legionary movement had planned an uprising. The constitution was suspended, and special legal decrees were promulgated daily. All Legionary newspapers were, of course, banned.

Nae Ionescu was arrested, as were nearly all of the Legionary leaders. Some time later I learned that they were in "forced domicile" in the former School of Agriculture near Miercurea Ciucului. In May, Codreanu and a large number of Legionary leaders were put on trial for high treason. This time Codreanu was sentenced to ten years in prison.

I continued to conduct my courses during these weeks of tension. The only novelty was the presence of several suspicious characters in the first and last rows of the Titu Maiorescu Amphitheater. One night the telephone rang. An unfamiliar voice warned me that "it would be better" if I didn't sleep at home that night. I knew that the searches and arrests were made in the nighttime, and I knew further that, once arrested, it was impossible for someone to get released. I had thought for some time about such an eventuality, but General Condeescu, president of the Society of Romanian Writers, had assured me that the only persons who risked having their homes searched or being given "forced domicile" were those who were actively engaged in politics. Since Condeescu was a friend of the youth and was also King Carol's librarian, I supposed he was well informed. But I must, at all costs, avoid arrest. A friend had come just then to see me. I proposed that the two of us go downtown to eat and then walk the streets till dawn. And so we did. At 2:00 A.M. we strolled past the house. The lamp on the desk was burning, the signal I had arranged with Nina to indicate that the search had been carried out but that it was still too risky for me to return. We passed the house again, three hours later. The lamp was turned off, and I went upstairs. Nina told me what had happened. Shortly after midnight two commissioners and an inspector from Security had come in and asked questions about me. She told them I had gone to the country. They began to rummage through the drawers and bookcases, searching for compromising documents. They read all my recent correspondence from abroad (the majority of the letters having to do with *Zalmoxis*, most of which was then with the printer), confiscating the letters written in English because they couldn't understand them. I wasn't sleepy after all the coffee I'd drunk that night, so I started leafing through the files of *Zalmoxis* and *La Mandragore* to be sure they had been left intact. However, I knew I had to find a place where I could hide until Condeescu would be able to straighten things out. I found it that same day, at the home of a father of one of Giza's classmates, in another part of Bucharest. I left with a pair of pajamas and a few books, thinking I wouldn't be staying more than a day or two.

I stayed nearly three weeks. Nina had seen General Condeescu (to whom, incidentally, she was related) that first day. The general had promised her that he would speak to Armand Călinescu, but he advised me not to return home until he sent me word. "Once he's arrested," he told Nina, "I can't do anything. *No one* can do anything. Not even the king. This was the condition imposed by Armand: absolutely no interference."

From the newspapers I found out not only about the trials and sentencing of the Legionaries but also particulars that concerned me personally: for instance, Nae Ionescu's dismissal from the university—that is, indirectly, my own dismissal also, as his assistant. Beginning in June, therefore, I lost my salary, and I wondered what we would live on, even though the owner of the apartment assured Nina he would grant me a delay in paying the rent. The article I had sent to *Vremea* had been censored, although I had chosen a neutral and rather insipid subject (something, I believe, having to do with Indian thought).[4] To my surprise and delight, the article written for *Revista Fundațiilor Regale* (The Review of the Royal Foundations) was allowed to appear, but it was the last one that year.[5] Fortunately, Alexandru Rosetti proposed that I translate a novel by Pearl Buck, *Fighting Angel*, and he advanced me a significant sum. For the moment, we weren't

4. Translator's note: The article meant is apparently "Un catolic excomunicat," which appeared in *Vremea* on May 8, 1938. It has to do with Ernesto Buonaiuti.

5. Translator's note: "Un savant rus despre literatura chineză" (about a book by the Russian scholar Basile Alexiev on Chinese literature), published in the August issue of RFR.

threatened with starvation. But I harbored no illusions. I sensed that, sooner or later, I would be "taken out of circulation," as some of my critics had wished me to be long ago. Even if I were to avoid the forced domicile, I knew I wouldn't obtain a university post again. I knew likewise that I would be unable to write and publish under a dictatorship. And yet I was neither grief-stricken nor disillusioned. In a way, I had been expecting something like this. Eleven years before I had written the article "*Anno Domini.*" I knew that I had lost the paradise I had known in adolescence and early youth: *disponibilité*, the absolute freedom to think and create. That was why I had produced so much, so fast; I knew that the leisure history had allowed us was limited. I had never imagined that we would find ourselves in such a situation due to a nationalistic student movement that in my university years I had viewed with indifference, and due to a young king whose coming to the throne I, like my whole generation, had considered providential.

I have never been curious to know beforehand "the sauce with which we shall be eaten." I did know, however, that there would come a day when history would prevent me from growing and becoming myself. I knew I'd be threatened with being swallowed alive and digested in the belly of a great monster. The thought consoled me that I had begun to write at least a part of the books I had dreamed of, and that I had published at least *Yoga*, although I was filled with regrets that I hadn't written *Viață nouă*, hadn't finished *La Mandragore*, and hadn't published volume I of *Zalmoxis*. If I desired freedom so much, it was, in the first place, to be able to complete at least the works begun. I suspected that, in a way, the cycle of "Romanian creation" was almost at an end. I was barely thirty-one, still very young— and I *felt* young—full of projects and possibilities. I told myself that I'd find a teaching position in Italy, where Tucci had invited me, or in the United States, where Coomaraswamy was urging me to come. I did not view exile as a cleavage from Romanian culture, but only as a change of perspective, or more precisely as a displacement in diaspora. I thought of exile with no bitterness or notion of revenge. In a few years' time I had had, in Romania, everything but wealth: fame, notoriety, prestige; I had been, and perhaps still was, the "head of the young generation." For all that had happened to me in the past few months I could not blame anyone, not even Carol or Armand Călinescu. I saw here the destiny of our generation: ten years of freedom . . . and then again to be "conditioned" by the historical moment. Things might have happened differently, but the sentence could not be revoked: at most, it could only have been postponed another two or three years. This time I knew, as did everyone, that war was near, that no matter what we might do, we too would be involved, that the only problem for the Romanians was, as Anton Golopenția phrased it, "how to hibernate."

In distinction from the majority of the youth, I did not believe that my generation had a political destiny, as the war generation had and as I hoped the generations to follow ours would have. Our destiny was exclusively cultural. We had to answer one question only: are we capable of being a major culture, or are we condemned to produce— as we had done up till 1916—a culture of a provincial type, crossed meteorically at intervals by solitary geniuses like Eminescu, Hasdeu, and Iorga? The appearance of a Vasile Pârvan, a Lucian Blaga, Ion Barbu, Nae Ionescu, and others confirmed my faith in the creative possibilities of the Romanian people. But it was necessary that our generation give its answer quickly to the question put to it. As I was repeating already in 1926, we must answer "while there is still time."

Never before had I sensed so concretely how little time we still had left. I must at all costs complete the first number of *Zalmoxis*; and I wrote, working night and day, almost all the book reviews that appeared in the first volume. Giza sent me, through her classmate, the books and notebooks I needed. After about two weeks had passed, Nina and several friends came to see me. Then, at the beginning of July, General Condeescu sent me word that I could return home. He had seen Armand Călinescu and had been assured that there were no accusations against me, that the search had been made out of an excess of zeal on the part of Security in order to ascertain that I was not harboring some fugitive and did not possess any "compromising documents."

I returned home, but at first I didn't dare show myself downtown. I hadn't the time, anyway. Day and night I worked on *La Mandragore*. Soon I received from the printer the galleys of the articles written by foreign contributors to *Zalmoxis*. I took them to the central post office and sent them to their authors in registered envelopes, to make sure they wouldn't go astray. This I did on the morning of July 14. In the afternoon an Italian student who had begun to translate *Maitreyi* came to see me. He had scarcely read a page when I heard the sound of heavy boots and hurried steps ascending the stairs, and moments later some six or seven Security agents and two gendarmes burst into the study. They had entered the building through all the doors at one time and had occupied all the rooms, even the bath, where they had left one gendarme on guard. The squad leader looked at me curiously, stared at my bookcases, and, after identifying the Italian student, said to me rather politely, "Come along with us to Security, to make a statement. But bring your pajamas and necessities. Maybe we'll need to have an interrogation."

*   ,   ,   ,*

The scene I had just remembered brought me to my senses, although I had heard no bomb explosion. Here's where it all started! I said to myself. The journey to the collective death which awaited me had begun on that afternoon of July 14. Certainly I had made some error, but I could not succeed in identifying it. It seemed absurd to believe that my fate had been sealed because, on that morning, I had sent to Pettazzoni, Coomaraswamy, and Przyluski the galleys of their articles by registered mail. It was true, as I found out soon afterward, that Security, in checking over the lists of registered letters sent that morning, had come upon my envelopes. I had, therefore, "foreign contacts"—behavior somewhat suspect at that time, and especially in my case: the assistant to Nae Ionescu and contributor to his paper. Still, I couldn't believe that such an incident could have put me on the road to a collective death. I knew I had made a fatal mistake, very probably in connection with my recent preoccupations (*La Mandragore? Zalmoxis?*), but I was incapable of understanding more.

"The all-clear's sounded!" Nina exclaimed, shaking me.

She believed, like all the others, that I had fallen asleep with my hands over my eyes, resting my head on my knees. It took me several minutes to understand what had happened.

"So, this time I've escaped with my life. *This time*," I repeated melancholically. "At any rate. . . . "

I had started to add, "At any rate I've escaped a collective death," but I stopped myself in time.

Notebook of a Summer Vacation (1937)

"I Am the Captain of my Soul!"

Observe carefully your traveling companions as soon as you cross the border. Before your very eyes, they change and begin to think of themselves as different people, important, handsome, free. They are embarked on an adventure! Watch them smoking as they walk up and down the corridors, see them leaning on the windowsills—their eyelids fluttering slightly, watching the fleeting landscape. What efforts they are making to try to combine indifference with excitement! Each passenger wants to seem to be, at the same time, the seasoned traveler, accustomed to distant places, and the connoisseur who doesn't miss a nuance. "I am the master of my fate, I am the captain of my soul!"—so they seem to be saying, all these eyes that look down on you from inaccessible heights, from the peaks where destiny or adventure has catapulted them. What a fantastic change of expression on the faces of all these people, on this summer night in which we are, in fact, only crossing a dreary Yugoslavian plain.

Fragment

I reread the lines above. Curious, how much the Bovaryism of my traveling companions preoccupies me.

I wonder what strange inferiority complexes are concealed beneath my passion to catch the "change" taking place in the people around me, their tireless *becoming*. At any rate, I follow these changes every chance I get, especially in the dining car (even if I'm only going to Ploieşti). I believe that nowhere is the transfiguration of the journey (at the departure, in the first hours on the road) more evident than in a dining car: a transfiguration, moreover, that is only approximate and ephemeral. I have learned now to distinguish species of travelers (my favorite author, Laurence Sterne, attempted this once, in his sentimental, sarcastic way), and it never ceases to delight me when I spot a youth who is passing the border for the first time, trying ever so hard to hide his innocence. I'd like to be able to watch all the mental films of those dreamers leaning on the windowsills, to overhear their fantastic, heroic inner monologues. How intense for everyone are the first hours of the journey! How responsible each one feels, how meaningful seems his existence, how fervently he experiences even the most insignificant happenings!

Passing Over

I believe I was wrong in speaking of "inferiority complexes" in myself or others. On the contrary, such a spectacle is very reassuring. The thirst for the fantastic, for daydreaming, for adventure has remained as unquenched as ever in the soul of modern man. With the most simple change of scenery, he begins to dream, he is ready to believe he's become *different*, richer spiritually, more real, more free. All these people around me, daydreaming—they aren't thinking of crimes, stealing, vicious acts, but, on the contrary, of deeds that are heroic (in the modern sense of the word, of course), manly, radiant. The adventure of which each one dreams, and which for some has begun with the crossing of the border, is, in any event, a desire for transcendence, for an anchoring in significant reality, in certain "ontological centers." People want, at all costs, to get out of neuter, non-significant zones. If I had the courage to carry my thought to its logical conclusion, I would say that people today, as always, long to go out of the "profane," neuter zones and attain the "sacred," that is, ultimate reality.

It is not simply a matter of the ancient desire of man for a "sacred" of a social nature. Such a simplistic explanation does not satisfy me. It seems to me that in man's general tendency toward the concrete, the sacred—in a word, his ontological instinct—there is betrayed the very meaning of existence: the *unification* (totalization) of the Cosmos, split in two (microcosm-macrocosm) by Creation. Only the One, the

Whole, can be sacred, real. My researches of the past year have put me on the trail of a new method for explaining the rites, symbols, and ideas of all archaic cultures. But about these "secret researches"— as Eugenio d'Ors says about his angelology—"for the time being, silence!"

Water—and Feminine Wisdom

At Vincovici, as always, rain. I make a calculation: I have passed through here five or six times, usually at night, and every time it has been raining. Probably a mere coincidence. But from such coincidences are born those subjective, "qualitative" geographies—the only ones that matter, actually. Cities, countries, rivers which we value or love for the image of a face seen in a station, for a glass of water that quenched our thirst, for an unknown fragrance—fantasies, images, things that struck us in the first moments, *ab initio*. "First" happenings have an exceptional, formative force. From a few such insignificant fragments we create our prodigious subjective geographies. But such fragments preserve their formative force only if they are encountered ab initio, at our first setting foot on foreign soil. All that happens after those first moments, after the miracle of cosmicization is past, is judged good or bad, as the case may be, *according to everyday standards*. I understand very well the psychology of those who agree to establish a family only on the basis of the virginity of the bride. *Prima noctis*, the beginning of a new existence, is like ab initio, the creation of a new Cosmos. Those infinite waters, the chaos before Creation, symbolize par excellence the feminine principle, the primordial motive force. *Ce n'est que le premier pas qui compte* (only the first step counts)—this maxim sums up a whole body of feminine wisdom.

Detective Novels

A new convert to the reading of detective novels: J. G. I found her tonight, comfortably stretched out in her compartment in first class— reading the volume I had loaned her a few hours earlier. Travel and convalescence: ideal interludes for the reading of detective stories. Time passes more quickly, and you forget the book an hour after you put it down. You are willing then to believe in absurd events, although you are incapable of accepting the pure fantasy of legends and fairy tales.

J. G. swears that she had never read a detective novel before, and I believe her. It takes a lot of courage to waste time in full view of the world. Ordinarily, people kill time in collective, legitimized, socially sanctioned amusements. Then, too, there is the unshakable belief that on a trip or during a vacation period we'll have the time to read more than in all the rest of the year. We go off on a journey with thick tomes, and then we return, as Aldous Huxley says, "with their secrets inviolate."

Huxley is in the habit of traveling, according to his own testimony (in *Along the Road*), with a volume of the *Encyclopaedia Britannica*. Short articles, unconnected to one another, which you can read in an hour of waiting in a station or in an overcrowded compartment—and which have the great merit of being quickly forgotten. This verifies once more my belief that the most important thing is to be able to forget—because to learn is infinitely more easy.

Fragment

At the Italian frontier, waiting for the train to leave, a signalman asks me where we are from. "From Romania," I tell him. "Bel paese!" (beautiful country), he replies.

Another person in the compartment, who is crossing the border for the first time, translates the signalman's response for me—and I thank him sheepishly, avoiding the embarrassment of confessing I know Italian.

Miramare

I once read some notes on Miramare written by a man enamored of it—a Romanian of course—who exclaimed with every line, "Mi-ra-ma-re! Mi-ra-ma-re!" distributing hyphens among the syllables to be able to express his ecstasy more adequately. That poem in prose— how much toil and how much joy it gave the author to write it! And how lamentable, how vulgar it was! It is dangerous to write under the enchantment of such a miraculous body of water as this gulf. An overwhelming vulgarity pervades the majority of pages of impressions of Italy whenever the author tries to describe nature *sur le vif*. Pages written on terraces, at a hotel window, or on a steamship—directly under the spell of the landscape—are especially horrible. Like every cry of possession, in fact; like the snort of a ravenous man who chews and swallows under the spell of his biology.

Memories

Every time I stop at Trieste, I remember the days spent here in 1927, with A. and C., waiting for money from home so we could return. We ate then in a popular tavern, full of students, and at each table there was one apple. We took ours down to the quay and ate it very slowly, as though it were the most precious fruit in the world.

Then, in December 1931, I waited here again for money to enable me to get home. I stayed at a hotel on the waterfront. My last traveling companion from the ship had left for Germany; I had accompanied him to the train station, feeling very melancholy. Winter had begun. I was wearing a thin trench coat and my hands felt frozen all the time. When no one was approaching me on the street, I would take them out of my pockets and blow on them.

This time, sweltering and stifling, we walk as close to the buildings as possible. J. G. tells me that Yugoslavian men are brazen, and she refuses to travel at night with one of them in her compartment. We buy some peaches in the marketplace: about 10 lei per kilogram. We walk along, each carrying a bagful, eating them as we go. At the station we meet N. and V. They also have a bag of peaches, and they ask us immediately how much we paid per kilo. They have taken a cab and have made a tour of the city. V. asks me if I've seen the tunnel. I'd almost forgotten about that tunnel which I saw another time, in quite curious circumstances.

Neighbors

They are certainly married, but she is still very young, whereas the husband is an old man, trying in vain to seem youthful. They are sitting as close together as possible on the seat. She is tall, blonde, and strikingly attired, with a big hat and a Sunday dress. The husband keeps putting his hand on her breast and whispering in her ear. He speaks so softly that I can't catch a single word. I think they're speaking in Italian. They have come to Venice, perhaps, on their honeymoon, or, at any rate, on a new adventure—because he can't take his head off the woman's shoulder.

From time to time she points at the palaces we are passing. They are, as usual, quite dark, except perhaps for a little attic room with an open window, dimly lighted.

The old man tries suddenly to lift his head, to identify a palace whose name, I suspect, the woman has whispered to him a little before. Who knows what memories are linked to that word, what books read in youth, what romances seen at the cinema or related by friends! For just a few moments he was able to hold up his forehead. I saw his eyes palpitating through the darkness. Then his head fell back again on the woman's shoulder, and she slipped her arm around his waist again, supporting him. They got off at the wharf the same way, pressed close to each other, arm in arm. The old man kept whispering in her ear, and his breath, strongly smelling of alcohol, opened a path for them through the lines that descended, silent, on the wharf.

Melancholy

How curious and confusing it is to wake up in a strange room, in a hotel! Sounds reach you almost without making sense; voices sound louder because they are unconnected to anything in the consciousness, and they seem to burst out close by, forcing you to come to your senses, to be alert, ready to defend yourself in case of danger. . . . And then, there is the melancholy that comes over you after any deep sleep, the feeling of the enormous vanity of all things. . . .

Venus and Vulcan

They were wrong—those Italian artists who made such noisy comments (trying sometimes to be funny) about certain canvasses in the Tintoretto exhibit (such as "Pesaro"). They came from Milan, the center of Futuristic experiments: an industrial city, acosmic ("Let us kill the light of the moon!"), fashionable (didn't Marinetti write a whole book on "How to Seduce Women"?). They have the most beautiful streets for automobiles in Milan, the most beautiful cravats; and there too the famous publisher Treves has grown rich selling large editions of such authors as Zuccoli and Ozetti, read especially by women.

Those artists had nothing to say about "Venus and Vulcan," a truly extraordinary painting (from the Munich Museum). And if they liked such a perfect nude, then probably they had renounced Futurism—if indeed they had ever participated in it. Tintoretto shows unprecedented courage in this painting. Venus has never had a more lascivious pose than here, nor has she abandoned herself so completely to the gesture of a god and the eyes of mortals. Behold Vulcan, bending over her, lifting with his left hand the narrow band of a veil that still covers the junction of the goddess's thighs. Venus herself is raising above her shoulders the other end of the veil: in her eyes half-hidden under sleepy eyelids, in her imperial body just awakened from sleep (because how else do you explain the gesture—too bold even for a Venus—with which she slowly spreads her legs?), pervaded, nevertheless, by a supernatural calm. In vain has Vulcan approached unawares and knelt close beside the bed of Venus, and bent over her, slightly lifting the veil, with darkened eyes, trying to penetrate the fiery essence of this "impermeable" body, self-enclosed as in a perfect cosmos (because the ancients imagined the cosmos perfectly enclosed, like a sphere); not one secret has been violated. Without fear, Venus once again leaves herself vulnerable to Vulcan's lusts, his jealousies, or—who knows?—perhaps to his restless curiosities. Because Vulcan was the god who alone knew the secret of metals and furnaces; he had mastered like no other the science of the inorganic world, the fire that melts stone and iron. Vulcan's jealousy must not be explained necessarily by his ugliness, his short leg, or the fact that he had for his wife a restless goddess like Venus. He was jealous because he was a master craftsman and a savant; that is, he had mastered the whole inorganic world and knew its laws. His jealousy toward Venus was nourished by his inability to understand the *organic* world, living nature, and to master its secrets and laws. This impenetrability of Venus, her impermeable and autonomous nature, naturally exasperates Vulcan, accustomed to penetrate things and unaccustomed to *resistance*, to autonomy (he was the god of fire, which melts, liquifies, unifies).

That is why he is so jealous and keeps watching Venus so closely, coming to her in the night to waken her from sleep, to gaze upon her once more, unveiling her, drawing near to her thighs—precisely to decipher some secret of this living world that is constantly "becoming," to find some "track." But Vulcan, god of the inorganic world and the subterranean fire, will never be able to comprehend the secret of the goddess who rules the organic world, the fire of biology and eros. Hence, the supernatural serenity of Venus, hence the somnolent indifference with which she reveals herself to the jealous gaze of the savant, her spouse. Vulcan, incapable of penetrating the secret of the goddess of the living world, contents himself with showing his distrust. On ocean and on the body of a woman one cannot trace tracks—said the Prophet. *Tracks*, when they are conceived of in the mystical sense, *vestigium pedi*, are the objects par excellence of magical knowledge, through which one can reconstruct the world or a certain cosmic event ("tracks," traces, fossils, documents, mediumistic writing—in magic, in the natural sciences and romantic history, in spiritualism). But if Vulcan cannot discover *vestigium pedi* on Venus's body, he succeeds in catching the adulterous pair in *flagrante delicto* in his iron trap. He had to use a tool melted and fashioned in his subterranean cave in order to obtain *proof* of the adultery.

But now Venus is alone. Her lover has gone. The amorous one is asleep beside her, with wings closed. Vulcan can approach without danger; he will guess nothing, understand nothing. . . .

And despite all this, Vulcan—as Tintoretto has painted him—is not repulsive. He looks like an old savant, eyes dimmed from long nights of thought, trying to penetrate the great secret of nature. How much he resembles Faust, sullen as he is, aged in the laboratory, curious, lucid, despairing!

The Girl and the Red Wine
That girl, though obviously a foreigner, strode through the garden restaurant with a splendid indifference: in one hand a sheaf of postcards, in the other a decanter of red wine. We watched as she passed by us and made for the most isolated table in the garden. There she sat down and began dreamily to write messages on the picture postcards. She had ordered the wine just to be able to write in peace in this sleepy garden restaurant. The liter decanter remained half full, and in the glass the wine turned warm almost untouched. A harmonica player came and stopped at the entrance to the garden. The sun penetrated even through the thick leaves on the trees, and the girl rested her head on her hand, balancing the pen timidly, hesitating. Was it so hard for her to write those few words on the last postcard?

Tintoretto
Stopping in front of "The Miracle of the Slave," the group of artists from Milan exchange rather loudly their ironic observations. "Look how St. Mark is falling, headfirst, with his hands stiff, his legs together! What a gross, crude miracle—that perfectly 'corporeal' apparition of the saint over the heads of the men torturing the slave!"

Indeed, this painting amazes and fascinates, above all for the courage Tintoretto has shown in his idea for representing the Christian miracle. A slave who, contrary to his master's will, has gone to see the relics of St. Mark, is condemned upon his return to have his eyes gouged out and his legs broken. When the slave utters the saint's name, a miracle happens and the saint descends. The executioner turns toward the master, showing him the broken implements. The executioner's helper falls on his knees beside the slave, who lies naked and exhausted on the pavement. At the top of the steps leading to the palace, where he is watching the punishment from a kind of throne, the master stares in amazement at the broken implements, the concrete proof of the miracle. Not one of those gathered around the slave and the executioner is looking at the saint. All have their eyes riveted on the concrete proofs: the assistant fallen to the ground, the broken implements, the snapped ropes. The woman with the baby in her arms, who was just about to leave, turns her head. One of those who are crowding around to see the slave whom the saint has liberated rests his chin thoughtfully in his hand; like a true Renaissance man he meditates on this inexplicable event.

And then I begin to wonder if all these people really *see* the saint, upside down, in the air above them; if St. Mark, like the phantom in *Macbeth*, is visible only to the spectators, the viewers of the painting, the actors in the drama being able to see only the *traces* of the miraculous apparition. How else to explain the surprise with which everyone is looking at the slave and the executioner, with his instruments of torture all broken—without anyone's raising his eyes even to the hand of the saint which hangs so close to them that it touches the executioner's turban? So, then, that perfect body, with muscles and veins and shading—which the actors in the drama do not see, and in no event *could* they see it in this way—is painted only for us, the spectators, just as the phantom in *Macbeth*, who appears in flesh and blood. The saint is shown as a robust man, conventionally dressed; only a halo around his head distinguishes him from the other personages in the drama. He is painted in this way so that it is understood that people don't see him, because, if he were represented as a flame, a cloud of smoke, etc., then his *presence* would be concretely visible to the others and the scene would have a wholly different significance. Tintoretto would have been forced to change the center of gravity of the drama; the personages would have been viewed from above, as happens in so many other paintings.

St. Mark descends again in another of Tintoretto's paintings, in order to save the one who pronounces his name—in "The Miracle of the Arab." At the moment his ship is wrecked an Arab calls upon the help of St. Mark, and the saint descends, lifting him by the armpits and carrying him (according to the legend) safe and sound to land. It is the same saint, with large-veined arms, with muscles tense from the exertion. And—exactly as in "The Miracle of the Slave"—the others seem not to see him. Even the Arab doesn't look at him, doesn't lift his eyes to see who has snatched him from the ship half swamped by the waves. But his clenched fists, his fingers stiff with fear, betray the emotion of the miracle.

From another point of view, one could say many things about the conception of miracle in Tintoretto's paintings. For example, the direct intervention of a supernatural power which nevertheless does not transfigure the real world around it is, in fact, in accord with the popular conception of the "fantastic." And today, in unspoiled folk cultures, things happen in like manner: two young men are walking toward a town in the evening, talking about love—and suddenly, without warning, without the slightest preliminary hallucination which would transfigure reality and make it accessible to miraculous events (as in Edgar Allan Poe), there intrudes the fantastic: the devil, a vampire, or whatever. The same concept, moreover, dominates Romantic literature, where a Peter Schlemihl suddenly meets with the "fantastic" without the reality of the world around him having been altered; or in *La peau de chagrin*, where Balzac begins and ends the story in a realistic manner, that wild ass's hide being found in an antiquary's shop (described very precisely, without any "transfigurations") and the hero continuing to experience real, nonhallucinatory events. When I wrote *Domnişoara Christina*, the critics judged it a failure precisely on account of its "realism," forgetting that this concept of the fantastic which intervenes directly and vertically into reality without transfiguring it, is an old "popular" conception; forgetting all about Peter Schlemihl, *La peau de chagrin*, and the whole Romantic fantastic literature.

With regard to Tintoretto—as well as to the other order of ideas—it is remarkable how much importance this genius of a painter accords to the *higher planes*. Up above, over the heads of the people, is where the true drama takes place; from there descends the whole significance of the scene. Those angels, holy gods, come from above in order to *transfigure* reality below, to annul proportions, shadows, weights. Take for example the angel in the altarpiece of St. Ursula (unseen by the people); the angels in "The Birth of John the Baptist" (unseen by the women); the angel who encourages St. Rocco (seen only by the saint). When St. Anthony, tempted by demon-women, calls on Jesus for help, the Savior descends, as does St. Mark, but this time Anthony sees him, but not the demons, because they are "people" here. In a great many of Tintoretto's paintings, the drama is located above, on high: the lightning that falls after the martyrdom of St. Mark ("The Theft of the Body of St. Mark"); the inanimate body of the saint in the higher register ("The Invention of the Body of St. Mark"); the rain of gold (Danae, the slave girl who stares upward, from whence the money is falling, and Danoe, who gazes at her, slightly aroused, sensing the erotic valence of the gold); the high steps on which the Virgin Mary climbs to the temple, the chief priest who waits for her there, at the top, seemingly preparing her apotheosis (because temple = mountain = center of the world, and whoever attains the highest terrace of the temple goes out of the "world," out of history).

Papini and Other Confessions
The blue covers of the first volume of *Storia della letteratura italiana* by Giovanni Papini greet me serenely, triumphantly in the windows of all the bookstores. A flood of memories: my first Italian readings in my attic on strada Melodiei, deciphering with the dictionary *Il tragico cotidiano* which I had found, tattered, in an antique shop. And the discovery that I made then: that you don't learn a language unless you love an author intensely. And the sadness, several years later, that I had read and reread Papini's entire *oeuvre*, and that there was nothing else of his left for me to read.

With difficulty I forget, especially here at Venice, that I too am a writer. I think sometimes that perhaps someone, just one youth, is following my writing with the same burning passion with which I have sought and read Papini's *oeuvre* for ten years. Even when his ideas failed to convince me, even when his poems failed to move me, I read him with the same joy, the same curiosity; there was not a new book of his I didn't buy the moment I found it in a window, and none I didn't read in a gulp that same night. It has been many years now since I realized Papini is not the great writer I had imagined him to be, that a good part of his *oeuvre* will not withstand the test of time. But my love, my curiosity, and passion for his writing and his life have remained intact. I'm interested in absolutely all he does, all he thinks, all he writes. I admire him and accept him *in his entirety*—and I don't believe there is any homage that pleases a writer more than this.

Those readers who know by heart a single book of mine, who have wept and dreamed on its pages, don't interest me. I don't feel that the person who has chosen certain of my writings, despising or ignoring the rest, is a friend. And if I was a little sad this year, perhaps my good friends bear a part of the blame—those good friends who consider me only an author or only a "thinker," who split up my writing, passing indulgently over the "erudition" and "culture" (as if I weren't capable of writing a single page of "erudition"; as if I weren't myself, whole, even on a page laden with notes and disfigured with Oriental terminology!).

I'm not interested in the total admiration of a person. What I am interested in is his *curiosity*, which requires him to be just as broad as I. A curiosity robust enough, at any rate, to be able to follow me in all I do and think—even if he criticizes me and rejects me in places.

Who can say he understands Laurence Sterne if he has not read his theological and moral preachments? How much has a reader assimilated of Samuel Butler if he contents himself with his novel and his *Note-books*, ignoring his treatises on biological philosophy, his pages on Haydn, and his theory about the *female* author of the *Odyssey?*

To a zealous reader of my literary works, I prefer the lucid but curious one, whom no erudite adventure terrifies, whom no abstract periplus wearies. A reader curious, young, enthusiastic—how often do I dream with him in mind, how many books have I addressed to him alone, like a long friendly letter!

Fragment

The train stops at Verona. And then at many stations, at which young couples get off, with suitcases, ready to spend a vacation by themselves. There are so many towns, so many villages, in which every house is guarded by a cypress or an elm. Oh, to be able to stay here a whole summer, near Verona, to forget all the bad literature you were forced to read in adolescence—and to leave the house every morning with a volume of Dante or Petrarch under your arm!

Milan

In the evening, seeking a cheap tavern, we walk along the street that runs from the Dome to the illuminated fountain. Tired, we sit on a bench, very near the entrance to the Opera House.

Group after group of excited people pass by, and we turn to look at the enormous signboard: *Madama Butterfly*. Trams stop a few meters opposite us, and the passengers seemingly pour out in torrents. The cries of the program-vendors seem desperate, frightened. In another five minutes this human river will have flowed past, and they will be left with bundles of programs under their arms. I seem to begin to detect in their cries a sadder, more discouraged note than their words and strident voices reveal.

A young woman walks past us, trying in vain to control her impatience. She is dressed in white; ordinary features—common, honest cheeks; enveloped in a sweetish cloud of cheap perfume. So many people are passing that she doesn't suspect that she could be noticed, that anyone could be following the movements of her hand as she passes it again and again over her handbag, her fingers sometimes clenched, sometimes relaxed. Now and then the wind is stronger than the force of the artesian spring in the fountain, and the spray is blown toward the woman, sprinkling her hat and her handbag of black patent leather. Her attempts to defend herself are truly pitiful. With her left arm lifted obliquely she tries to cover her head, and with her right she clutches the purse to her breast. But she moves only a few steps away from the fountain. Here, undoubtedly, is the place of the rendezvous. Here the lights are brightest. And perhaps at the very moment she took refuge on the sidewalk, in the shadow, her sweetheart would pass by the fountain, hurriedly, without seeing her.

Only a few people are left outside now. A couple are arguing vehemently, walking away from the ticket office. The woman tries several times to pull free, to save herself—but the man has seized her arm and is gripping it savagely. It seems that a tragedy will begin at any moment. The woman struggles, but without raising her voice. The man grips her arm harder and whispers something gruffly in her ear. Still arguing, they pass by the traffic policeman, who regards them questioningly, puzzled, as he stops a whole line of cars with his arm.

I have time to glimpse once more the pale face of the girl dressed in white, before she decides finally not to wait any longer. She starts toward the entrance with a brisk, automatic gait, without looking back at the fountain.

Berne
A remarkable discovery today in the window of a toyshop. Not only lead soldiers of all sizes and poses—but also a large number of tanks. Some of them are quite realistic, with machine guns in the turret and

wheels encircled with tracks. Locomotives are no longer in fashion today, in children's toys—not even in Switzerland.

Portrait

Lucian Blaga, at his pension at Riedweg 17, points out to me, in the
dining room, an elderly Swiss woman who is eating alone. Obese,
with puffy cheeks and gray hair. She smiles sometimes, involuntarily,
through a simple memory of the muscles. She has been senile for
many years, he tells me. Her guardians pay the pension and leave her
only a few francs spending money a day, exactly enough for her to
take coffee with cream at the most beautiful restaurant in Berne every
afternoon.

She is the first to come to the table, always. And she eats in a
frenzy, perspiring, without looking up from the plate. She speaks
with none and recognizes almost no one. And yet this total stupidity
has not robbed her of the charm of the gentle femininity of an indul-
gent and wise grandmother. Her adherence to biology, her ravenous
hunger, has saved her.

Fragment

I return to our room late at night after long walks and wonderful conversations with Lucian Blaga. How much I admire his courage, his
regal indifference to "specialists"!

Although I have a number of "discoveries" in mind, I lack the
courage to write them down and publish them, until I verify all the
data and consult all that has been written on the problem. In this way
I spend five or six years on a book of science which I ought to have
written in three months. The superstition of verifying everything,
of reading everything, of knowing everything that has been done before your work—as if all this could improve in some way your own
idea. . . .

But maybe it isn't just a superstition—the terror of "method," etc.
My passion for erudition means, perhaps, the passion of man for vanity, for worthless, ephemeral, minor aspects of life. Other men waste
time with small talk, insignificant adventures, sleep—while I waste
time on erudition. It is the same triumph of the futile and ephemeral,
the same participation in the somnolence and mediocrity of the human condition. When the instincts no longer succeed in putting a
man to sleep, in conjoining him with insignificant becoming, then the

abstract, noble passions come into play. Any kind of instrument serves equally well for the degradation of man, for bringing him down from his higher hours, for benumbing him in absurd passions for the insignificant and the perishable.

Isidora

Last summer, Isidora Blaga spent a whole month in a village in Transylvania. In a barn, a cow was about to give birth. Isidora, who was then six years old, went into the cowbarn alone to see if the calf had come. The cow rolled her big brown eyes toward her, staring in surprise.

"Maybe she thinks I'm her calf," Isidora said.

Old Women

Someone told me once—and I believe this is the unanimous opinion of all Romanians—that the most beautiful women in the world are to be seen in Bucharest. In Bucharest, as in other cities of Romania, the Balkans, and Eastern Europe in general, old women go about very little in public. You see them in limited numbers on the street, almost not at all on the trams, and extremely rarely in a tavern. This gives the impression of the youth, frivolity, and luxury of the "beautiful women" of Bucharest.

The old women of our cities stay in the courtyards, on the porches, or, at most, in front of the houses in the slum districts, seated on chairs. They have worked all their lives, and now, in old age, they are happy to be allowed to rest on a chair in the courtyard, watching life and the street through the fence. The last traces of the gynaeceum.

On the other hand, the farther west you go, the more you encounter elderly women. They too, have worked all their lives, but now that they have no more cares, they go out walking, they see the world—or at least they see the city in which they had all too little time to walk before they saw their sons espoused and married off their daughters. In Switzerland and Germany the parks are full of old women; and their drab clothing, of dull colors, gives an air of sadness and desolation to even the most splendid gardens. In England, the presence of old women can be overwhelming. The trains, ships, busses, "historic" churches, and art museums are full of elderly Englishwomen who cannot renounce life, who travel and learn and amuse themselves as they had no time to do in their youth. I shall not soon forget

those few hours I spent on the ship from Ostend to Dover, surrounded by a hundred elderly ladies, all lying on deck chairs, each
with her detective novel in one hand and a pack of cigarettes in the
other. Nor the ride from London to Oxford in a third-class compartment, elegant but "taken over" by an old woman with gray hair cut
pageboy style, who smoked one cigarette after another and talked,
trying to be coquettish, for three hours straight.

In this respect, at least, the East and Southeastern Europe are preferable to any "civilized" city.

Freiburg

We find ourselves suddenly in front of a cathedral, although we had
started down this little side street at random. There are ragged clouds
in the night sky, and from time to time gusts of wind whistle through
this wide square.

Am I imagining things, or do I indeed hear an organ and the faint
voices of a choir, rising and falling? And yet the cathedral is dark, inanimate. Slowly circling it, I keep hearing the same sombre sound of
an organ.

Rehearsals for a concert tomorrow evening, I am told at a nearby
tavern. We won't be able to hear it. But these fragments, half-scattered
by the wind, seem to me more sacred, more mysterious coming
through the night over the empty square. . . .

Frieburg

Long walnut boards nailed along the walls, deer antlers of all sizes
between mirrors, above coatracks, over paintings. And throughout
the tavern there hovers a strange odor, the smell of a German kitchen,
a clean house, wine. Now I realize the source of this emotion nourished by so many memories: there is a world from before the war
here. The world of German provincial beer halls in which professors
and pensioners meet in so many novels. And yet, the memories come
from even farther back: these men with thick, curled moustaches resemble my grandfather and my uncles. The same placidity of 1914, the
same easy humor, the same abundance. Their life, sheltered from
worries and tragedies, flowed precisely like the life of these men
around me, who eat their Praguer sausages and drink their Rhine
wine, without being aware of what's happening in the world, of
what's in the offing. . . .

Frieburg

I can hardly recognize the square now, in the daylight. It is full of booths where women sell vegetables and fruits.

We pay 15 pfennings to visit the cathedral. In our group are two old ladies who exclaim every time our guide (the sexton) mentions any "historic" name. Only after leaving the cathedral do I realize that I looked at them more than at the stained-glass windows. Two faces that remind me of the elderly sisters in the film, *Mr. Deeds Goes to Town*. I believe their delirium was this: they no longer reacted to anything but the sound of historical names, and then they reacted excessively, almost hysterically, as if their ruined femininity were trying to know for the last time ecstasy, stimulated by the glory of heroes and artists of other centuries. When the guide pronounced the name "Cranach," the old ladies sighed, choking, clasping their hands, wringing them. Probably Cranach was the famous person they had most recently come to respect, perhaps they had learned about him on this very trip—and the pronouncing of his name provoked the inevitable.

Titisee

How do you resist these children who ride their bicycles alongside the train, and signal to you with their hands, and shout and call out to you? The train seems to have an air of festivity, of vacation time, because the morning is clear, the valleys covered with firs echo with the shouts of hikers, and the tunnels are so close together that they seem to have been dug deliberately to make passing through them a game.

Almost half the passengers get off at Titisee. The lindens are still in bloom here. We all set off in the direction of the lake, on a broad road. Several Englishmen stop at a place where wooden canes are for sale, in tall woven baskets. They begin to make their selection, proceeding very seriously, very intently, almost respectfully. They test the cane, bending it, twirling it in the air, twisting the handle. Very close to us the fir forest begins. Borne by the wind from unknown corners, shouts and cries are heard.

Titisee

There is a large stone here, on the edge of the lake, half in the water and half on the beach. Couples come and climb on it, doing their best to keep their balance, holding hands, while a friend takes their picture. Scarcely can man get beyond the mystique of "the peculiar," the fear or admiration for a curious object which differs from others! Thousands of years ago such a stone would have been worshiped for its supposed magical or sacred virtues. It is too strange, too different from all the others, half in the water as it is. Today, "the peculiar" attracts the attention and devotion of people in another way: couples photograph one another, keeping their balance with difficulty on top of it, with their arms linked. The mystique—or, if you will, the magic—of the stone has remained the same.

Sigmaringen
Overcast sky. The princely castle dominates the wide valley in which the lindens still haven't shed their blossoms. How disquieting this small town is for a Romanian! I have the impression of having been here before, long ago, at the time of my first schoolbooks.

Two trains start out from the station at the same time, side by side. I am in the last car, and I can see the castle for a long time. In the other train, several girls are pressing their foreheads against the window and gaily shouting to the conductor to hurry, to get ahead of us. The two trains run alongside each other for almost two minutes. Then they separate dutifully, and the girls at the other window threaten us in jest and scold the conductor for letting them fall behind.

I don't understand the source from which there wells up suddenly in my soul such a great love of life, so much faith. The sky remains overcast.

Ulm
In our family album filled with picture postcards there was one I especially liked: the card with the cathedral at Ulm. I believe I fell in love at an early age with that medieval city, just because of the name. When I was six and promised myself I'd see the whole world, my mind focused first on Ulm.

And today, when I see it for the first time, memories come and go, melancholically. I think especially of my parents, who stopped in Ulm on their last trip abroad. I remember too the many afternoons I spent looking at the viewcards in that huge album with green covers which was kept on top of a little stand.

It is too late now to be able to walk along the streets, down to the

Danube. I enter a restaurant, full of soldiers, in the vicinity of the station. A three-man orchestra is trying to put some life into an exceptionally large room. Then the Kapellmeister announces to the audience the beginning of the cabaret numbers. A female vocalist appears, dressed in black, holding a red flower in one hand, and sings a love song. She is still young, and her voice is good enough. How has she ended up, so soon, in this provincial German beerhall? There is nothing tragic in her face or the timbre of her voice. She betrays no sadness, no melodrama, no destiny. A perfect inertia—even in the red flower which she brings to her lips as she thanks the audience for its applause.

Ulm
This cathedral—about which I have learned that it was begun in 1377 and was worked on, intermittently, until the sixteenth century, and was restored and completed in the nineteenth—is the tallest in the world. It has some of the most beautiful stained-glass windows in Germany. Even the modern ones are of a perfect purity and intensity—as if they had been made by Adrian Douglas in Ronald Fraser's novel, *Marriage in Heaven*. In particular, the blue windows on the right side of the altar resemble closely those of Adrian Douglas. And he would have enjoyed working here alongside the many Dantesque heads of medieval knights and bishops, all sculpted from severe, opaque stone. The paintings of Schaffners, especially "St. Elisabeth of Thuringia," would have shown him the secret of combining a dead purple with a dusty gold.

On the vestments of the bishops: stylized oak branches, leaves, stems, and flowers. The same motif of the "tree of life," which one can sometimes discern intact beneath the floral fantasies that cover it. With what strength this symbol persists: the tree of life, the tree of immortality, of good and evil! See it here, on an altar door, in a famous cathedral—after it had adorned thousands of Mesopotamian bas reliefs, after it had given birth to Asiatic decorative designs from the Caspian Sea to China and Siberia! The tree of life emerged long ago from the biblical framework. It has been transformed now into oceanographic trees, with long entwining stems like those of an underwater plant. It has become a common ornament in the baroque style, sometimes suffocated by a recent inspiration, and it has been preserved in ceramics studios of the last century, rising up sometimes on dessert plates. . . .

What a long life a symbol has!

The Unicorn

Look! On the left door of the altar, between trefoils and dancing flowers—there bursts forth a winged horse with a single horn on his forehead: my precious unicorn! If I hadn't read recently a whole book about the legends and symbols connected with this unicorn—in the Orient, the classical cultures, and Christianity—I might have passed over this door without noticing it. But *The Lore of the Unicorn* by Odell Shepard was one of the most fascinating books I've read in the past year. From whence comes this symbol so rich in meanings, found in China, Mesopotamia, and the Near East? Pliny and Aelian considered the unicorn an emblem of solitude. In pre-Christian times it was the symbol of sovereignty. Christianity transformed its pagan significance and sanctified it: the unicorn became, in turn, the symbol of monastic life (pagan solitude), of Christ, and later the emblem of the Holy Virgin. Medieval legend said that the unicorn could not be caught by man or touched by a weapon. This wild animal which loves solitude and purity, comes at night to a spring and sticks his horn in the water. If someone has poisoned the water, he makes it safe to drink for the other beasts of the forest. (For that reason, in the Middle Ages, cups for tasting poisoned drinks were made from horns alleged to be those of unicorns.) The most beautiful unicorn I have ever seen is the one kneeling at the feet of St. Justina in a painting by Moretto (1530) in Galerie Belvedere, Vienna. It is white, serene, noble. And it has a precise significance, because, say the legends, the unicorn cannot be tamed save by the presence of a virgin. If, when it comes to drink at a spring, it finds there a chaste girl, it approaches her and falls asleep with its head on her lap. Then the hunters come and lead it with pomp to the court of the king (a scene shown often in medieval miniatures).

Odell Shepard proposes eight hypotheses to explain the origin of the legend of this splendid animal. It would not be at all hard to find others. Worthless hypotheses, in my opinion. Symbols aren't born as simply as that. And neither do they perish, ever, no matter how skeptical and superficial men become.

Ulm

The Danube is turbid as it passes here. Only under the bridge, around the piers, where the water eddies, does it become clearer. We walk a long while on the river bank, below the city wall. On our left the battlements and terraces of reddish and golden-brown stone rise up.

I try in vain to catch the images precisely. I haven't the eye—or the mind—of a sketch artist. I don't differentiate, don't measure, don't compare. My visual memory does not even retain lines and forms— only colors. I'm like this Danube flowing beside me: turbid, pellucid only in spots—where it is cleft by the piers of stone underneath the bridge.

I'm not at all like the city on my left, the harmonious city in which so many forms are set side by side without running together. And yet, how melancholic I feel as I gaze at that paradise of facades and roof-tops, of which I shall retain, a few moments from now, only the colors!

And how sad I always feel watching a swimmer—that body "which becomes night in the amorphous mass of water" (Eugenio d'Ors) without losing its autonomy, rhythm, or spontaneity. I have never been a good swimmer. Water fascinates me, fatigues me, assimilates me. Its massive and totalitarian rhythms resemble my own rhythms so closely that it affords me no resistance. I can't distinguish myself from the water. At best, I can drown. . . .

Dialogue

I reread the page above. I reread it after finishing just now a letter to C. N. In this restaurant dining room, with so many honest smells which enable you to reconstitute the menus, to classify and judge them—I'd be dishonest if I let myself be satisfied with a mere for-mula. A self-portrait made in *plein-air* will not resemble one drawn indoors. Here, everything pushes me into controversy, dialogue.

Perhaps, I do not, indeed, possess an aquatic nature, as I re-discovered (for the nth time) this morning. It's true, I'm a mediocre swimmer. And I have just as mediocre a memory for shapes and masses. But maybe it's because none of these interests me as a reality of the first order. Like all European nationalists, I don't believe that form, line, and proportion are the only categories of culture. Beyond these worlds of forms—which fascinate a Paul Valéry, a Eugenio d'Ors—there exists a "purer" world of a more stark spirituality, *the world of symbol.* My eye, which cannot retain for long the *design,* quickly seeks and discovers back of the forms and lines—the *symbol.*

I don't know who divided the field of vision into "design" and "landscape." I believe, however, that this visual field is pierced and impaired by the amazing intervention of the symbol, of transcendental meaning, which dissolves a landscape in the crown of the tree of life, and shatters the economy of a design in order to single out a cross, a spiral, or a vortex.

It is impossible for me to preserve intact the precise image of this marvelous medieval city of Ulm. But in a great many places I have seen, stifled, the spiral—ancient symbol of the center—surviving today as a simple decorative motif, without anyone's understanding its meaning.

Heidelberg

In a preliminary stroll around the city before nightfall, we discover new neighborhoods with almost modern houses, and we walk along the "Philosophers' Lane." Here, C. N. could saunter every evening, meditating. Perhaps he would stop at this tavern, leaning against this ivy-covered wall, or resting on the bench beside it. Another twenty steps and one sees again, through the trees, the Neckar flowing in the valley.

On this Philosophers' Lane C. N. would feel conjoined with a long and glorious effort to achieve knowledge and wisdom. He, who loves norms so much that he sacrifices gladly the only precious thing youth possesses—spontaneity—would regain here his creativity and melancholy among these many shadows and philosophies. Actually, he's right. If one reads more profitably in a rich library and learns horseback riding better at a riding school, why wouldn't one think with more precision and responsibility in a "Philosophers' Lane"? This location, in all probability, has not been chosen at random. Everything here conduces to meditation, to concentrated interiorization, to sobriety. Everything: the environs, the prestige, the memory. . . .

There are all kinds of geographies in the world. There are islands that reveal the meaning of Paradise; there are others that raise vice and orgy to the rank of necessity and the dignity of categories. Everything collaborates, in such a venereal geography, to the dissolution of your being in vice, despair, and dream: everything—from a too-hot sun to flowers of noxious beauty, from ultrasoft vowels to a too-broad culture, in which mysticism can become physiology and vice-versa. In a venereal geography, the evanescence and dissolution of your being have the necessity of a destiny and the significance of a metaphysical concept. Because, you are not simply annihilated by events, as a man is annihilated in Bucharest: drinking, sleeping, making love, forgetting himself. You are annihilated "with meaning"; you are destroyed because the unworthiness of the human condition has been demonstrated to you; your life is taken away to keep you from ascribing value to it. Every spiritual geography is a lesson, an instruction. Whether it opens for you a gate to Paradise—through colors, the density of the sky, the purity of the air—or whether it puts at your disposal the enchanted barque of loss of self—the *lesson* remains the same. From the myriad landscapes—as many as exist on the face of the earth—a few, a dozen, a hundred are detached and become, in certain circumstances, *revelations*. At Bethel Jacob slept with a stone at his head and he dreamed of a ladder to heaven, on which angels were ascending and descending. That place was *sacred*, in the sense that it had ceased to be "landscape," it had been separated from the laws of space; it had become the "gate of Heaven," a mystical zone, the only one in which man can *see God*, in which he can endure the Revelation.

There are other places on earth where you are forced to sense and think about the aesthetic, which only then reveals itself to you as a category of the real. Spiritual geography differs from concrete geography precisely through this transfiguration of the landscape, through its transformation into category, into call, into instrument of revelation.

In Heidelberg, the landscape suddenly ceases to be itself, becoming in this shady area a "philosophers' lane." Anyone who doesn't feel obligated to walk here, meditating solemnly and academically, doesn't have the vocation of philosopher.

"The Red Ox"

After getting directions, we set off for the famous student beerhouse "The Red Ox." We arrive too early. At the wooden tables—long, old, badly scarred, with rickety benches along the sides—there are seated only a few soldiers, intimidated by the collegiate tradition of the place. The windows are still open; night has barely begun to fall—a peaceful summer's eve.

The walls of the room are covered with all sorts of signs and posters, partly pulled off and pasted over by several generations of students.

The posters hang from the walls, the ceiling; crowded together, one atop another; with no order, no plan. Tattered posters, their paper yellowed, printed in old-fashioned letters, bring back memories of the 1880s. Also a great many photographs are on the walls: groups of students with peaked hats, lightly tinted by the photographer, holding full glasses and steins of beer. The oldest photographs are almost faded out; the faces of the students of 1870 can scarcely be seen any longer. Only their muttonchops and thick moustaches allow you to identify their era. Each one is carrying a placard indicating by arrows and block letters where he will spend the rest of his life: New York, Stockholm, St. Petersburg. In other photographs, friends gaze at one another pensively, each seated on his valise, resting his chin on his fist. Their student caps are set at a less rakish angle, still leaving the forehead uncovered, but not revealing shocks of wavy hair beneath the bills. You imagine that these caps, which up to now have lived a life of adventure, are preparing to enter into memory, to detach themselves from life, to be hereafter invested with the prestige of souvenirs.

The Engaged Couple
After making a quiet entrance, a young German couple have seated themselves unobtrusively at our table. Like the soldiers who were here when we arrived, they too are intimidated by the collegiate anarchy and intellect of the atmosphere.

They have asked for wine, and are drinking it with the grace of adolescents. Neither of them is particularly good-looking. But they are engaged, and timidity transfigures this future bearer of babies and this polite athletic type with shaved neck. I know very well the source of the bewilderment and tragic hesitation of these angels forced to eat from plates. Their embarrassment is neither sentimental nor erotic. These two young people sit facing each other, silent, smiling— without suspecting the personal apocalypse that awaits them. Two creatures, two separate *natures*—and they, poor souls, believe that it will be easy for them to live together. Two people cannot live together without being turned into demons, or else having their beings enhanced with angelic substance. Man does not remain *man* except in isolation.

Living together with another person leads man, *of necessity*, to an angelic or demonic level. In most instances, the first meeting of the two natures is "possessed"; if the love isn't strong enough for you to feel secure in *giving* yourself, the opposite ordinarily happens: you try to merge the other person into yourself, to absorb the other after first having decomposed him or her.

Actually, for the man who has ceased to be alone, there remains only one path to salvation: *to give himself wholly,* without reserve. This, at least, preserves him on an angelic plane (not in the metaphysical sense of the word, but in the moral-ascetic sense: the angel does not have instincts, is no longer selfish). Because, if he doesn't do all in his power to give himself—he is *taken,* he is decomposed by the demonic presence of the other, he is absorbed in an almost physical way, without dignity, without glory. While if his demon is the stronger, and he succeeds in *taking* instead of being taken, the result is the same: decomposition.

Hence, the bewilderment and hesitation of the engaged couple at our table. This state of unnatural suspension in timidity foreshadows the conflict that could come. The two beings, the two "natures," stand face to face in unknown depths, awaiting the struggle. The young people are far from suspecting the destiny that can rapidly turn them into angels or devils. The girl has finished half her glass of Rhine wine. She smiles, flushing.

Americans at Heidelberg

In a little while, the room has become too small. It has been invaded in the past fifteen minutes by several students, a brave businessman, an English family, and then by two touring groups of American girls with their guides and several older ladies. The wooden benches are all occupied, down to the last space. The occupants are all persons of limited means—students, ballet dancers, functionaries—traveling on limited funds. They drink only beer, and they order it only after asking the price and converting the amount into dollars. All are smoking cigarettes, and because they are at Heidelberg they amuse themselves like students.

Who gave the signal? When did that tall, dark, attractive young man with the harmonica and student cap come in? At first, the group of local students, crowded in one corner, sang choruses they didn't know very well. They laughed first, hoping the others would laugh too, and join in the singing. Then the American girls began—old songs, perfumed with the memory of the first "talkies," well-known love songs, amazing for their frank vulgarity. And then, suddenly, the whole room was in commotion: strangers talking to one another across the tables, newcomers being greeted with shouts. The windows were shut tight, and with great spontaneity the youth next to me began throwing cardboard and cork coasters at the most innocent caps.

The student with the harmonica walked among the tables, moving with difficulty, accompanying the song begun by a group of friends in the back, grinning in surprise whenever he encountered along his way another song, started on other initiatives. We thanked God in our minds that he had sent us a whole crowd of non-wealthy American tourists. We might have run into a group of Englishwomen—those awkward, overly-spontaneous Englishwomen, such as I have met frequently in my travels. They would have tried to amuse themselves just as noisily in Heidelberg—but with disastrous results. And this glorious student gathering, instead of being, as it was now, alive with youth and beauty, would have been frozen between steins of beer and lighted cigarettes.

They have a wonderful candor—all these girls who think it's smart not to understand German. And their beauty is truly amazing, as is also their nobility—although, probably, they are only daughters of grocers and workingmen. But how magnificent is the triumph of the prestige of culture and tradition! How quickly they have become "students," and how sincerely they have respected the unwritten law of this university city—to sing, drink beer, and "have a good time"! Probably, the barbarians behaved the same way at Rome, when they got drunk on wine they didn't like, cheered enthusiastically at games they didn't understand, and bought sandals that hurt their heels.

And these girls have an odd, barbarian beauty. Shut your eyes a little while and think: don't you see in that blonde with the large, unspiritual eyes a paleo-Scandinavian who finds herself, by some miracle, within the walls of Rome? Mark well how she drinks her beer. She has drunk, undoubtedly, plenty of beer in her own country. But now she's at Heidelberg, and she sips from her stein as if it were a magic cup. All these girls are enchanted. They became "merry" the minute they entered the magic circle of culture and tradition. A little longer, and they'll understand the first act of Faust. But only the first act. . . .

De praestigiis daemonum

We visit the old university. In our group: an elderly professor from across the ocean, with his family—the wife, a daughter suffering from astigmatism, and a retarded son, the innocent victim of syphilis or parental debility. The poor child, with monstrous shoulders, misshapen face, lifeless hands, and the dull eyes of an idiot, has been brought along on this vacation trip, because, probably, the parents couldn't bear to leave him in an asylum in America.

The old professor is still rather vigorous, and he is, it seems, a student of political science. He is the only one in the group who asks any questions. The guide—at first, a female student, then some sort of assistant—speaks in English, mainly for his benefit.

The first thing shown us is the student jail. Two or three rooms, each with an army cot and no sheets, in which student brawlers used to serve their sentences. In order to make the time pass faster, they drew their portraits on the wall, using a mixture of bread crumbs and ink; they wrote elegies, curses, and funereal inscriptions; they even signed their names, in order to participate in the glory of the disorder. When they were released, the other students made a great demonstration of sympathy, parading them in triumph through the streets of the whole city. Since these occasions of triumph and organized drunkenness didn't happen too often, the students were careful to space out their periods of incarceration, in order to be sure of having times to celebrate.

I must acknowledge that there is nothing stronger in this world than the glory of disorder. This jail is not admired for the tradition of university discipline is represents, for the nostalgia everyone knows is connected with Heidelberg, or for its historical or caricatural curiosities. The "popularity" of the student stockade is explained by the prestige enjoyed, especially today, by the Demon, the spirit of anarchic freedom, reckless courage, juvenile rebelliousness, arrogance, insurrection, and *je-m'en-fichisme*. Laughing heartily at the jokes of some intelligent students, we admire not only this jail—which by the way is painted with much imagination and good humor—but we admire any anarchic initiative. The prestige of the demon has overtaken even countries of great and ancient culture. We Romanians admire Domnul Gol ("Mr. Emptiness") because he is clever, but we admire even more the young man who thumbs his nose, laughs at his professors, plays hooky, breaks off five engagements, doesn't pay his rent, and doesn't keep his word. And perhaps it is an exaggeration to say that only we Romanians do this. Everywhere disorder is "popular" and fascinating. Maybe we applaud the adventure of the anarchic youth because we ourselves could never do such a thing. When you hear about a boy who has deceived a girl, has broken his promise, and run away when he was in a predicament—you applaud, either because at the bottom of your heart you envy him ("he was smart"), or because you're ashamed to protest. *You are ashamed to seem to be moral,* even if you live, in fact, a morally serious life. However paradoxical it may seem, morality has no prestige.

A man who is decent, good, clever, etc. exercises no "magic." Moral perfection brings you no comrades, not even any "admirers." (This is probably the destiny of living a moral life: to live alone.) However, it is enough for the news of your "anarchy" to leak out, and you find obstacles falling before you, you sense the admiration of others directed toward you.

It is purely and simply a matter of prestige. That is, in a word, of *magic*. Any anarchic act fascinates, amazes, attracts. This is true everywhere in the order of reality. Nothing attracts us, nothing interests us, nothing holds sway over us—but that which differs from the rest, even if it is only a matter of an accident.

One can't resist the prestige of the demon. Every man carries around inside him millions of repressed acts of liberty and libertinism. How could we fail to admire someone who has had the "luck" or the "courage" to carry them out? But, let us suppose that you have so perfected yourself that you no longer live under the terror of repressed freedoms. You live, nevertheless, under the blackmail of intelligence. Again, the demon has a perfect technique: he can easily persuade you that the anarchic act is, by the same token, a victory of "personality" over the "law of the herd," or a revolt of fantasy against bourgeois morals, and so on. And because you believe in your prestige as a free and intelligent man—you let yourself be persuaded. Without realizing you are "under a spell," you too become a victim of that formidable, luciferic *prestige*.

Fragment
The man who has not been seriously concerned, at least once in his life, with theological problems, is irremediably mediocre. From a man's reactions to theology you can gauge his spiritual dimensions. There is

nothing more depressing, nothing more alarming, in the present condition of the West, than the "triumph of intelligence" over theology. (Actually, of course, it is more a matter of the triumph of the clever man over the thinker.) Of all the depressing spectacles I've witnessed in my lifetime, nothing has distressed me more than the "intelligent" observations of a friend at the start of a theological conversation.

One is ready to believe that the contemporary man has deteriorated irremediably, and that no historical power can regenerate him and restore his lost dignity.

The more that theological problematics is ignored or demeaned in a culture, the more its spiritual level is lowered. There have been times in modern Romania when it was so shameful to pronounce the word "theology" that even the clergy avoided it. People talked then about "force and matter," "moral energy," and the "ideal." Those were the years of the lowest spiritual level our unfortunate modern culture has known. The spiritual sterility of America, its overwhelming vulgarity, goes hand in hand with the secularization of theology, with the transformation of a stunning system of metaphysics and Revelation into innumerable systems of ethics, hygiene, social policies, birth control, etc.

But, at the same time, how true is the obverse of the coin! How irremediably mediocre is the man who has never in his life known melancholy! Who has known only the feminine sadness of memories, or sentimental Moldavian nostalgia; who has lamented that he was no longer seventeen, or wept on finding a flower pressed in a book many autumns ago. . . . Not in these tears and nostalgias is melancholy revealed. Melancholy, a major instrument of cognition, the only one capable of disturbing and shaking the imperialistic security of theology. . . .

French Students at Heidelberg

On the way back to our room last evening, passing along a main street, we meet two girls, French students, arm in arm, bareheaded and wearing shorts, walking boyishly and humming a merry tune. They belong, no doubt, to the group of French students who have come to take courses at Heidelberg. But it is amazing to discover, suddenly, how much the street has been changed by their passing. They are a "hit," an "instant sensation." These placid Germans smile at one another, as if they consider themselves fortunate to have witnessed such a spectacle. The women, especially, are moved, following with their eyes the nimble, skipping step of the two French girls with bare knees. And they can't keep from exclaiming to us—with maternal admiration, but also with a note of regret—"Those French! Those Parisians!"

This reminds me of what happened last summer at the Berlin Olympics: the spontaneous enthusiasm that greeted the French athletes, the total admiration for their jokes, their "manners," their jerseys and berets. There were spontaneous demonstrations of Teutonic enthusiasm whenever a bus carrying French athletes passed on the street. Undoubtedly, this is no chance happening. Germans, despite the frantic pride of their race, suffer from a curious inferiority complex when it comes to the French. The admiration the great German creators have always shown for the French genius is shared fully by the man in the street. Of course, this admiration is manifest in complex and diverse ways, according to circumstances. "Good soldiers, those French!" the German businessman who fought in the war tells you. "*Dass war etwas* prima!" the young couple recalls who visited Paris. And the one who knows a poem by Lafontaine, learned in school, recites it for you. In a sense, it is a title of glory for him to be able to do it, and he realizes it.

Such incidents reassure you. You realize that the whole of Europe is nothing but the result of the jealousy, confrontation, and collaboration—willing or unwilling—of these two great stems, the Germans and the Latins. The Germans' sentiment of inferiority toward the French has nothing degrading about it; it is not the repression of an envy or a fear, as are the inferiority complexes of the colored races in a state of slavery or semislavery. Rather, it is the permanent homage which the Germans make to qualities they do not now possess or have never possessed: grace, casualness, irony, the freedom to be frivolous.

Neckarstein

Almost three hours by boat on the Neckar. As soon as we leave Heidelberg the landscape begins to change. The vault of the heaven seems to enlarge, the hills recede. But there's something else: the resonance in the air over the valley, a resonance that grows increasingly clearer. It reminds me of a certain piece of Grieg's—because musicians, too, as someone has rightly said, have their landscapes. And perhaps something more: the work of each of them preserves a hidden correspondence with the hours of the day. Why is it always morning when you hear Grieg's "Lyrische Stüke"?

We get off at the dock and proceed immediately into the forest, toward the ruined castle. We ascend a well-graveled lane; the last building is a shed, from back of which comes the muffled whine of a buzz saw. The forest is dense now. Ten steps more and everything is swallowed up; the whir of the saw can scarcely be heard. A quarter of an hour further on, following first one path and then another, we come to a "private" lane. We set off toward a different part of the forest. And suddenly, without any warning—the ruins of the castle. The weeds and ivy have grown vigorously on the heaps of rubble and stone. For a moment I have the impression that these ruins are completely ravaged. But soon I discover a few benches, well-hidden under the leafy boughs. A couple is resting on one of them, looking rather solemn. On a wall, a woman of indefinite age, frowning in concentration, is focusing a camera, holding it to her chest. The ruins are abandoned to the vegetation, in order not to spoil the landscape. But tourists are also taken into account. The benches are skillfully distributed; no matter where you look, you see no more than one at a time, well-camouflaged. I write this without any irony. In this way, the castle retains the melancholy of its solitude. On the walls, the boulders, the ruins—no one is now to be seen. (The benches are out of sight.) You understand better the melancholy of these stones, which ceased to live several hundred years ago. The structure returns to its primordial condition: stone, the mineral matrix.

Stones and Death

This reminds me of an old aphorism which I've never had the courage to pronounce. There is only one form of "death" known to the mineral kingdom: to be removed from the telluric matrix and integrated into a structure devised by the spirit of man. Stones displaced in this way from their natural mode of being begin to participate in a new destiny: that of the human condition—tragic, mortal, ephemeral. A block of stone dislodged from a city wall and fallen into the valley, stays there, "dead." It is out of place there; it was not born and did not grow in that landscape. It succeeded in being animated by another life, a spiritual one, only so long as it remained integrated in a structure. Amorphous in itself, the block of stone participated then in a form. Placed by the hand of man in one way or another, it became transparent and alive—because a building reflects a whole cosmology.

This condition, noble but unnatural, is certainly an ephemeral one for the stone. Once it *says* something which was not implied in its mode of being, it falls under the law of time. And when the living body of the building is shattered, the stones cannot return to their prior forms (the telluric matrix, the landscape). They die, then, the same debased death as that of the great majority of men. Actually, to carry my thought to its conclusion, what man does in building something of stone constitutes a *temptation* for the mineral kingdom. He wants to modify the mode of life and expression of minerals and stones, and he succeeds. A rock in its native environment *says* something; squared or rounded, in a building or a wall, it says something utterly different. In the latter case it participates in the expression of ideas, norms. It lives more intensely and speaks more precisely—but it does so *temporarily*, because the work of man's hands knows death. I believe further that one could attempt a comparison between this temptation of the mineral kingdom by man, and the temptation of the latter by Lucifer—but we have gone far enough. One thing is certain: any temptation changes and "ennobles" the natural mode of being . . . but at a price!

Ferns
We can see from here the Neckar, looking very silvery in the valley far below. We can distinguish easily the ship on the run to Heidelberg. Somewhat farther upstream a dredge is about to begin work, dragging its scoop along the bottom of the river.

We return to the forest. And because it is still too early to go back to the dock, we sit down on the edge of the path. Time passes slowly, without any spurts. I discover close by me great bunches of ferns. Perhaps I'm obsessed by my most recent readings in folklore, or maybe it's only a fancy—but these ferns suddenly absorb my attention, like something miraculous, full of mystery. I can't get it out of my mind that the seeds of a fern—according to Germanic beliefs, especially— make man invisible. The seed of a certain fern, collected in the proper way—on a certain night, with a certain ritual—was enough to enable the hero in a legend to make himself invisible at will.

I look at these ferns with some suspicion, smiling. I have the impression that they're concealing something, that there resides within them, unused, a strange power which no one knows how to appropriate. A light breeze is blowing in the direction of the river, and the intricately laced leaves tremble. Are they answering my doubts? I spy a black worm twisting and turning at the root of the fern. By remaining still for a long time with my eyes close to the ground, I find the space around the ferns beginning to change. A whole world comes to life, acquiring depth and proportion. And the fern, with its impenetrable, well-hidden secrets trembles with infinite grace.

Once I spent several nights in a row observing closely an ivy-covered wall. I had learned the ancient mythology of those plants, and I came every night to probe into it. What if those fantastic beliefs, buried today in antique tomes, were true? I asked this of myself hesitantly, somewhat in jest. Not long before I had seen a film about vampires, and I had been troubled by the remark of the doctor in the film: "This is the luck of the vampires, that no one believes in them any more!" What if all those *powers* that once upon a time terrified the mind and soul of man, and in which almost no one in our day believes, still continue their magic, unbeknown to anyone, in a world hermetically sealed?

Mainz

From Heidelberg to Mainz—about two hours by train. We arrive in time to catch the boat that cruises along the Rhine. We pass through the little city without seeing much of anything except the old black cathedral, from whose lacy pinnacles eyes continually look down on you. An endless promenade, lined with evenly spaced linden trees, runs along the riverbank. The water here no longer has the green-gold color sung about in ballads. A huge bridge in the middle of the city links the two banks. Ships and barges pass by quietly, without haste.

Our boat, which will take us to Cologne, delays its departure for several minutes because another, full of Italian students, is approaching the landing. The noisy and restless excursionists can be clearly seen. At the moment their boat docks, they burst out with "Giovinezza!" Several thousand people are waiting there to welcome them. Hundreds of children from the *Hitlerjugend*, with their blond heads, easily sunburned, are milling around. Someone begins to speak. We can't hear him. Our boat pulls away with surprising speed, and without getting too far from the bank it makes for the big bridge. Its movement is rapid, despite the deceitfully weary-sounding engine. We pass the principal bridge and then we meet another, connecting with an enormous, wooded island.

Rheingau

In this part of the river we are continually coming upon large, green islands, with ancient trees that cast reflections on the water's surface. We are in the famous Rheingau. The vineyards here, spreading out as far as we can see, conform to the caprices of the terrain: the depths, the curves, etc., then climb the folds of the gently sloping hillsides, as though happy to be able to respect, at least some of the time, the Germanic spirit of order. There, on the right, is Eltville, with romantic ruins on the heights behind the town. Beside it, almost adjacent, is Erbach; and in the background, on the mountain, lies Raumental. Here in the Rheingau, the best Rhine wines are made, we are told: merely looking at these sunny banks makes us want to taste them. One becomes euphoric just listening to their names and hearing about their pale gold color, their marvelous sparkle, and the long-stemmed glasses in which they are served. Everything here partakes of a definite and very discreet delirium of light colors and blond nuances. The grain in sheaves along the riverbanks, the stems of the vines, and the gentle sunlight (although this is the middle of summer) promote the same noble, fertile, and nevertheless gracious color: yellow.

Suddenly I feel a solidarity with this region of blond glories, where even the wine from the glass sparkles golden and clear, discreetly assuring you that the toxins have been purged along with every other noxious, opaque mineral residue. Everything is *European* in the valley of the Rhine, standing under the sign of gold. For once I have escaped from the obsession with dark, barbarous, mineralized hues. I recall that ten years or so ago I published an article, "Fragment monden" [in *Cuvântul*, October 11, 1928] in which I confessed wonder that European style and taste promote a tyranny of black and shades of brown. These dark colors demonstrate once again how powerful the non-European barbarian influences are—because Europe has always sung the praises of "la Dame Blanche," "Donna Bianca," and "Blanchefleure." Jazz, the snobbish fashion of Negro art, Expressionism, and solar heresies have promoted dark, opaque, mineralized skin as the new prototype of European beauty. Our contemporaries want to be "tanned," to have a copper-colored or even swarthy skin, without realizing that this return to the lustre of minerals has nothing glorious about it.

My article didn't convince anyone at the time. Actually, there's nothing surprising about that. It's no accident that this mineral pigment is so much desired by everyone. It corresponds to a solidarity with metallurgical magic from which the whole Euro-American culture suffers. That steel which we have tried to make our slave was stronger than we—and it is taking its revenge.

Modern man no longer wants to become tempered like steel—but he is tempted by the gleam of the steel, which he has appropriated in his eyes, his epidermis, and his manners and morals.

But here, thank God, we are in the Rheingau.

Romanticism and the Bicycle

At Rüdesheim a young English couple get on the boat. They are visiting the Rhine Valley in stages. They travel for a few kilometers on the excellent road that winds, neat and clean, along the right bank of the river. Then, as night approaches, they board a boat, in order to sleep in a "romantic inn."

The truth is that their plan has unexpected benefits. They started from Mainz, riding bicycles belonging to some German friends. They seem familiar with this whole region, although they speak deplorable German. But there is something touching in their love for the Rhine, the German landscape, and Romanticism. The young woman is carrying in her hand a little book of a kind sold in kiosks at railway stations and even at the little bookshop on this boat. It is a booklet of medieval German legends. Actually, the reputation the English have for being sentimentalists and lovers of "romance" isn't just a bad joke of the Continentals. The English family, famous for its "hearth," is a very serious, very responsible thing. And lovers who end by getting married find in Romanticism the only possibility for their survival, because it transforms the bourgeois stages of their marriage into so many occasions for nostalgic reminiscences. This simple journey of theirs through the Rhine Valley, which a man who took it by himself would forget after a few years, will become for them, as youth passes, an increasingly legendary episode.

It is by no means accidental that the most "romantic" Europeans are the English and the Germans—peoples solidly anchored in familial morality. And I do not try to explain this coincidence by what is called "repression"; that is, that because their family life is so monotonous and devoid of adventure, such people desire absolute love, adventure, miraculous marriages. This opinion, however intelligent it might seem, is nevertheless superficial. In fact, the power of man to transform his life and his surroundings to the point of transfiguration is unlimited. It is a real power, not an illusion. The man who loves transforms his beloved into a Beatrice or an Isolde—and then it is only one step further to the transfiguration of the banal "hearth" into the most perfect medieval stage setting.

From the same reason—their anchorage in marital and civil reality—there derives, perhaps, the love of the English and the Germans for the Middle Ages—which, from a theological point of view they would deny, good Protestants that they are. Catholics, as well as men of adventure, are not obsessed with medieval charm; in France, Italy, and Spain the Middle Ages is present only in proximity to cathedrals, while educated people speak very little of that era. The *romantic past* is more active in the life of men who have decided not only to remain serious—but who respect their destiny completely.

Lorelei

Everyone has come out on the upper deck to admire this famous cliff. It is indeed magnificent: tall, steep, rugged. The river flows faster here, even though the water is very deep near the base of the cliff.

I don't remember Heine's verses, and I'm not going to try to find out from anyone what they are. However, I'm fascinated by what an expert in Rhine lore is saying back of me. He asserts that this rock, beautiful as it is, became famous only as a result of Heine's poem. Foreign travelers of a century or more ago scarcely noticed it. In any event, the Lorelei did not have then the romantic aureole which it obtained following the publication of Heine's verses.

Poetry, as well as culture in general, *adds* something to nature. It contributes not only to the beautification of the Cosmos, but also to its "signification" (if I may be allowed such an expression). Things not only appear more beautiful after they have been sung about by a great poet, but they appear to us, above all, with signification. They begin to speak to us, so to say, "coherently." A little ordinary poetic magic and this steep cliff, this scowling chunk of basalt, is transformed at once into a companion who never tires of conversation.

In this situation you realize in what the much-lauded solitude of the Romantics consists: in an exhilarating conversation with the enchanted landscapes of nature.

"If You Think This Is Something . . . !"
One of the most tedious and unbearable things about a trip is the inevitable conversation of your traveling companion, who keeps talking about places more beautiful than the one through which you are passing. Or else he tells you how much better this place looks when seen in more favorable conditions (from an automobile, with an interesting group, at a festival time, in May, on a moonlit night, etc.). As a matter of fact, the majority of us are guilty of this sin—even the most sober and generous of us. Very few can withstand the temptation; very few have the strength to be *present* in the place where they are. Traveling in the Danubian delta, someone speaks to you of the Riviera; and in the same way your companion on a nocturnal Mediterranean voyage dampens your enthusiasm and tempers your emotional thrill by saying that nowhere is the sea more beautiful than in the Gulf of Mexico. It goes without saying that the same person, if he were with you in the Gulf of Mexico, would talk about the Aegean or the North Sea.

No landscape is imposing enough for such persons. When you stay at home and read their travel impressions about faraway lands, you become convinced that these persons traveled in a kind of hypnotic state, utterly fascinated by the surroundings and the mystery of the place. But in most cases, it doesn't happen that way. The fact that the Red Sea seems to you like something out of a fairy tale, doesn't prevent a great many others from telling you about the beauties of other oriental seas—at the time you are crossing it. In colonial regions, especially, the conversation on the train pertains almost always to countries other than the one in which you are traveling. No matter how moving India is, you hear people on the train talking about Papua or New York—even if you're in the midst of the most incredible scenery in all Asia. At Calcutta, the conversation, full of nostalgia, centers on Singapore, while at Singapore you will hear people talking in heartrending tones about Paris or London. No place is beautiful enough or extraordinary enough; the spirit of man is always hankering for something else, it is continually being reminded of other places and longing for them.

Perhaps things aren't so simple or frivolous as they seem at first sight. Perhaps it's more than just a need for braggadocio on the part of your traveling companion. It is difficult for man to endure great beauty, just as it is difficult for him to endure any "great" thing (that is, any *absolute* thing: faith, love, heroism, morality). In the presence of a deeply moving landscape, his subconscious helps him to fly away, helps him not to be *present*, impells him to think of something else—anything to keep him from imbibing fully the beauty of the present moment, which would overwhelm him. The recollection of other beautiful scenes is a means of self-preservation. Because, if man were to experience intensely all the things that happen to him—that is, if he were to remain *present* in every moment—he would be consumed like a burning candle.

. . . Et Altera Pars

But maybe another explanation is truer. A trip, no matter how modest it may be, is connected in our consciousness to earlier trips, even if a whole series of years has passed since the last one. In other words, all our journeys constitute an organic continuum, qualitatively different from the massive intervals of time in between them, which in a sense belong to "profane" time, neutral and nonsignificant. One trip is joined to another, just as, in a sacred calendar, one holy day is connected with another directly, without the intervention of profane days. In the mystical corpus of liturgical time, one Sunday is connected directly to the preceding Sunday or other religious festival day. Liturgical time constitutes a continuum which has nothing to do with profane time; the two are on different planes. The last hour of a Sunday is not connected to the first hour of Monday, but to the first hour of the following Sunday. (I have oversimplified my example a little, in order to facilitate understanding. In fact, on the other days of the week there are sacred, liturgical hours also, which are linked to one another in the same way, without being separated by profane hours.)

So, then, it is not at all surprising that the majority of travelers remember—especially in optimum moments and in deeply moving landscapes—fragments from previous trips. It is a natural continuation of a little miracle. Because, whether it be a matter of a hike in the mountains or an expedition to another continent, the journey remains in a certain sense a miraculous thing.

Even if it were nothing more than the sentiment of the *reality* of life, a sentiment induced by any detachment from an environment neutralized by too long a residence there, one can speak of a "miracle." The function of the latter, as is well known, is to place man face to face with reality. In the presence of a miracle, you realize that all you have known before was an illusion, an insignificant spectacle, mere vanity. . . .

But, of course, all this doesn't make any less annoying the conversation of your traveling companion who prates to you of other places, more beautiful than these.

The Inimical Brothers
Over there, very close to the river bank, on two mountain peaks, two ruined buildings are visible. They are the remains of castles, glorious in their romantic ruination: Liebenstein and Sterrenberg. Or, as people hereabout call them, *Die feindlichen Brueder*. At the foot of the mountains, reflecting its reddish walls in the waters of the Rhine, is a monastery: Bornhofen.

We have a few minute's time to look at these stark ruins, proud in their petrified desolation. The slow movement of the ship helps you to contemplate them, somehow animating them, turning them slowly before your eyes. As if they were taking their nickname seriously, they seem to be defying each other across the gorge, in spite of crumbling walls and deserted turrets. Their only greatness that has remained is this: to illustrate in stone the most depressing formula of life: the inimical brothers.

And since I am disposed to find hidden meanings everywhere, it doesn't surprise me at all that precisely at the foot of these mountains whose peaks contain these enchanted ruins—precisely here is found a humble monastery. As if to remind passersby that the formula of life can be corrected by Revelation, by Christianity; that those inimical brothers on the mountains are nothing but a terrestrial copy of the ancient models, Cain and Abel—annulled, however, by another passion, that of the Savior.

I have the sentiment that I do not err in identifying elements of the human tragedy in nature and in ruins of works erected by the hand of man. Any religion is a book sealed with seven seals for the one who doesn't understand that witnesses to the beliefs and thoughts of ancient man are to be found always in nature. The fall of man into history brought with it the participation of nature in history. Nature does not merely imitate works of art, as Oscar Wilde's paradox puts it; sometimes it imitates also human dramas—yet not the greatest ones. . . .

Castles

The sky begins to darken. Imperceptibly, the landscape changes. We have left the mountains behind. From Boppard the Rhine curves sharply till it reaches Oberspey; then, again, it bends obliquely toward the left, passing the famous Stolzenfels Castle, restored at the beginning of the last century. Before it arrives at Koblenz the last mountains crowd together around the Lahn River. We hear nothing but famous names: Marksburg, Laneck, Wallfahrtskirche. The Marksburg Castle looks intact, although it was built more than a thousand years ago. It was known already in 882, I learn.

You are overwhelmed by the castles which line both banks of the river. Then you discover suddenly that you know almost nothing about them, that their sight evokes for you at best a Germanic Middle Ages of colored cartoons and serial novels—and you vow then and there to inform yourself seriously, at the first opportunity, about this important segment of European history. The truth is that any trip throws a bright, startling light on the gaps in your education. You realize your ignorance nowhere more than in a museum or in a country where history has left its traces at every step.

It suffices for this sentiment of *history*, of the past, to come over you, to cause the Rhine to acquire suddenly a completely different significance. Besides, that pleasant light of morning has gone, and the sonority of the air is no longer the same. The air is heavy here. The day is coming to an end. A large part of the sky is covered with clouds. And that chill wind, with the smell of rain in it, which is striking you, reminds you that the river can detach you; that its waters, mixed with blood, participate in history. The scenery gradually loses its supremacy.

From whence comes this obsession with tragic history, in its primordial sense of struggle and cataclysm, which only the medieval castles, out of all the moments of the past, leave with you? Men have butchered one another in other times, not only in the Middle Ages, and not only in this Occident overrun by barbarians. Rome became the sun of the ancient world only after first having become its master—on rivers of blood. And yet, in spite of that fact, the ruins of Rome, as well as those of Athens and Egypt and the ancient East, evoke something else entirely than struggle, the will to victory, and tragic history. You are amazed or mournful in the presence of Roman or Hellenic ruins. In Egypt, Mesopotamia, and India you gaze upon the remnant of the "glorious past" with an aching heart; so much grandeur, so much mystery, so much melancholy! You are reminded of the evanescence of people and things, of the secrets those obscure master builders took with them to their graves. In any event, you don't see the struggle, the competition, the desire for victory which you sense as soon as you look intently at a medieval castle.

The history you sense in ancient Rome or Athens has a collective flavor: it is impossible not to think of armies when you see all those triumphal arches; and the theatres, the arenas, the forums—all these spaces your imagination fills with crowds. You have again the impression that all traces of warfare and bloody conflict were washed away once the armies reached the city walls. The castle, on the contrary, has in its very architecture the gesture of the fighter. Ortega y Gasset has shown this rather well. But, apart from the warlike style, from whence springs this oppressive sentiment of *history* which one feels looking at medieval castles? When you are around them you sense that man is not free on earth, and that this lack of freedom is not a biological law but a consequence of man's participation in history. You sense here man's responsibility to his nation, to his dead. The medieval castle reminds you that you haven't come onto the earth to be happy or to perfect yourself, but to obey and serve. And this consciousness of belonging to a certain collectivity is oppressive, suffocating. You have here the somber revelation that such an attachment presupposes a ceaseless struggle, a ceaseless awareness. A castle knows but one state: the state of vigilance.

It is oppressive, it is tragic—but you realize there's nothing else to be done. For the time being. . . .

Koblenz

Just ahead of us there rises up the bridge with the great arches, supported on only three gigantic pillars. The city of Koblenz extends along the left bank, where the Moselle pours into the Rhine. The diminished light, the threatening rain, neutralize the charm of this city famous for its wines. The Rhine is more turgid here, and the wind is blowing harder.

At dinner, a young couple is seated opposite us. The man orders a bottle of wine immediately and examines the label closely. Then, victoriously, he shows it to his companion.

"I didn't think they'd have it," she says, smiling with a very discreet irony.

The young man takes her hand and kisses it gallantly.

"But that doesn't mean anything," the woman adds.

They both begin to laugh. He leans toward her and speaks fast, in a whisper. I hear only snatches of this hushed declaration. The noise of the engines erupts suddenly, and the boat leaves the dock, rocking. I cast my eye out the window momentarily and catch sight of the Kaiser Wilhelm statue situated close to the extremity of the city, where the Moselle flows into the Rhine.

"Let's write them a postcard from Bonn," I hear the young man say. "They were awfully charming."

The woman is staring absently at the river bank. I turn my head to look too: the Ehrenbreitstein Castle.

"We could stay a day longer," the man adds, following her gaze. "I see how much you like it."

Their eyes meet suddenly and they begin to laugh.

It seems that this secret allusion has dispersed the young lady's melancholy. And yet, as seen from here, that tall, massive fortress built by the Franks in the fifth century has nothing sentimental about it. It is, on the contrary, an enormous mass with truncated walls and no towers or balconies. But who knows how many romantic strolls have been occasioned by this ancient fort? Lovers are always bolder in the shadow of history. Maybe this zone of heroic ruins amplifies their masculine virtues. Or maybe the very tangible evidence of the nothingness of man and the evanescence of human life creates a state of total acceptance in the woman's mind. When you feel intensely how completely and swiftly all things human *pass*—power and glory, youth and beauty—what is the use of resisting, of postponing, of keeping yourself pure? The sentiment of the past frightens, and at the same time it awakens a terrific desire to consume the present, to exhaust the moment. Haven't you noticed that in all the novels whose plots unfold in Italy, sensuality and sin find their most dependable stimulant in the contemplation of the grandeur of the past?

Laurence Sterne

The only book I have brought along with me is Sterne's *A Sentimental Journey*, in a pocket edition from the series "The World's Classics." Sterne was, at one time, my "favorite author," as people say, and I used to read *Tristram Shandy* at least once a year. I find it amazing, however, that this writer who enjoyed such exceptional popularity on the Continent at the end of the eighteenth and first half of the nineteenth century, is today very little relished in certain European countries.

In England, on the other hand, he has remained to the present day a popular author. His two most famous books have been reprinted in numerous editions, and all editions are sold out in a very short time.

He is indeed an author who cannot be relished unless he is *read*. There are many classics from all literatures of the world that can be known, relished, and cited in conversation—without having been read in their entirety.

A few sonnets of Petrarch, for example, suffice to enable one to speak intelligibly about his art and flavor. Other classics are known and present in culture thanks to collections of excerpts or to reworkings, or even to musical librettos ("Faust"). Everyone has read *Don Juan* in a condensed version. The same can be said about Rabelais. With respect to the French classics, the educated person "knows" them from school or from anthologies. Actually, these excerpts collected in anthologies are always very readable. Anyone who has read a few chapters of Montaigne, or a tragedy of Racine, or a few pages from Pascal is aware of what each author is about. To be sure, it is an inadequate, superficial knowledge, but at least it is something.

In the case of Sterne, however, you don't understand him, you don't relish him, you don't even realize "what he's about" unless you've read him in his entirety, and several times. He is a difficult author. But that isn't the only thing. He is an author who becomes great only after you have finished reading his last page. Until then, you don't realize the magnitude of his genius. He stubbornly resists summarization, fragmentation (although his work is made up of thousands of fragments), and being published in "selections." You can't extract anything for an anthology, you can't illustrate anything with a "selected page," you don't find anywhere the diamond which would convince the reader of the quality of his genius. He has written his books, moreover, not only to be read to their last page but also under the conviction that he would follow each of them with numerous other volumes. Neither *Tristram Shandy* nor *A Sentimental Journey* is finished. One could even say that they are scarcely begun! In his autobiography, *Tristram Shandy*, there is no mention yet of the hero, it is only about his parents, about events in their lives, and about that unforgettable Uncle Toby. The nine books of the novel, consisting altogether of six hundred pages of small type, barely introduce the reader into the life of the Shandy family. It would require another forty to fifty books—some five or six volumes of the same size—to exhaust the autobiography of *Tristram Shandy*. If he hadn't been brought down by tuberculosis, Sterne would have continued to write and publish as many as two small volumes per year. It was not only a glorious affair but also a profitable one. Editions sold out rapidly and the whole world of book readers of that time waited impatiently for the next installment of the novel.

Sterne never finished *A Sentimental Journey*. This little volume, comprising two books, hardly equals the length of a small novel of the seventeenth century. Not only is nothing finished with the second book, the last sentence is not even completed. Everything remains suspended—as was the intention of the author, who lived long enough to have finished at least the last paragraph.

I advise the reader to approach Sterne's art through this *Sentimental Journey* which, obviously, must be read in the original. Sterne is one of the few untranslatable English classical writers. He is, moreover, inimitable, and he did not create a "school." No one could start out from his stopping place. The freedom of the narrative in *Tristram Shandy* is bewildering. No other author, not even Proust, has had the courage to narrate so randomly and with so many digressions. The whole book, in fact, from the first page on, is nothing but an open-ended digression.

Now, when the rain is beginning to fall and the Rhine is turgid, it is time to open *A Sentimental Journey* and read it again, slowly, repeating certain passages out loud.

Eliza Draper

I have a subnormal memory, but there are certain details I can scarcely forget. I will always remember, I believe, the name of Eliza Draper, the "Belle Indienne" whom Laurence Sterne, it is said, loved in a mysterious and innocent way. And among the items I regret never having seen in the collections of the British Museum is the miniature painting of this adventuress—who married in Bombay a man twenty years her senior, who came to England in order to put her children into school, who met Sterne and was loved by him with a passion for three months, and who then returned to India. Sterne never saw her again, but he wrote a *Journal to Eliza*, from April to November 1767 (the year he met her) in which—a spicy detail!—he copied also a goodly number of old love letters he had written to his wife!

How could I ever forget Eliza Draper! One of the most pathetic, most "sentimental" letters I've ever read is one written by Sterne to "Dear, dear Eliza." This man who had studied theology and was approaching fifty years of age, the most liberated author, considered in England a classic humorist—poured out a continual stream of tears thinking of the fate of Eliza, of her slight indisposition which made her face pale, of her loneliness.

And that isn't all. He talks about her everywhere he goes. In one delightful letter he relates how he became friends with old Lord Bathurst, the drinking and conversational comrade of Pope, Swift, and many other famous persons. Lord Bathurst was eighty-five when he invited Sterne to dinner—and he spent the whole evening listening to Sterne talk about nothing but Eliza. "A too-sentimental afternoon we spent together, lasting until nine," he writes to her. "But you, Eliza, were the star that guided and illumined our conversation."

At that time, the suffering Eliza kept Sterne's portrait above her little writing desk. This detail moved the cynical author to tears. It is true, however, that the beautiful Eliza, once she had arrived back in Bombay, recognizing once more her change of feeling for her husband, ran off with a John Clark of the navy. She returned to England some seven years later, and from that point on her biography becomes obscure. Seemingly, she went from bad to worse before she died. Sterne himself had died in 1768, a year after Eliza's departure for India. It is probable that he never found out about the adventure with John Clark "of the navy"—and he never even suspected the moral degeneration of his beloved "Belle Indienne." Eliza Draper died in 1778, exactly ten years after Sterne.

I imagine her as Sterne describes her in his letters: without being beautiful, with an air of "vestal" melancholy, "intelligent, animated, gentle." Sterne anticipates here the whole atmosphere of Romanticism, and even the destiny of the romantic heroine.

Portrait

Opposite me now a German, of indefinite age, with a bundle of newspapers and reviews, has taken a seat.

He has ordered a bottle of mineral water, and now he is drinking it slowly from a glass, sighing. He does this without any enthusiasm, as though he were following a doctor's prescription. Then he unfolds very carefully each of the periodicals and runs his eyes over the advertisements. In his right hand he hold a big red-leaded pencil with which he circles heavily certain notices. From time to time he casts a glance out the window and consults his watch. He doesn't dare become bored.

He continues reading ads in the papers and magazines, occasionally comparing certain items with his pocket notebook.

This continues for better than an hour, until we are nearing Bonn. He becomes more and more downcast, but he doesn't quit until he has checked the last review with the same attentiveness and ill humor. Then he wipes his brow pensively and stacks up the papers and magazines. All at once he gets up from the table, without paying his bill. The boy who served him bows deeply, helping him to the door. Someone sees him in front of the captain's cabin and runs after him, calling out, "Herr Direktor!"

At the dock at Bonn, in the rain, two blond youths are waiting, making signals with their hands while we are still a good distance away.

/ / /

Published originally in five installments in the Romanian periodicals Vremea *(August 15, September 12, and October 10, 1937) and* Universul literar *(July 29 and August 26, 1939).*

16. Detained by Destiny

I HAVE recalled many times my obsession of that night of September 9 when the famous Blitz was launched against London. I did not understand then (and I doubt I have ever understood in all its implications) the enigma of the collective death which linked my destiny to that of Nae Ionescu and yet at the same time separated it from his. Neither did I understand my certainty on that night that all that had happened after July 14, 1938, had been due to a "fatal error" which I had made then or a little while before. I had committed, certainly, many mistakes, both before and after July 14, but none of them seemed to carry in its consequences the explanation for my enigmatic obsession with the collective death that awaited me from one day to the next.

I was escorted to Security headquarters and locked in an office, with a guard beside me. At night I slept on the floor. I had difficulty falling asleep because I wasn't allowed to turn out the bright light bulb that hung from the ceiling. But soon I became accustomed to it. I remained in that office for almost three weeks. Probably, precise orders had been received concerning me, because, outside of the fact that I slept on the floor, I couldn't complain of anything. However, I could hear the screams of other prisoners being interrogated in the basement, especially in the nighttime, after the music from the nearby cinema had ceased. I realized that I was being treated as a privileged person when I was informed that I could receive food from home and even books and manuscripts. Since the announced interrogation kept being postponed, I set to work in earnest. In those weeks I wrote "Magic, Metallurgy, and Alchemy." It was, in fact, a considerably augmented elaboration of several chapters from *Cosmologie și alchimie babiloniană*. It appeared later in *Zalmoxis* volume I, and also separately, as the first of the "Cahiers de Zalmoxis."

On the evening of the day I was arrested, Nina went to see General Condeescu. He seemed devastated by what had happened, and he promised her he would speak to Armand Călinescu. Several days later he spoke with him, but Călinescu shrugged. "Show me the dossier you have on him," Condeescu said, "so I can see for myself why he has been censured." "He's Nae Ionescu's man," he replied, "isn't that enough?" Then he added, "He's a symbol." "What does he symbolize?" Condeescu insisted, "India? The history of religions?" "He symbolizes all that is capable of frustrating me in my struggle to safeguard the monarchy and democracy in Romania." "Let's quit kidding around," the general broke in. "Fair enough," Călinescu replied. "I have nothing against him. In fact, I like what he writes. Let him sign a declaration of dissociation from the Legionary movement, and he'll go free."

The "declaration of dissociation" was the latest discovery of Armand Călinescu. He considered—probably with good reason—that such declarations, published by the whole press, would contribute greatly to the discouragement and disorientation of the Legionaries and their sympathizers. The series of dissociations was inaugurated by a priest, the former confessor of Corneliu Codreanu. Since I did not consider myself a "political man," I refused to sign any of the declarations presented to me by an inspector of Security during various phases of the interrogation. Because, after a week or so during which, probably, they hoped I would lose my patience or my courage, the interrogation began. I was brought to the office of the inspector, or else he came to the office where I was being held. He rudely ordered the guards to wait in the corridor and began to ask me questions: When was the last time I had seen so-and-so? What had Nae Ionescu said when Codreanu's circular appeared on the Iorga article?—and others of the same sort.

In comparison with the beatings and tortures of other prisoners, and especially in comparison with the assassinations that would follow—not to mention the terrors of the Soviet and Nazi extermination camps later on, or the terror and genocide which were to descend on Romania after 1945—the afflictions I suffered were child's play. But in the perspective of the year 1938, they were rather grave. I had been tracked down and arrested for my friendship with Nae Ionescu and because I was a contributor to his newspaper—which had reappeared with the full consent of the government. Thousands upon thousands of men were arrested because they belonged to a *legal* political party with which Iuliu Maniu had not hesitated to conclude an electoral pact. They were accused retroactively for a political stance which, prior to the winter of 1938, the constitution had guaranteed them. The dictatorship of Carol anticipated all that was to happen seven or eight years later, after the occupation of the country by the Soviets. Like the terror unleashed by the Communist party after 1948, the one ordered by Carol and put into effect by Armand Călinescu was undertaken in the name and for the defense of "democracy." Carol's only originality was his certainty that he could permit himself anything because the "people" would not react—a certainty based on the very low opinion he held about the Romanians. Since he had never known any but dishonest politicians and men with no backbones, Carol considered all Romanians to be cut from the same cloth. He showed his political intelligence when he chose as advisors Puiu Dumitrescu and Ernst Urdăreanu instead of Nae Ionescu. The rest—honor, respect for promises, "personality"—depended on the decision and caprices of Elena Lupescu. Avaricious himself, Carol saw in Romanian politicians nothing but money-lovers, swindlers, and poltroons. Since all his maneuvers succeeded, since he was successful in shattering the unity of the Liberal and National-Peasant parties, he could permit himself anything. And probably he died convinced that he had not been mistaken.

In 1937–38 his only fear had been the possibility of a rebellion provoked by the Legionary movement and supported by the army. But he took care to assure himself about the army, removing all those who did not agree to be his tools, and to reinforce the general security and the gendarmerie. On the other hand he knew that Corneliu Codreanu would not launch an uprising at a critical moment, when there would be danger of inviting the intervention of Soviet troops. (This was a year before the Russo-German Pact, when the Spanish Civil War was in full swing.) He knew, finally, that the "masses" would not react if the terror was imposed upon them gradually. The almost complete success of the Carol dictatorship was due, primarily, to the tactics adopted by Armand Călinescu—which would be those also of the Communist parties in Central and Eastern Europe after 1945. At first, nothing spectacular, just minor, continuous harassment. Then the suspension of the constitution, massive arrests, and several sensational trials, but without death sentences. Finally, when the Legionary movement was disoriented if not suffering from heart failure, with all its leaders in prisons or camps, the final blow: that is, its decapitation.

I don't know how Corneliu Codreanu will be judged by history. The fact is that four months after the phenomenal electoral success of the Legionary movement, its head found himself sentenced to ten years at hard labor, and five months after that he was executed—events that reconfirmed my belief that our generation did not have a political destiny. Probably Corneliu Codreanu would not have contradicted me. For him, the Legionary movement did not constitute a political phenomenon but was, in its essence, ethical and religious. He repeated time and again that he was not interested in the acquisition of power but in the creation of a "new man." He had known for a long time that the king was planning to kill him, and had he wished he could have saved himself by fleeing to Italy or Germany. But Codreanu believed in the necessity of sacrifice; he considered that every new persecution could only purify and strengthen the Legionary movement, and he believed, furthermore, in his own destiny and in the protection of the Archangel Michael.

In 1937–38 the most popular theme among the Legionaries was death. The deaths of Moța and Marin constituted the exemplary model.[1] The words of Moța: "The most powerful dynamite is your own ashes," had become like a Gospel text. A good part of the Legionary activity consisted in worship services, offices for the dead, strict fasts, and prayers. And the most pathetic irony of that spring of 1938 was that the crushing of the only Romanian political movement which took seriously Christianity and the church was begun under the administration of the Patriarch Miron.

I don't know what Codreanu thought when he realized that in a few hours he would be executed. I am not thinking of his faith, but

---

1. Translator's note: Ion Moța and Vasile Marin were two Legionary leaders who were killed in January 1937 in Spain, where they had gone as volunteers for Franco in the Civil War. Eliade was acquainted personally with both men, who were about the same age as he.

of his political destiny. He had assured Armand Călinescu through numerous circulars that the Legionaries would not react, even if hung by their feet and tortured. He had given strict orders for nonviolence, even for renunciation of passive resistance, and he had even dissolved the party, *Totul pentru Țară* (all for country). Călinescu's tactics succeeded: all the Legionaries had let themselves be trapped and were now in cages, waiting, like rats, to be drowned alive. Probably Codreanu, like so many other Legionaries, died convinced that his sacrifice would hasten the victory of the movement. But I wonder if some of them didn't see in their imminent death, not necessarily a sacrifice, but the fatal consequence of a catastrophic error in political tactics. I know only that Mihail Polihroniade, who was one of the very few leaders concerned with political victory rather than with the salvation of souls, said once to his wife in the prison at Râmnicul Sărat, after the execution of Codreanu: "See what all our liturgies and offices for the dead have gotten us!" In less than a year he too would be executed—he who did not even have the consolation of liturgies and requiems. But he died no less serenely than the others, the believers. He asked for a cigarette, lit it, and walked smiling to the wall where the machine guns waited.

*   *   *

In the summer of 1938, to be a Legionary or a Legionary "sympathizer" entailed the risk of losing everything: job, freedom, and perhaps, ultimately, life. It is easy to see why, for someone like me who did not believe in the political destiny of our generation (or in Codreanu's star), a declaration of dissociation from the Legionary movement seemed not only unacceptable but downright absurd. I could not conceive of dissociating myself from my generation in the midst of its oppression, when people were being prosecuted and persecuted unjustly.[2]

Thus it was that, by refusing to sign the declaration, after about three weeks of detention at Security headquarters, I was sent to the camp at Miercurea Ciucului. I had finished in the meantime the article "Magic, Metallurgy, and Alchemy" and had begun to translate Buck's *Fighting Angel.* I utilized many of my memories from the Security headquarters and Ciuc in *Noaptea de Sânziene,* and I regret now that I

2. It should be recalled here that in the three months of the government of General Antonescu and Horia Sima (September to December 1940), Legionary terrorists committed numerous horrible crimes.

did; it could leave the impression that Ştefan Viziru is an alter-ego of mine, which isn't true. But the events of 1938, as well as those of the years I spent in London and Lisbon during the war, put at my disposal, somewhat ready-made, a rich body of narrative material—and I succumbed to the temptation. From a certain moment on, instead of continuing to invent the life of Viziru, I constructed it by using my own experiences. I need to make this point in order to explain the lack of enthusiasm with which I write about events of the summer and fall of 1938; I have the impression that I have told them all before.

The prison camp was located in a former agricultural school, some ten kilometers outside Miercurea Ciucului. It was a building from the turn of the century, four stories high, with spacious rooms, in each of which from five to ten prisoners slept. There was a courtyard, some hundred meters long and thirty wide, surrounded by a barbed-wire fence, guarded by gendarmes armed with machine guns. In the four corners were wooden watchtowers, with machine guns positioned to fire directly into the yard. Here we walked, conversed, and early each morning, under the direction of an instructor, did gymnastics. Eastward from the camp the plain extended to the mountains of Odorhea, which we contemplated with melancholy, profiled against the purple horizon. A single highway came from the direction of Ciuc, but seldom was any motor vehicle seen. When a car did come our way, passing the first cordon of gendarmes a hundred meters off, the whole camp would begin to murmur. It was a visitor: the mother or wife of some prisoner. Although the meeting took place in front of the major of the gendarmes, the commandant of the camp, still a certain amount of news from outside filtered in. Otherwise, the only news we received came from the recently arrested. Newspapers were forbidden, but we had a few books—which were passed eagerly from hand to hand.

I had been allowed to bring *Fighting Angel* and several other volumes, including *The Complete Works of Shelley,* a book which I gave to Nae Ionescu when, a few months later, he was about to be moved to the military hospital at Braşov. I was allowed, further, to bring writing paper. Compared to the camps of later years, life at Ciuc in the summer of 1938 was quite bearable. We were isolated from our families and the rest of the world, but we were free to walk about, to discuss, and to read, while our food was no worse than that of an average army camp. It is true that sometimes the macaroni had worms in it and the cheese was often moldy, but they gave us plenty of borscht, fried potatoes, and sauerkraut. Nevertheless, in 1938 we were the precursors; we were in a situation that would worsen and become general later, in Romania and in other countries as well. Perhaps that is why we felt so "persecuted": what was happening to us was something *new*, it was a diabolical innovation in Romanian political mores and thus something corrupt. Moreover, no one knew what would happen the next day. A dictatorship cannot maintain itself very long in even a minimum of humaneness. (I had learned this in India.) Those machine guns weren't pointed at us merely for symbolic purposes.

For the time being, I was glad to have escaped from those four walls of the prefecture and the ever-burning light bulb, to be able to walk around the courtyard, and above all to discuss things with Nae Ionescu. I had my army cot taken into his room. Also with him were Nellu Manzati, a young priest, very witty, and a doctor, also young, who was suffering with a heart condition and knew that his days were numbered. Perhaps this explains why he was always jolly, droll, full of funny stories and sayings. The schedule was simple: rise at 6:00, roll call in the courtyard at 7:00, tea at 7:30, lunch at 12:00 and dinner at 7:00 P.M., followed by another roll call and group prayers at 9:00. The only exception: Friday was fast day when, except for those with chest ailments, we ate nothing but the evening meal. For the rest of the time, everyone did what he wanted. When I arrived, various "courses" had been organized: Nae Ionescu had given several lectures on metaphysics, and I was asked to improvise a course on the history of religions and to speak about Gandhi and the Indian nationalist movement.

All kinds of men were included among the prisoners: university professors and lecturers, doctors, priests, elementary-school teachers, laborers, and peasants. Intellectuals constituted the majority. In the evenings, the group prayer service was concluded with the moving "God Is with Us!" sung by three hundred voices. On the top floor there was a room set aside for "constant prayer." Continuously, day and night, a prisoner prayed or read the Bible for an hour, not stopping until his replacement entered the room. The most difficult hours of watching and praying were, of course, from three to five in the morning—and there were many who requested to be put on the list for those hours. Seldom in the history of modern Christianity have the fasts, prayers, and blind faith in an omnipotent God been rewarded with more blood. . . . And later, when the tragedy had been consummated, one of the things that fascinated me most was to discover the same steadfast faith among the few survivors of the massacres. There were enough encounters of this sort for one to understand that the Legionary movement had the structure and vocation of a mystical sect, not of a political movement. Moreover, Puiu Gârcineanu repeated this to me in our conversations, maintaining that the supreme end of the Legionary movement was no longer individual salvation through possible martyrdom, but the "resurrection of the nation," obtained through a "saturation of torture and a sacrifice of blood." The one massive refutation of the well-known refrain that the Romanians are not a religious people (the only Christian people without a saint, we are continually being reminded) was made by the behavior of those several thousands of Romanians in the years 1938–39, in prisons or camps, fugitives or free. All the more grave is the responsibility of those Legionary leaders who nullified the "saturation of torture and sacrifice of blood" by the odious assassinations of November 30, 1940, when, along with many others, Nicolae Iorga and V. Madgearu were murdered. But this tragedy too belongs to the destiny of the Romanian people, a people without luck, which was not even allowed to preserve undefiled the most recent of its innumerable sacrifices.

Nae Ionescu was unchanged: serene, optimistic, scintillating; the same as at the university or in his office at *Cuvântul*. The majority of the prisoners let their beards grow and went about in ragged clothing. Nae Ionescu, on the contrary, shaved every day, always wore a clean shirt with his legendary big bow tie, and changed outfits as often as possible (he was allowed three suits, a vest, and several pullover sweaters). He declared that, as long as he would be permitted to do so, he would dress and behave in the camp just as he had dressed and behaved at the palace, on the street, or at the university.

I don't recall ever having seen him sad, downcast, or discouraged. Sometimes, when we were alone or in a small group, he spoke to us about the books he had decided to write: a "Commentary on the Epistles of St. Paul" and "The Fall into the Cosmos," the latter consisting of a series of letters, the majority of them addressed to C. D., his great love of those years (and his last). Nae Ionescu considered St. Paul the most important Christian thinker: not because he was a greater philosophic genius than, for instance, St. Augustine, Origen, or St. Thomas, but because he had shown in what sense one can think philosophically, in a critical way, after the Incarnation. I don't know how much he had actually written of his commentary, but I saw and discussed the plan of this book with him and several other former pupils of his (Mircea Vulcănescu, Dinu Noica, and others) at our weekly gatherings in this house at Băneasa in the winter of 1940. As for the texts which would have composed "The Fall into the Cosmos," which he wrote in 1938–39, they still existed during the war years.

Nina came to see me at the beginning of September; but in the presence of the gendarme major, the commandant of the camp, she was unable to tell me very much. However, she brought me news from family and friends, a supply of coffee and cigarettes, and heavier clothing for fall. As far as my situation was concerned, I understood that it was "stationary." Armand Călinescu had repeated to General Condeescu that no one would be released from the camp without a declaration of dissociation.

I had finished translating *Fighting Angel* when I began to be obsessed by the theme of a novel. For several days I fretted and stewed, searching for a quiet corner, moving from one room to another, trying in vain to find a place to write. At last I located on the top floor a little unoccupied chamber in which, until recently, a prisoner suffering from tuberculosis had slept. Now he had been taken to the military hospital at Miercurea Ciucului. I brought in a little table and started to write that very night, by the light of a smoking kerosine lamp. Gradually the camp became still; nothing could be heard but the sentinels patrolling beyond the barbed-wire fence and, on the hour, the footsteps of those coming and going from the prayer room. Toward midnight I made myself a cup of coffee, and I continued writing until 2 or 3 A.M. It got cold at night, though, and since the room was unheated, I put on two or three sweaters and draped Nae's topcoat over my shoulders.

I started writing the novel in the middle of September. Gradually I became aware that it had become autumn; the forests behind the camp had turned russet and the mountains of Odorhea were becoming more difficult to see, being covered with hoarfrost. Then the rains began; at first timidly and seemingly far off, so that I wondered if it were really rain or just dry leaves being rustled by the wind. But soon there came the fine, steady rains of autumn, which I could hear falling gently on the roof—as though trying to tell me that we were nearing the end of a year, of a cycle, perhaps of a life, and I would have to hurry in order to finish the novel while there was *still time.*

Nina succeeded a second time in obtaining permission to come to see me. Again she brought coffee and cigarettes and another, even heavier suit, for winter. Since she had learned at Bucharest that many prisoners had contracted tuberculosis, she brought me medicine also, adding that General Condeescu, N. I. Herescu, and my other writer-friends "implored" me to "take care of myself," not to tire myself, so as to be able to "hold out as long as possible." Naturally, I didn't dare tell her I was writing at night in the room of a consumptive whose severe and repeated hemoptyses had forced the major to evacuate him to the hospital.

From time to time Nae would ask me, "How is it going?" I told him I was visualizing a love story which would not resemble anything I had written before: about a love which was, and would have remained, perfect had there not intruded a mystical element, the desire to prolong it indefinitely in a biological-temporal duration, making it "fruitful." The theme was, in appearance, simple: two men, meeting by chance on a hunting trip, tell each other, on the same night, the story of their great romance. The confession is begun by the younger man, a novelist, Mavrodin, probably because his companion asked him about what he was writing, and he answered, "Marriage in Heaven." He said it was a book in which he would ask the forgiveness of Ileana, whom he had loved and whom he loved still, who had vanished without a trace a year before. I told Nae what I wanted to do, but without summarizing the novel; it seemed to me that any kind of summary would betray it, annulling that which constituted the essence of the story. It was, of course, a story of love, relived at a distance of some years, by two men; but the tragedy which, both times, cut short their "perfect love" had not been provoked by incidents pertaining to the profane world. In fact, neither of the two men—who, in the beginning, do not suspect that they are speaking of the same woman—understands why he was abandoned. That is why, for a long time, they can't believe that Ileana has really left them forever. Although very different from each other, neither of them had any doubts about the "perfection" of his love; the mystical, nuptial dimension, which Ileana anticipated as a final fulfillment, remained inaccessible to them, though for different reasons.

"But why do you call it 'Marriage in Heaven'?" the Professor asked me once.

I didn't know how to answer him properly then. I ought to have said: Because "Marriage in Heaven" expresses the ambiguity of the whole situation. In asking forgiveness of Ileana, the novelist tried, by this title, to justify his behavior: assuming his duty to be a creator in the realm of the spirit, the writer hoped that the marriage of which Ileana dremed would still be fulfilled somewhere—in a transcendent world, in Heaven, *in aeternum*. But if she were to have found out about this title, Ileana would have understood it differently; she had lived from the beginning a marriage in heaven; for her, *this* had been the "perfect love": an endless bliss, a rapture, a perfect union which in itself lacked nothing, and to which nothing more could be added. But for Ileana, such a "marriage in heaven" was but the indispensable condition for a later fulfillment which only she foresaw. It was not, as Mavrodin mistakenly thought, a matter of a specifically feminine instinct, that of maternity, because then it isn't understandable why Lena leaves her husband after he asks her to have a child. (She also wanted to have a child, "But not this way, haphazardly," she had said to him once. She sensed that their "perfect love" was threatened from all sides and she knew that the last chance of saving it was the child.) Not maternity, as such, was involved here, but the desire—of a mystical nature—to *incarnate* the "marriage in heaven," to integrate it into the sphere of life; in a sense, to sanctify life anew. But, obviously, neither of the two men had any way of perceiving all this; Ileana never told them about the mystical element. Nor would she have known how to tell them, because not even she knew that it was indeed a "mystical element"; it was, simply, her mode of being, the same as that of all women, but only rarely assumed totally and definitively—this time by Ileana.

In a sense, I was trying in this novel to catch "the eternal feminine," as it could be intuited by a Romanian with an ordinary understanding of the sacramental meaning of existence. With the exception of Ştefania in *Viaţă nouă*, whom I had begun to portray, my feminine personages up to then had been presented two-dimensionally; they had not revealed their deep dimension, their own mode of being. They were reduced to "psychology" and "events." On the other hand, the deep dimension of masculinity had engrossed me; that is why, perhaps, so many of my masculine characters seemed demonic, possessed of an exasperating and sterile egocentrism, leading to the craving for "freedom" and "authenticity," and further to cruelty and irresponsibility. I believed at that time that the banality of the masculine condition could be transcended only by the absolutizing of certain tendencies specific to the male (in the first place, the need for freedom), or through a paradoxical experience (for example, Pavel Anicet's attempt to love two women at the same time, with equal sincerity, and totally).[3]

In October it became rather cold, and since the little room where I was writing remained unheated, I was able to work only with great effort, and only for a few hours each night. Toward midnight I had to return to my sleeping room, where there was a stove, to get warm. Soon I developed a cough: a dry, nagging cough, which eventually made all my roomates anxious. One of the doctors listened to me and asked the major to send me to the military hospital in Ciuc for an X ray, especially since he had discovered a suspicious temperature (probably I'd had it for some time but had not been aware of it). The major had to telephone Bucharest to obtain permission for the X ray. As might be expected, the news soon reached Armand Călinescu, who was agreeable to my being sent to the hospital. But soon afterward, General Condeescu also found out, and he interceded again with Călinescu, asking that I be placed in a sanatorium for diseases of the chest. I don't know how he succeeded in persuading him; probably the hemoptyses which I had had the previous week influenced his decision. I was, in any event, a privileged person, and the major was quick to realize this. Among the dozens of consumptives he had had in the camp, I was the only one concerning whom Bucharest asked to be "kept informed." The others were evacuated to the military hospital at Ciuc only when the hemoptyses became threatening . . . and after that no one asked to be kept informed about them.

In those last weeks at the camp I wrote Part II of *Nuntă în Cer* (Marriage in Heaven). I knew that this manuscript, as well as that of the translation of Pearl Buck's novel, *Fighting Angel*, would have to be turned over to the major for censorship, but I hoped they would be restored to me quite soon. However, I didn't know what to do with the journal I had been keeping since I arrived in camp—on pieces of toilet paper, to be able to hide it more easily. (I had even hoped to be

3. But although *Nuntă în Cer* was very popular with both the critics and the public, I don't believe many readers saw anything more in it than a love story (which, undoubtedly, it is). The extent to which Ileana incarnates a Romanian "eternal feminine" was destined to remain imperceptible, or more precisely unrecognizable, beneath the gentle fervor and balanced serenity which characterizes all Romanian modes of being in the world.

able to slip it into Nina's hand some time, but I gave up that idea after I found out that we would be searched before being conducted into the visitors' room and that the major was always present.) At last I decided to compress it, to reduce it in size as much as possible, and attach it directly to my body, underneath my shirt. I reasoned that special agents would come from Ciuc or even from Bucharest to accompany me to the sanatorium, and in that case the major would content himself with a summary search.

It turned out as I had imagined it. On October 25 a captain in the gendarmes came from Braşov in a Security car. The day before, the major had informed me I was leaving and had asked me to give him my books and manuscripts. To my great surprise and relief, he handed them back to me as I was getting into the car. It was a dark, cloudy day. All the prisoners came out into the yard to watch me pass by the guards and the barbed wire, and leave the camp. They were sorry to see me go, but since they considered me seriously ill, they were glad I'd be cared for in a sanatorium.

I was to see again only a very few of those men who gathered in the courtyard to salute me. Some time later, a part of them were sent to the camp at Vaslui. Ten months later about a third of those at Ciuc and Vasliu would be executed. Suffering from a heart condition, Nae Ionescu was placed in the military hospital at Braşov soon after my departure, and we were not to see each other again for almost thirteen months.

I didn't dare be happy when I saw the camp blurring and disappearing in the distance. The warrant officer rode beside the driver while I, in back, sat silent alongside the gendarme captain. At Braşov we boarded a train, riding in a reserved compartment, and got off at Predeal. Here another car was waiting for us, which took us to the sanatorium of Moroeni. We arrived at nightfall, after traveling several hours through forests. The sanatorium gleamed from a distance as if it were a palace bathed in light.

I couldn't believe my eyes when I discovered that I had a large room, with a bath and a terrace, and, alongside, an anteroom where a warrant officer of the gendarmes—sent from Sinaia to guard me— was to sleep. It was the last room on the fifth floor, at the end of the wing on the right, chosen specially to impede any possible attempt on my part to escape. From the window I could see nothing but forests, while high up and, seemingly, very close, was Piatra Craiului, as I had never seen it, white with snow.

The next morning the analyses and X rays began. Only after several days did the doctors understand—and then I realized how lucky I had been. They discovered that the hemoptyses were not of pulmonary origin, but were from some veins in my throat which had ruptured during my frequent coughing spells. Nevertheless, I continued to run a fever, and listening through the stethoscope they heard those suspicious sounds which had misled the doctors at the camp. Another series of X rays identified the cause: I was suffering from an inflamation of the pleura, on the verge of becoming pleurisy; if I had remained a month longer at the camp, without doubt I would have been infected with tuberculosis, as had happened with many prisoners. I had left the camp just in time. The doctors assured me that after two months at the sanatorium I would be fully rehabilitated—if I respected the regimen: that is, if I spent four or five hours a day lying on a chaise longue out on the terrace, if I ate heartily, and if I did not smoke. Insofar as I was able, I held to the schedule. I could not, however, give up the hours of work at night. I had to correct and put the finishing touches to the two manuscripts. I wanted at all costs to publish *Nuntă în Cer* before Christmas. I needed money, and I wanted to reassure my friends and readers by showing them that what had happened to me in that year had not paralyzed my literary creativity. In addition to this work, I had to transcribe my journal. The thin pieces of paper, of a depressing color, written with pencil as small as possible, had become almost illegible, especially after I had tried to reduce their bulk, folding them and pressing them with the heel of my shoe. I didn't dare to undertake to decipher and transcribe these notes except at night, after I was sure my guard, the warrant officer, had gone to sleep. I burned the original papers as I copied them, and hid the transcribed pages among the pages of the novel. This task took almost two weeks. Shortly after that, Nina came to see me and I gave her the manuscript, suggesting she try to get the novel published at Cugetarea. To my surprise and delight, Georgescu-Delafras accepted *Nuntă în Cer* and sent me word that it would appear before Christmas.

One day, some three weeks after my entrance into the sanatorium, the guard told me that he had received orders for my release. I couldn't believe it. I was free! I telephoned Nina the great news, then went out for a walk around the sanatorium. Only about four months had passed since I had gone walking without worry, but it seemed like an eternity. Only then did I sense how miraculous is this act—apparently so simple—of *living*, of being alive. I told myself that never would I forget that I can be happy by virtue of the simple fact that I am free to leave the house and go walking on the street, that no sorrow would be able to withstand that bliss. But of course the euphoria of freedom did not last very long. A few weeks later I had resumed the routine of my everyday existence. But with one important difference: now I could not forget how precarious freedom is, and, ultimately, life itself. And sometimes, when I was overwhelmed with worries, it was enough for me to remember the room at Security, the courtyard at the camp, or the gendarme who slept in the room beside mine, for me to recover the serenity and joy of *living*.

Nina arrived the next day, and the sanatorium director allowed her to stay with me. She had brought with her, among a great many other letters and messages from friends and colleagues from the Society of Romanian Writers and the university, a very moving letter, signed by many of my students. In it they assured me that they were "lined up" in front of the bed where I was lying, breathing slowly ("practicing *prānāyāma*," they said), and, meditating in a concentrated way ("*ekagrata*," concentrated on a single point), they saluted me. Obviously, I had no way of knowing then that in a sense they were saying good-bye to me, that they were saluting their professor, together, for the last time. Some of them—very few, actually—I would see again, but only individually. The "class" which I had built up over the past few years would no longer be accessible to me.

I had been a professor only five years, and yet for a long time afterward I kept discovering with emotion and pride how powerful was the memory of my courses. Many years later, in 1956–57, the Italian ethnologist Ernesto de Martino, after having spent several months in Romania doing folklore research, told me that he had found everywhere the echo of my lectures and seminars of 1933–38, and he congratulated me that I had left a *mark* which adversity had not succeeded in destroying. I was impressed especially by this detail: a researcher, who was working with him at the Folklore Institute, asked him if he had ever met me.

"Yes," de Martino replied. "I met him this very year, at Rome."

The young man gazed at him a long time, and then began to cry. But de Martino didn't remember his name.

17. The Great Departure

I STAYED at the sanatorium only until November 12, although the doctors had told me at first I'd have to remain at least two months. But after the gendarme guard left and I was no longer "detained" and therefore the responsibility of the state, I had to pay the sanatorium. And although the president and the secretary of the Society of Romanian Writers, General Condeescu and Professor N. I. Herescu, assured me that the society would contribute with a subvention ("Aid to the Ill"), the sum was too large for my income; for the time being we had nothing to go on but the advance promised by the Cugetarea Publishing House.

I returned with excitement, but also with melancholy, to the apartment on strada Palade. My work table was covered with hundreds of letters received during my absence, as well as the last of the proofs of the journal *Zalmoxis*, waiting since August for my final approval. Beside the desk, piled on the floor, were dozens and dozens of packages of books, the majority of them from abroad. Some of them remained unopened for a long time, because, no matter how eager I was to "read in freedom," to my heart's content, book after book, I knew I should have to concentrate exclusively on works already begun (first of all, *La Mandragore*) and to limit my reading to books about which I could write reviews or articles.

It was with joy, however, that I was reunited with family and friends, beginning from the evening of my return. Father, to an extent I had never seen before, couldn't hide his emotion. He had heard so many rumors about my illness (advanced bilateral tuberculosis) that probably he had ceased to hope he would ever see me alive again. Mother, on the contrary, was the same as always: serene, confident (convinced that "truth will out" in the end and that right always triumphs), full of hope. Corina and Ticu, probably to keep from betraying themselves, kept exclaiming over and over that they'd never seen me looking so robust, that I was the "picture of health." Nina came with me; the events of the past several months had had at least this one positive result: Nina was now part of the family.

My friends, both those of the "right" and those of the "left," showed themselves just as devoted and sincere as I had left them. And because they knew our financial situation, they invited us to dinner frequently and brought gifts when they came to call. They knew that since May I had received no salary from the university, and that since my arrest Nina had lived on money she had borrowed, on advances Rosetti had given her, and on the Aid to the Ill Fund of the Society of Romanian Writers. But while the repayment of the loans could be postponed, the printer of the Official Monitor had been waiting a long time for the remainder of the 60,000 lei (a considerable sum, not only for my means) in order to print the first volume of *Zalmoxis.*

Fortunately, Alexandru Rosetti, whom I saw the second day after my return, assured me that I could resume contributing to *Revista Fundațiilor Regale,* and he advanced me a significant sum. Soon afterward, General Condeescu found a way of covering my debt to the printer, and *Zalmoxis, Revue des Études Religieuses,* volume I, appeared a few months later. Before Christmas *Nuntă în Cer* had been issued, and the first edition of 4,000 copies sold out rather quickly. The novel was, as was said then, "well received by the critics and the public." But although it was reprinted twice, it never attained the popularity enjoyed by *Maitreyi* and *Huliganii.*

Nevertheless, in that winter of 1939 I began to realize that no matter how many articles I might publish in weekly periodicals and the *Revista Fundațiilor Regale,* no matter how much I should gain from the republication of my older novels, I still would not be able to earn enough to allow us to live decently. It is true, the landlord was not pressing us to pay the rent for the last quarter, but that debt would have to be discharged some day. From a letter of Ananda

Coomaraswamy I understood that due to the influx of refugee scholars from Nazi Germany, it had become almost imposible to find faculty openings in American universities. I knew also that all the positions at the Royal Foundations had long since been filled. For the distribution of volume I of *Zalmoxis* I had spent already many thousands of lei, but the publisher in Paris received the foreign subscriptions, while in Romania the number of subscriptions was negligible.

The solutions to which I had to resort were many and varied: from short-term loans and unsigned translations, to correction of poorly translated texts and proofreading. Because the advances I had received had long since consumed the potential royalties for *La Mandragore*, Alexandru Rosetti suggested I collect in book form the studies and review articles I had published in *Revista Fundațiilor Regale*, and at the signing of the contract I could realize a rather tidy sum. The volume, entitled *Insula lui Euthanasius* (Euthanasius' Island), was given to the publisher in the winter of 1940, but due to changes in the leadership of the Royal Foundations which occurred soon after that, it could not appear until 1943, three years after my departure from the country.

In the spring of 1939, quite unexpectedly, General Condeescu died from a heart attack. I had lost my most important "protector," to whom, in spite of the differences in our ages, I had become closely attached in the past several years. Writers and men of culture had lost a supporter without equal. Thanks to him, the Society of Romanian Writers had funds available now and had been able to help a great many writers, young and old, poor and ill. It was he who had introduced to the Royal Foundations Mihail Sebastian, Păstorel Teodoreanu, and many other writers and critics. General Condeescu knew well the precarious nature of the writing profession in Romania, and he never forgot his promises. His wife told me that, in his last days, between two heart attacks, he had repeated to her several times that he had promised me a subvention for the printing of the second volume of *Zalmoxis* and still had not succeeded in sending it to me.

The next day, among those attending the religious service conducted in the general's own room, in front of the bed on which he lay, were King Carol, Elena Lupescu, and Armand Călinescu—and so I saw them, for the first time. Friends of the writer who were there included N. I. Herescu, Alexandru Rosetti, Mihail Sebastian, and myself. No one, not even D-na Condeescu, had known that the king would come, accompanied by the Lupescu woman and the prime minister.

A short while later, at the general meeting of the Society of Writers, Professor Herescu was elected president. The post of secretary thus became vacant, and Herescu persuaded me to accept it. This, too, was part of the plan he and General Condeescu had worked out for reintegrating me into "normalcy," that is, from removing the stigma of having been "detained." The position of secretary was not remunerative, but neither did it require much work. I only had to go to the Society's center three or four times a week in the evenings, and spend less than an hour working.

The only decision for which I was responsible was the distribution of texts—in almost all cases, translations of dialogues from foreign films, which had to be corrected from the standpoint of grammar and style. The film houses paid 1,600 lei for each text corrected. The society paid the one who did the correction half the sum, the other half going into the Emergency Aid Fund.

I have never regretted those hours spent at the office of the society where, besides the bursar, I always found several older members—especially Corneliu Moldovan—along with young poets and writers, more or less gifted, but uniformly poor, who had come to see if they could "get a film" (the correcting of those few typed pages took at most half an hour, and nearly all the work was done on the premises or at a nearby café). I listened to all sorts of recollections of the older men, and I found out about the latest scandals, intrigues, and jealousies from the younger ones. (And by just listening to them talking about their problems, I realized I had no right to complain about being poor.) It was my only experience of "café literary society," although, of course, only an approximate experience, because undoubtedly the young men didn't dare say in front of me all they would have said in a café.

I had to distribute the films in such a way as not to show partiality to anyone. Sometimes, when I couldn't assign a film to a certain young writer because he had had two or three already that month, and the man declared that he needed the money to be able to eat that evening, I would take the bursar aside and persuade him to advance him an amount from the fund for emergency aid. (And sometimes I would find out that the young man hadn't told me the truth, that in fact he needed the money not for dinner but for a party with friends in some cheap tavern. But, of course, we all expected this—and we weren't upset.)

*   *   *

That summer we hiked in the Bucegi Mountains, just the three of us: Nina, Giza, and I. I don't know why we didn't go with a group of friends, as we had done so many times before. Perhaps because Nina wanted by all means for me to spend a day or two at the Moroeni Sanatorium, to be examined by the doctors who had taken care of me the previous fall. I didn't suspect then that I was climbing for the last time those Bucegi Mountains which I had loved since adolescence, and of which I was so often reminded in the Himalaya region: watching the sun set from the hotel window in Darjeeling, walking on the rocky banks of the Ganges at Rishikesh, or climbing through the jungle at Lakshmanjula.

I returned with melancholy to the Moronei Sanatorium. The results of the medical analyses, at least, pleased me: the pleura was almost healed and, *sauf imprévu*, there was no danger of pleurisy developing. I was given permission even to smoke and drink coffee, things of which I had great need. We returned to Bucharest after a week, tanned but, at least in my case, without the euphoria I usually felt after coming down from the Bucegis. I sensed, like everyone else, that the cycle which had begun in 1918 was about to end—perhaps any day now. After the Munich accord and the annihilation, by stages, of Czechoslovakia, no one could doubt the imminence of war.

For those who, like me, believed that in this century at least the smaller nations could not shape their own destinies, the chief problem was: how could we survive, ethnically and spiritually, in the historical cataclysm that was coming? For my part, I put all my hope in the skill with which the Romanian people, in the past, had succeeded in withstanding the "terror of history." But this time it was not only a matter of the survival of the religious and spiritual traditions of the people, but also of the safeguarding of the culture which had been created in the past two or three centuries by the elites, that is, by a handful of thinkers, poets, and visionaries. I was thinking then of "methods of camouflage," or more precisely of "occultation," which could be put into application by the elites in case we should be condemned to undergo anew, perhaps for several centuries, the darkness of the Romanian Middle Ages. I was no pessimist, but neither did I harbor any illusions. I had been convinced, long before, that in History we Romanians are a luckless people. "History" allowed us a scant twenty years of national unity and political autonomy: from 1918 to 1938. In that interval many good things had been accomplished in Romania, but the only creations I was sure would survive were those of a spiritual order. Only these could assure our ethnic identity and cultural continuity with the past. The model of this type of survival through culture is illustrated admirably by the history of the Hebrew people. Indeed, after the destruction of the Jerusalem Temple, the Jews were threatened with disappearance as an ethnic and cultural unity, but they survived, thanks to those primary schools founded by Johanan ben Zakkai at Ybna, which safeguarded the fundamental values of Judaism.

,   ,   ,

I resumed working, with fury, on *La Mandragore*, but I managed to write no more than two additional chapters. On September 1 the German troops invaded Poland, conquering half the country in a few weeks, the other half being occupied by Soviet divisions. Then followed *la drôle de guerre*, which decieved many naive people. For my part, I strove to put the final touches to a part of what I had pondered and prepared in the past few years. That fall I collected in *Fragmentarium* a series of articles and recent notes.[1] Also in 1938–39 I wrote several essays on the idea of *coincidentia oppositorum* in the history of religions, commenting especially on the myths and symbolism of the androgyne and the dialectics of the integration of opposites in the structure of certain divinites. These texts appeared in various reviews and were completed and reunited in the volume *Mitul reintegrării* (The Myth of Reintegration), published in 1942. Some examples and conclusions from this book I was later to use in the *Traité* (called in English, *Patterns in Comparative Religion*) and *Méphistophélès et l'androgyne* (also called *The Two and the One*).

At that time also I delivered to the printer volume II of *Zalmoxis*, which contained that famous study by Ananda Coomaraswamy, "Janua Coeli," plus an article of mine on aquatic symbolism, later published, revised, in *Images et symboles*. At the end of the autumn of 1939 I wrote my first play, *Iphigenia*. Soon afterward I presented it to the committee

---

1. Many of my observations and interpretations relative to magico-religious symbolism are contained in this little book.

for review of texts at the National Theater, and it was accepted. But I never saw it performed. It was staged early in 1941, but in spite of an excellent cast of players, it was not successful. I was told I didn't have "dramatic vigor"—which probably is true. If *Iphigenia* has any merit, it must be sought in other directions.

In the winter of 1940 I was pleasantly surprised to be reunited with Nae Ionescu. He had been released from the military hospital at Brașov, and he came to see me on strada Palade. Although he had not regained his chair at the university, he was allowed to see, once a week at his villa at Băneasa, a group of young philosophers and disciples: Mircea Vulcănescu, Mihail Sebastian, Ioan Gherea, C. Noica, and others. It is unnecessary to evoke the interest, variety, and passion of the discussions. For the first time I felt that Nae was resolved—I should say even *impatient*—to write his *Metaphysics* which he had presented in many courses.[2] At our meetings I do not recall that we ever discussed "politics," not even the mysterious military immobility on the Western front.

In that winter of 1940 I was tempted by a fantastic novella—which I proceeded to write at a frenzied pace—"Secretul doctorului Honigberger" (The Secret of Doctor Honigberger). I wanted to utilize certain facts (the historical existence of Honigberger, my personal experiences at Rishikesh), camouflaging them in a fantastic story in such a way that only a forewarned reader would be able to distinguish truth from fantasy. The novella appeared in *Revista Fundațiilor Regale*, and the director of Socec Publishing House suggested I compose another story in the same genre and publish the two as a book. So I wrote "Nopți la Serampore" (Nights at Serampore) where the camouflage could be readily discovered by anyone familiar with Bengal: for in fact there was no forest anywhere around Serampore.

At the beginning of March we learned, much to our dismay, that Nae had suffered another cardiac attack. Our weekly meetings were canceled. We heard all sorts of rumors: that he was out of danger, that he had died, that he had been poisoned at the restaurant where he had last dined with friends. Then, on March 15, the telephone rang and Nina told me:

"The Professor's dead!"

2. A part of these courses appeared posthumously, edited by Mircea Vulcănescu and Constantin Noica, but these books do not represent the final and systematic form of Nae Ionescu's thought.

It was of him, of Nae Ionescu, that I kept thinking that autumn of 1940 while following, as best I could—from the newspapers, the radio, and telegrams received at the legation—the course of events in Romania. I wondered what Nae would have thought about King Carol's abdication and the "National-Legionary State" proclaimed by General Ion Antonescu and Horia Sima, vice-president of the Council of Ministers. If he had lived, probably he would have been appointed to an important post. But for how long?

In the middle of September in 1940 we moved, together with Danielopol and Vardala, to Oxford, into a modest boarding house, the "Oxoniensis." Shortly after the abdication of Carol, the minister, V. V. Tilea, was recalled to Romania, but he refused to return and instead settled, with his family, in a village near Oxford. Thus, the counselor Radu Florescu became chargé d'affaires. I went in to London about twice a week to meet with colleagues or foreign correspondents and to find out any news that might have been received at the legation (not always by coded telegram). The rest of the time I read, took notes, and elaborated the plan of a vast synthesis of morphology and history of religions, a synthesis which I glimpsed instantaneously in an air-raid shelter during an alarm. I shall return later to this book, *Prolegomena to a Comparative History of Religions* (which became *Traité d'histoire des religions* or *Patterns in Comparative Religion*). For the time being, I note the fundamental idea: hierophanies, i.e., the manifestation of the sacred in cosmic realities (objects or processes belonging to the profane world), have a paradoxical structure because they *show* and at the same time *camouflage* sacrality. By following this dialectics of hierophanies to its ultimate consequences (the sacred revealed and at the same time concealed in the cosmos, in a human being—the supreme example: the Incarnation—in a "sacred history"), it would be possible to identify a new camouflage in modern "cultural" practices, institutions, and creations. It is well known, of course, that important biological functions (eating, sexuality, fertility), the arts (dance, music, poetry, the graphic arts), occupations and trades (hunting, agriculture, construction of all sorts), techniques and sciences (metallurgy, medicine, astronomy, mathematics, chemistry) had at their origin a magico-religious function or value. But I wanted to show that even beneath its radically desacralized forms, Western culture camouflages magico-religious meanings that our contemporaries, with the exception of a few poets and artists, do not suspect.

,   ,   ,

But the "terror of history" was becoming increasingly evident all the time. With horror I learned of the assassination of Nicolae Iorga and V. Madgearu, plus a group of "detainees" awaiting questioning at the Văcărești Prison. By these assassinations on the night of November 29, the Legionary squads who committed them believed they were avenging Codreanu. In fact, they had nullified the religious meaning of "sacrifice" held by the Legionaries executed under Carol, and had irreparably discredited the Iron Guard, considered from then on as a terrorist and pro-Nazi movement. The murder of Iorga, the great historian and brilliant cultural prophet, would be a blot, for years to come, on the name of Romania.

For the first time I was glad Nae Ionescu was no longer alive. His early death had spared him this painful spectacle: the murder of all those men (even if some of them were not without guilt) without trial or sentence. As for N. Iorga, he was—and had remained—the great teacher of Nae Ionescu. No matter how many errors he made, N. Iorga could not be attacked. As Nae Ionescu had said: "When Nicolae Iorga errs, he is like a drunken priest with the holy chalice in his hand. If you strike him, you spill the chalice and profane the Holy Eucharist."

I relived that period of terror of January 1941, when the Legionary rebellion broke out—an action hard to understand, because Horia Sima was vice-premier in General Antonescu's government, together with other Legionary ministers. The information I received was, certainly, sketchy and much of it inaccurate. Nevertheless, I learned of the excesses and crimes of the Legionaries (examples were cited of pogroms: in particular, one at Iași). Soon after the crushing of the rebellion by the army, which had remained faithful to General Antonescu, I learned of the massive influx of German troops into the country, with the mission of training certain elite Romanian divisions. Many members of the legation wondered how much longer the British government would maintain diplomatic relations with Romania.

After Christmas, along with Danielopol and Vardala, we moved into a large house rented by Mrs. Sassoon, a friend of ours. To defend myself from despair, I buried myself in my work. It was chilly in my study, because both coal and electricity were being conserved as much as possible. Nevertheless, I began writing a chapter of *Prolegomena*. But, although the food improved after we moved to Mrs. Sassoon's, I still felt as weak as I had at the Oxoniensis. The doctors I consulted recommended mineral supplements (calcium and phosphorous) and rest. However, I realized I had become almost useless to the legation: my activity consisted in summarizing "cultural" reports (book reviews and bibliography about Central Europe) which I passed on sporadically to the chargé d'affaires.

So I was glad when I received the telegram informing me that I had been appointed cultural secretary at Lisbon. Radu Florescu advised the Foreign Office about my transfer and requested that two seats be reserved for Nina and me on the plane which was still making regular flights between England and Portugal. I left my library in the care of Mrs. Sassoon (but when I met her again in Paris in 1946, I learned that the majority of the books had been lost on the occasion of her moving), and I began making preparations to leave. But, of course, the Foreign Office had no reason to hurry. Very probably the severing of diplomatic relations had already been decided, and they were waiting for me to be evacuated along with the other members of the legation who wished to return home.

My intention, anyway, was for us to spend a week or two at Bucharest before settling ourselves in Lisbon. This was not only in order to see family and friends again, of whom we knew nothing, but also to allow me to obtain an audience with General Antonescu. V. V. Tilea had requested me to transmit certain things to the general. For my part, I wanted to tell him the following: (a) whereas the Romanian government believes that England will lose the war and is behaving accordingly, the more time passes the more improbable England's defeat appears; and (b) nevertheless, even on the hypothesis that England will lose, Romania cannot dispense with her (in 1918, following Germany's defeat, the most important diplomatic post, after Paris and London, was Berlin); therefore, the way England was being mocked in the press and on Radio Bucharest was not only ridiculous but also dangerous for the political prestige of Romania. But I wanted to convey to General Antonescu one thing further: London had been saved by the home guards, that is, by civilians. The only possibility for withstanding massive bombardments is through the organization of the civilian populace.

At the beginning of February Radu Florescu announced that we had seats on the plane to Lisbon for February 10. On the seventh we finished making preparations for our departure. On the ninth we left Oxford in Florescu's auto. We lunched at the Savoy with all the colleagues from the legation, who then accompanied us to the train station. At 3:00 we caught the train for Bristol.

I copy here several excerpts, and summarize others, from the *Journal*, written in Lisbon: "Carefully I guarded the sealed valise, although I was told it contained nothing important. We spoke to each other hardly at all the whole time on the way. We were both very anxious, and we hid our feelings from each other. We didn't know if we'd escape bombardment, because Bristol had been violently attacked in recent weeks. We didn't know if we'd be safe, even on the plane. We arrived in Bristol at night, during an alarm. The station— almost destroyed. No porter, no taxi. A fine rain. With the greatest difficulty we managed to get out of the station and onto the platform. We set our suitcases on a trolley, put the bouquets of flowers we had received on top of them, and waited. After a quarter of an hour, seeing that the "all-clear" had not been given and that no taxi was in sight, I left Nina with the luggage and set off in the darkness.

"Now and then there came the sound of antiaircraft batteries, but I was used to that. Finally, I found a taxi. The driver hesitated to take me, but I promised him ten shillings extra. We arrived at the hotel at 10:00 P.M. The restaurant was closed. All we could get were two sandwiches and some tea. I didn't realize that the hotel where a room had been reserved for us was the only one that had escaped bombardment—or, more precisely, one wing of it only had escaped! I went into the bathroom, but no sooner had I begun to draw the water when bombs began falling nearby. We slept half-dressed. We had to be up by 6:00, because the car was coming to get us at 7:00.

"We left in the dark. In front of me sat an officer with tired eyes, smoking. (He was the one who would search me later.) As soon as the car set off, we began to be aware of the extent of the disaster caused by the bombings. We passed through ruins. Here and there, a building was still standing, but through its windows the sky was visible. A sinister sight, which haunted me for a long time afterward.

"We arrived at the airport at 8:00. There were just the two of us, plus a young Englishwoman (a secretary at the Madrid legation), a young foreign man, and the crew. We were left for the last. We waited in a large room, with a reservist beside us, dressed so oddly, with a uniform too large for him, that I wondered if he were a Secret Service agent who knew Romanian, put there to eavesdrop on our conversation. I was called, alone. I took the diplomatic case with me.

"When I showed the service passport to the functionary who was sitting at a table beside the captain, he pointed out that cultural attachés are not included in the official list of the accredited diplomatic corps. I could not, therefore, enjoy the benefits of diplomatic privilege. He asked for my billfold, but found nothing compromising in it. The captain left the room and turned me over to some special agents who proceeded efficiently to a body search. When I found myself naked, I felt humiliated and experienced a moment of silent indignation, but I kept my temper and I don't believe the agents noticed anything. Their attention was concentrated on the search. They examined everything so painstakingly and with such dexterity that I'm sure that if I had made a mark with a pin on one of my shoestrings, or if I had dotted my tie with imperceptible points, I'd have been arrested as a spy. Nothing could have escaped them. They removed the heels of my shoes, they scrutinized the buttons, the stitching, the lining—in a word, everything.

"On the plane later I found out that Nina had suffered a similar radical body search. At the same time that she was being searched, in another room her toiletries were undergoing examination: the toothpaste, powder, lipstick, and other things were pierced with pins, taken apart, etc. Our baggage, too, as we learned only at the airport at Sintra, had been opened and gone through, piece by piece. The bags had been repacked and closed with some impatience—because the search had lasted almost three hours, and absolutely nothing compromising had been found. In the haste to close up the suitcases (the plane had been delayed two and a half hours beyond its schedule), the handle had been torn off one bag and the stitching on the valises was damaged.

"When the captain reappeared, he told me that, not being a part of the diplomatic corps at London, I could not take the sealed briefcase. I refused then to leave. But he pointed out that without me the plane would not leave, and in that case he would have to sign a legal document obliging me or the legation to pay the sum of 1,000 pounds. I asked to telephone London. Impossible. He allowed me to send a telegram. For the briefcase he handed me a receipt which I have kept; it's rather amusing. On a piece of paper with the heading "British Air Mail" it is stated that they have received from me a sealed valise.

"I met Nina, in tears, and we ran to the airplane. The captain followed us, now very affable. He wished us bon voyage, and held out his hand to me. There, in the sight of all, I had the satisfaction of not shaking it. It was my only revenge."

The flight lasted almost nine hours, because the plane veered first sharply toward the Atlantic and then headed for the Portuguese coast, to the right of the city of Viana de Castello. I was obsessed again by the enigma of collective death. This time the enigma seemed reducible to a *malentendu* (of a political nature, of course). I was the first Romanian to leave England, a besieged fortress. Those whose business it was to know, knew about my connection with Nae Ionescu, considered by many the most intelligent (and therefore the most dangerous) Germanophile. If the "specialists" had arrived at the conclusion that my whole pro-Allied attitude and activity in England were part of a second-rate system of deception, my return to a Romania occupied by German troops would entail a series of inconveniences. Obviously, I didn't know any "military secrets," but I could have given information about the results of the bombings. Above all, I would be able to make negative propaganda, speaking of the food shortages and other privations. I wondered why just *this* airplane was nearly empty, when we had been told repeatedly that for weeks before no seats were available in any plane going to Portugal. The crew, which was Dutch, and the young legation secretary going to Madrid might have been sacrificed. . . . But there was yet another possibility: that our plane would be shot down by German fighters. The same collective death, although provoked by another *malentendu*. . . .

We arrived that evening at Sintra, and after I had telephoned our legation, we caught a taxi. We couldn't believe the profusion of lights in the city. At the legation, the chargé d'affaires, Cămărășescu, was waiting for us, together with Jean Antohi, economic minister, and the consul Bastos. The evening newspapers carried the information that Great Britain had severed diplomatic ties with Romania.

"This explains everything!" exclaimed Cămărășescu. Then he telegraphed the foreign minister that my diplomatic case had been confiscated and I had been subjected to a body search.

A room had been engaged for us at the Hotel Suisse-Atlantico, in Cascaes, where we would remain for almost three months. Next to the lights of the city, our greatest surprise was the menu at the hotel restaurant: sixteen different dinners to choose from!

18. Lisbon

LISBON won me over from the first day, just as the Lusitanian provinces did as I came to know them. I had begun to learn Portuguese during my last year at Calcutta, but only now, in the spring of 1941, did I study it methodically and enthusiastically. I read several newspapers daily, because I had replaced the press attaché, Aron Cotruş, who had been transferred to Madrid. Mornings I spent at the legation, discussing "events" with Cămărăşescu and Antohi, trying to make myself useful (for example, I wrote short press bulletins and corrected Cămărăşescu's reports).

The rest of the time I discovered previously unvisited neighborhoods, or, in our room in the Suisse-Atlantico, in the village of Cascaes, I read books—with dictionary in hand—until well past midnight: for example, the novels of Eça de Queiroz (fortunately, immediately after *O primo Basilio*, there fell into my hands the admirable *Os Maias*), the historical monographs of Oliveira Martines and Alfredo Pimenta, or the massive *História de Portugala* by João Ameal. But my secret desire was to concentrate on the life and work of Camoëns. In time, I bought all the annotated editions of *Sonêtos* and *Os Lusidos*, and, one evening in late spring, I had the luck to find at an old bookshop the famous monograph of Carolinei de Vasconcellos, long out of print. Camoëns attracted me for another reason also: his biography and poetry were linked to a region of India which I had not known: Goa and the Malabar Coast. I planned to write a book about Camoëns and Portuguese India. To me it seemed interesting (and somewhat "symbolic") for a Romanian who had lived and studied in Bengal to present the greatest Lusitanian poet who, three centuries earlier, had lived on the other coast, the western, of India. But this book, like so many others, has remained in a projected state.

At the Janelas Verdas Museum I discovered, alongside many canvasses by Hieronymous Bosch, that prodigious painter Nuño Gonzalves. Only in the museum in the little town of Vizeu, when I found myself that spring suddenly before the paintings of Vasco Fernandes, did I experience again the thrill that left me mute in front of the triptych of Nuño Gonzalves. I returned often to Janelas Verdas, and I filled many pages of a pocket notebook there, as I did also on my walks around the city. Along with some other papers, these notes were lost. I have found only a few fragments, which I transcribe and include as the Appendix to this chapter.

∕   ∕   ∕

In the first week I realized from the telegrams received from the Ministry of Propaganda that I should not be able to go to Bucharest and therefore I should not be able to meet with General Antonescu—a meeting to which I, as well as V. V. Tilea, had attached a great many hopes. I had received a diplomatic passport, and I was obliged to remain in Lisbon as cultural attaché and, temporarily, press attaché as well. The chargé d'affaires, Cămărășescu, seemed delighted at this appointment, since he had not gotten on too well with Aron Cotruş. I believe, moreover, that I was of use when, at the beginning of spring, the deposed King Carol and Elena Lupescu fled Seville and took refuge in Lisbon.

Predictably, General Antonescu telegraphed Cămărășescu, instructing him to protest directly to Salazar. The secretary general of the Foreign Ministry replied to him, saying that the Portuguese government considered Carol a political refugee, and that this being the case he could not make any commitment. General Antonescu, then, sent a message for Carol, warning him not to attempt any political activity, since his first gesture would endanger the dynasty itself.

Cămărășescu told me in detail how the audience went. Dressed in a frock coat as Urdăreanu had requested, he presented himself exactly at the appointed hour and was taken to a drawing room in the house of the former Romanian minister to Lisbon, Jean Pangal. He waited some five minutes; then Urdăreanu appeared, and took him to another drawing room. Finally, they went to a third drawing room where Carol was waiting, standing (according to Cămărăşescu, looking "aged, tired, without *éclat*"). Carol asked him, "What do you want?" and Cămărăşescu read him the general's message. "Tell the Romanian government that I shall respect the pledges made," replied the former sovereign. Cămărăşescu started to withdraw, but Carol invited him to be seated and they conversed for a quarter of an hour (Cămărăşescu repeated, very impressed, the king's lavish words of praise for *Maitreyi* and *Yoga*). Carol assured him that he would remain for some time in Portugal, as he was intending to write a history of the Bragança family, to which he was related.

After this audience, unexpectedly, without anyone's suspecting anything—and, according to Pangal, without his paying him the salary of $1,000 per month which he had set—Carol embarked with Elena Lupescu on an American transatlantic liner with South America as its destination.

In the middle of April, Nina returned to Romania for a visit of several weeks. In the meantime, the new minister, Iuraşcu, arrived, and I was obliged to accompany him and his wife on a long journey around Portugal.

On April 28, from the balcony of the Ministry of Finance, I witnessed the massive popular demonstration in Praça de Commercio in honor of Salazar. I transcribe a few lines from the *Journal:*

"He is dressed in a simple, gray suit, informal, and he smiles, saluting with his hand, coolly, without other gestures. When he appeared, baskets of rose petals were emptied from above—red and yellow, the colors of Portugal's flag. I watched him then as he spoke. He read, warmly enough, but without emphasis, raising his eyes from time to time and looking at the throng. After he had concluded his speech and the crowd had given him a tumultuous ovation, he inclined his head and smiled."

Three days later I participated with the whole legation in the ceremony of the presentation of the letters of accreditation of the minister Iuraşcu. This was the first time I had taken part in such a ceremony and the first time, too, that I had worn a full-dress suit. From the Hotel Aviz—where Iuraşcu was staying—to the presidential palace, our cars were escorted by motorcycles. I was the only one not wearing decorations—except, of course, Salazar, who accepted every kind of decoration, but never wore any. The president, the old General Carmona, listened, leaning on his saber, to the text read by Iuraşcu, nodding his head significantly every time he heard the word "Latinity." I transcribe from my *Journal:*

"Salazar, beside him in a frock coat, seemed exceptionally modest, as if he were one of the president's secretaries. He listened without making himself conspicuous. Now I have seen his eyes well. They are not sparkling and they do not pierce you, intimidating you, but they pass through you without hostility."

In the latter half of May, Nina returned from Bucharest, bringing Giza. She had seen several friends, and also Alexandru Marcu, Bădăuţ, and other functionaries at the Propaganda Ministry. All, though for different reasons, insisted upon one thing: that I remain in Lisbon. I was the only one who had known England under siege, under bombardment; I had connections with several writers and journalists, and I followed the English press. I must by all means keep the ministry up to date on the news and commentaries of the British newspapers which arrived regularly, by plane, in Lisbon. Soon, however, this mission was entrusted to Gh. Munteanu, who had come from London. Thus, by the start of summer, I was free to focus exclusively on the Portuguese press and culture.

A friend of Cămărăşescu, the attorney Costa Pinto, had a small villa at Cascaes, the picturesque fishing village near Estoril, the most luxurious town on the littoral. I rented this little house in June for the entire summer. Every morning I took the train from the village and in a half-hour I arrived in Lisbon. Ordinarily, I would stay at the legation until evening, or even late at night, but sometimes I returned to Cascaes around lunchtime. By the end of June the heat was intense. I returned with joy to Costa Pinto's little house. In the largest room, with windows opening on the patio, there was a plain wooden table and several bookshelves. There I set up my library, consisting in the main of Portuguese and Spanish books.[1]

Whenever I could—on free afternoons, Sundays, nights—I would shut myself away in my workroom. On May 7 I had received from London, sent by Vardala through the diplomatic pouch of the Swiss legation, the package of notes and manuscripts confiscated at Bristol. I rejoiced to find—along with *La Mandragore* and notes for *Prole-*

---

1. I had procured from Madrid all that was to be found of the series *Clássicos Castellanos* and the first twelve volumes of the *Obras completas* of Menendez Pellayo, a favorite writer of mine from student years.

gomena—the "journal" of the novel *Ştefania* (the first part of *Viaţă
nouă*) which I had begun in the Oxoniensis boardinghouse on November 5, 1940, and had interrupted on December 10. I read those 75
pages I had written, and to my amazement they seemed good. That
same night, May 7, I began working again on the novel, and in a week
I had written 120 pages. But on rereading this manuscript whole, I
realized it was unusable. So it was necessary that I begin another version. I took advantage of the solitude of Cascaes and wrote every
night, with the exception of the inevitable interruptions caused by
meetings and events which I shall mention shortly. In the "journal"
of the novel (which I had the good inspiration to continue), I find that
by August 21 I had arrived at page 201. But at the beginning of September, after she had typed the first 70 pages, Nina seemed disappointed. Many months later, in order to take a break for a few
hours from the exhausting work to which I had harnessed myself (I
was concluding then the book about Salazar), I reread the new version of the novel. An immense melancholy came over me. I had to
admit that I had failed again this time. The novel seemed monotonous,
with no sparkle; too long and drawn-out. I abandoned it then, hoping
to be able to rewrite it later. But since then I have never reopened the
manuscript. And so the cycle *Viaţă nouă*—begun with *Întoarcerea din
rai* and continued with *Huliganii*—has remained unfinished.

I wondered later if contributing to this failure was not the fact that,
with the extension and intensification of the Second World War, the
world of *Viaţă nouă* had come to seem to me both outdated and devoid
of psychological interest. In *Huliganii* I had presented—rather skillfully, I thought—the behavior and ideology of a youth which, through
its violent rupture from the moral values of contemporary society, anticipated the "angry young men" of the 1950s. But the proportions I
visualized for *Viaţă nouă* (about 2,000 pages), the number and variety
of characters, obliged me to evoke, at a leisurely pace, a world of the
1930s that had already become dated.

On June 22, 1941, I was on the beach at Guineho when Nina brought
me the news of our entrance into the war against Soviet Russia. That
evening I wrote in my *Journal:* "I realize that I didn't expect this war in
1941. I believed the so-called Russo-German collaboration would last
longer. This means that the Germans realize they can't win the war
this year and are preparing for a long conflict. In my opinion, the attack is a sign of weakness on Germany's part."

I left immediately for the legation. But I learned little from the telegrams received that evening. And only on June 29 did the first German communiqués of the war appear. They were impressive, to be sure, but they did not lead us to foresee a lightning victory. I shall not recall here the episodes of the first months of the war, nor the emotions, hopes, and doubts they provoked. For my part, I didn't allow myself to be optimistic. I knew the strength and determination of England and, like many others, I could not believe that sooner or later the United States would not intervene directly in the war.

Obviously, I couldn't do anything then. I spent the time at the legation reading all the newspapers, waiting for telegrams, or making the rounds of the newspaper offices where I had a good number of friends, explaining "Romania's position," trying to learn from the Anglophile journalists the reactions of British public opinion. Sometimes at night, in my work room at Cascaes, I tried to find myself again by writing a page or two of the novel. But even this defense against the pressure of events was denied me in the first weeks of July, during the visit of Pamfil Şeicaru.

Şiecaru had been sent by the Antonescu government on an official mission to Marshal Pétain, Franco, and Salazar. I hadn't seen him for many years, but, from a distance, I had admired his success in making himself useful, in turn, to Carol and to Antonescu. I thought of the destiny of Nae Ionescu, of Armand Călinescu, of Iorga; Pamfil Şiecaru's triumph, I said to myself, must surely have a symbolic significance. But in this tragic moment, Şiecaru too could be of use to the country. The minister Iuraşcu had obtained audiences for him with Salazar, President Carmona, and the Patriarch. In those eight or nine days, I escorted him to all the newspaper offices, I introduced him to António Ferro, the minister of propaganda, to António Eça de Queiroz (who held an important post in the Press Department), the directors of newspapers, and all the journalists with whom I had become acquainted. I insisted on publicizing his visit to Portugal as much as possible. While he was there, I spent almost the whole time with him or arranging for his interviews. I accompanied him in the minister's car to Coimbra; I smiled, sometimes, finding myself next to him at Alcobaça, Batalha, and Busacco. But, I said to myself, we're at war, the most terrible war in the history of Romania. In anticipation of the collective death which I couldn't manage to forget about, I was doing my duty.

In those weeks I decided to concentrate my efforts on a book about

Salazar, and immediately after Şiecaru's departure I began to reread the documentary material I had accumulated and to look for other sources. (I managed to continue working on the novel at night, however.) But in the first days of September I fell ill, and the flu persisted for a long time. The rains had begun, and the little house at Cascaes was now as damp and chilly as a cellar. Thus, on October 1 we moved to Lisbon, to a roomy and comfortably furnished apartment on avienda Elias Garcia, number 147, fourth floor.

/ / /

In the four and a half years I spent in Portugal, I kept a rather elaborate journal, especially between 1942 and 1945. If it should ever be published in its entirety, the reader will find many facts and much information useful for understanding the era. I shall not try to summarize them here. I shall content myself with remembering just those events which played a role in the trajectory of my life, and to indicate the changes, revisions, and—finally—the renewal of conceptions and hopes that I experienced before leaving the country.

That autumn unfolded under the sign of war. Nevertheless, we attempted occasionally to escape from the terror of contemporary history. I remember, for example, how eager I was at the beginning of October to meet Reinaldo de Santos, director of the Museum of Modern Art. Eugenio d'Ors had spoken to me about him at Madrid; when I asked him to what extent it is still possible today to be a *uomo universale* of the type of Leonardo da Vinci or Leibniz, Eugenio d'Ors cited the name of do Santos: the best surgeon in Portugal, an honored historian of the arts, and an innovator in the criticism of aesthetic ideas. At that first meeting with him we talked for two hours—in particular about Camoëns and maritime civilizations. I returned home reinvigorated, but also melancholic; I knew that the next day I must return "to duty."

In November the minister Iuraşcu was recalled to Romania and replaced by Ambassador Victor Cădere, professor of law at the University of Cluj. In the last two weeks of November, many farewell receptions were held. Nina and I, too, had to have such a ceremony in our apartment on avienda Elias Garcia: a new step in my initiation into the mythico-ritual scenario of the diplomatic corps.

For many months I concentrated almost exclusively on the book *Salazar şi revolutia în Portugalia*. I had at hand now a considerable quantity of published material to which I added many unpublished facts gathered from journalists and historians, such as Manuel Murias, Silva Dias, and Correia Marquez. On November 19 I began the writing. I wrote every night, till three and four A.M. By proceeding thus, in a month's time I had some sixty typed pages. Sometimes, for relaxation, I would write long articles for the review *Acção* ("Latina ginta e regina," "Camoëns e Eminescu," etc.). The subjects I discussed in the book as well as in the articles were interesting, but, with the exception of a few of the essays, they were not integral to my literary "project." I wrote them to promote Portuguese-Romanian ties of a cultural and at the same time political nature.

The great surprise of December was the Japanese attack on Pearl Harbor and the entrance of the United States into the war. From that moment on, Portugal was a different country. People were nervous, suspicious; after the first Japanese naval victories, Lisbon seemed panic-stricken. Iuraşcu had gone, and the new minister, Cădere, had not yet arrived. Cămărăşescu had been transfered long before to Rome. The chargé d'affaires was a young legation secretary, Totescu. In company with Leontin Constantinescu, the new press counselor, I helped Totescu as much as I could to carry on his mission in a critical situation which no one had foreseen.

After the arrival of the minister Cădere and after I had shared with him my projects of cultural propaganda, I doubled my hours of work: the Salazar volume had to be written as quickly as possible, and then printed immediately. In January of 1942 a cold prevented me from leaving the house for several days, thus enabling me to write, feverishly, some fifteen pages. I did not interrupt the work until mid-February, when, along with D-na Cădere and the Leontin Constantinescu family, we traveled to southern Portugal: to Algarva, the only province I hadn't visited previously. I saw then, for the first time, almond trees in blossom and orange trees laden with fruit.

A few days later I was at the home of Alfredo Pimenta, historian, scholar, and famous polemicist—one of the few Portuguese intellectuals who, owing to his intransigent anti-Communism, supported the Rome-Berlin Axis. I admired his library immensely, and, even more, his courage to be unpopular. Toward the end of March I met, at António Ferro's place, Ortega y Gasset; I was to see him again many times, fascinated always by his presence and his provocative observations which transformed every conversation, however banal, into a philosophical dialogue.

I wrote furiously, sleeping just four or five hours per night, as in my early youth. But a "heart attack" (actually, as it was proved later, the attack was vascular) forced me to cut down on my hours of work. I was working so stubbornly because I sensed that, very soon, I would find myself detached from this book; from long experience I knew that after that, every page written would demand a tenfold effort. Indeed, I did not succeed in drafting the last chapter before April 30, the day Nina and Giza returned to Romania for a visit of several months.

I finished *Salazar și revoluția în Portugalia* at the end of May. A few days later N. I. Herescu telegraphed me from Bucharest to inform me that he had listed me among the candidates for the chair of Philosophy of Culture, recently created. The news made me glad and sad at the same time. On the one hand, I was being invited, after a three-year absence, to rejoin the Faculty of Letters and Philosophy in Bucharest; but on the other hand, an enigmatic melancholy overshadowed me: is it not too late? In any event, I asked the minister for a two-weeks' leave of absence and decided I would leave on July 10. The legation obtained a place for me on a Lufthansa plane which made the flight between Lisbon and Berlin twice weekly. As soon as I received the ticket, my spirits brightened: I was reminded, with a sudden fervor, of the collective death.

*   *   *

On the evening of July 6, António Ferro telephoned, informing me that the next day, at 5:00, I would be received in audience by Salazar. Being unable to find a taxi, I arrived at the Palace San Bento almost running. The doorkeeper asked me whom I wished to see. "Señhor Presidente," I told him. He pointed to the stairs in back. "Two flights up, on your right." This was how one gained entry to the dictator of Portugal! In the few minutes I had to wait, I gulped down a glass of water; my mouth was so dry I was afraid I wouldn't be able to talk.

I transcribe from the *Journal:* "I enter the office and he receives me at the door, pronouncing my name very precisely. A modest office, with a wooden desk bare of even one file folder, and to the left of it a little stand for the telephone. [. . .] He is less rigid, seen at close range. There is something candid, fresh, virginal in this face so finely chiseled and so masculine. His eyes are moist, shadowed, and they seem to be looking at you from a great distance; now and then his glance glides over you and passes beyond. He has a warm, soft voice, different from the one I have heard many times on the radio." He asked me about the studies I had done in India and about my Portuguese experience. When I spoke to him about *Salazar și revoluția în Portugalia,* which I had just finished, he seemed surprised by the documentary information and my interpretation of the creation of a "New State" (*Estado Novo*).

The audience was to have lasted fifteen minutes, but when the secretary came in and announced that a quarter of an hour had passed, Salazar waved him away. He returned fifteen minutes later and withdrew immediately. Finally, when fifty-five minutes had elapsed, I made as though to rise several times. Salazar stood up all of a sudden, wished me a safe trip, and calmly shook my hand.

Back at my apartment, I recorded in the *Journal,* in detail and at length, all that I considered interesting in that long audience. Reread now after forty years, some portions seem extremely valuable. It would not be worthwhile to summarize them here, however.[2] On a separate page I noted all that had reference to the current situation in Romania and, especially, to the problems and crises Romania would face after the conclusion of the war. I realized that, in an ingenious way, these considerations constituted a personal message addressed to Marshal Antonescu. "If I were in his place," Salazar had said in essence, "I'd keep my army within the country as much as possible. Marshal Antonescu is not a politician; he did not obtain his position through the support of a political party; his only strength is in the army. Why then scatter it on the Russian steppes? By keeping it at home, or as close to the borders as possible, I would be able to have the support of the army to cope with any difficulties that might arise." Obviously, Salazar was suggesting the marshal follow the example of Finland.[3] I reread this page several times, almost learning it by heart, and I included it in the diplomatic case I carried with me to Bucharest. But, owing to circumstances I shall relate later, I considered it prudent to destroy it ultimately.

As might be expected, my long audience with Salazar, and especially the fact that three days later I was leaving for Bucharest, did not escape the attention of certain secret services. The minister Victor

2. The complete text will be included in a possible selection from the *Lusitanian Journal* (1941–45).

3. It is useless to discuss here to what extent the polices of Marshal Mannerheim could have been imitated.

Cădere informed me confidentially that I was already being followed by Gestapo agents, adding that the situation would become even more complex after I had been received by Marshal Antonescu and Mihail Antonescu. He insisted that I be "as cautious as possible."

I stayed two days in Berlin, spending all my time with my colleagues of the press service. I noted in my *Journal:* "After five years, I find Berlin more sad. Few people on the streets, and all seem to have a 'preoccupation' in their eyes." I took the train for Bucharest, and twenty-four hours after I had set foot on the platform of the North Station, I was summoned for an audience by Mihail Antonescu, vice-president of the Council of Ministers.

The audience took place at 8:00 P.M. Mihail Antonescu "begins by telling me that he knows me from *Cuvântul,* when he came to see Nae Ionescu, and that he is not in the habit of forgetting people he has known 'in an earlier time'" (*Journal*). We talked for about an hour, sitting in armchairs facing each other in front of the desk. I transmitted to him the "message" from Salazar to the marshal, but with some difficulty, because he kept interrupting me. He liked to talk; he said a great many things—not unintelligent, but rather commonplace and, above all, oratorically expressed. After the way he spoke about the military ("They have a pragmatic spirit and don't know how to run a country") I doubt he ever conveyed Salazar's message to the marshal.

The very next day, on my way to the Propaganda Ministry to see the new minister, Professor Alexandru Marcu, I realized I was being followed. Thereafter, every time I left any place—home, the residences of family members or friends, or the ministry—I identified those two or three agents who were attempting to fulfill their mission discreetly. (Sometimes I identified them immediately; sometimes it took me a few minutes.) Thus, I had to be, as V. Cădere put it, "as cautious as possible." For that reason I met with very few of my old friends: Mircea Vulcănescu, Constantin Noica, Dan Botta, and some others. I met with Professor Alexandru Rosetti only once. I avoided seeing Mihail Sebastian, and this fact, which pained me and grieved Sebastian profoundly, was to have grave consequences many years afterward.

I stayed as much as possible in my study on strada Palade (putting the final touches to the articles which constituted the little volume

Mitul reintegrării) or with members of my family. Corina and Ticu were just as I had left them; their son Sorin, however, nearly five now, no longer resembled the shy and listless toddler of the spring of 1940. My brother Nicu had been mobilized on the spot, in the chemistry laboratory he directed. My parents seemed older to me. I perceived, however, that they were happy in the knowledge that I was far from the country, far from the front.

From the few discussions I had with friends, from all they told me, I gathered that the marshal was not very popular and that Mihail Antonescu was detested—or, at best, he wasn't taken seriously. As for the war in the East, I believe few Romanians were conscious of the disastrous consequences of a defeat. That week spent in Bucharest has remained in my memory as a melancholy dream, punctuated by nightmares. And yet I could not have suspected then that—except for Corina and Sorin—I would never again see my family, my country, or the majority of my friends; while my library, manuscripts, and files of notes would remain inaccessible to me, stored in the attics of the houses where my parents and Corina lived over the years.

I breathed easily only when the train pulled away from the platform of North Station. Up to the last minute, I had been afraid of being detained on some pretext or other by the Secret Service—as had happened with some of my colleagues who had gone to Bucharest on missions or on vacation. The page on which I had written Salazar's message I had burned as soon as I saw how vigilantly I was being followed. For the same reason, I didn't dare take with me the journal for the years 1928–40, which Nina was to entrust later to N. I. Herescu, and which would be lost a few years afterward, along with many of Herescu's own manuscripts and correspondence.

We stopped in Berlin for two days. One of the press attachés, Goruneanu, escorted me to the residence of Carl Schmitt, in Dahlem. Schmitt at that time was finishing his little book on *Land und Meer*, and he wanted to ask me some questions about Portugal and maritime civilizations. I spoke with him about Camoëns, and, more particularly, about aquatic symbolism. (Goruneanu had given him volume 2 of *Zalmoxis*, where my "Notes sur le symbolisme aquatique" had appeared.) In Schmitt's perspective, *Moby Dick* was the greatest creation of the maritime spirit since the *Odyssey*. He hadn't been very impressed by *Os Lusiados*, read in German translation. We talked for three hours. While accompanying us to the Metro station, he explained why he considered aviation a terrestrial symbol.

, , ,

As soon as I returned to Lisbon I resumed—at least apparently—the schedule interrupted two weeks before. I had been named cultural counselor, which required me to read only one newspaper per day. The rest of the time I could devote to study and writing. Thus I was able to rework a long passage from the still unfinished *La Mandragore*, which was to appear in volume 3 of *Zalmoxis*. Also, I began writing in French a volume published in 1943 (in Portuguese) under the title *Os Romenos, Latinos do Oriente* (The Romanians, Latins of the East). The historian João Ameal had invited me to contribute to the series *Gládio*, which he directed. I was continuing, as is evident, the effort at drawing Portugal and Romania closer together—an effort begun with articles in *Acção* and the book about Salazar. At the same time I had organized a series of cultural exchanges. It was inaugurated in October by N. I. Herescu, who was invited to lecture at the University of Lisbon.[4]

I was not always successful, however, in maintaining my serenity. The news reports from the Eastern front were not encouraging. I sensed that catastrophes and radical changes were in the making, and I wondered to what extent the spiritual values in which I believed could survive. I sought support in meditating on several mystical and metaphysical texts, and in contemplating works of art. For that reason I was happy to accompany N. I. Herescu to Madrid. Nina and I stayed some ten days in Spain. The new cultural counselor, the art critic and historian of the arts, Alexandru Busuioceanu, guided us around Castile; we revisited Toledo; we discovered the charm of those famous towns Segovia and Aranjuez. I spent much time in conversation with Eugenio d'Ors, preparing with him a selection of his writings which I had in mind to translate into Romanian. I verified what I had discovered long ago: the best defense against the terror of history, next to religious experience, is spirituality, creation, culture.

Like many of my contemporaries and many other Europeans, I interpreted the landing of American troops in North Africa as an en-

4. In the following two years other Romanian savants lectured, a play by Fernandei de Castro was performed in 1943 at the National Theater in Bucharest, and George Georgescu was invited in 1944 to direct a series of concerts in Portugal.

couraging sign. The United States had recognized the priority of European problems. But the operation did not have the expected results: the campaign dragged on until April 1943.

Just before Christmas I received Carl Schmitt's little book *Land und Meer*. I had sent him somewhat earlier the third volume of *Zalmoxis*. From a letter from Goruneanu I learned that Ernst Jünger had borrowed volume 2 of *Zalmoxis* from Schmitt and had taken it with him, in his knapsack, when he was drafted and sent to the Eastern front.[5] In January 1943, I was invited by the rector of the University of Munich to participate in the inauguration of the Sven Heddin Central Asiatic Museum. But pretending to have a stubborn case of the flu, I didn't go. I was obsessed by the agony of the armies encircling Stalingrad, where there were several Romanian divisions. Sleep was impossible without sleeping pills.

I defended myself as best I could. I defended myself especially by writing. I began writing a novel entitled, provisionally, *Apocalips*, whose principal character was a half-educated mythomaniac. In that year I interrupted and resumed work on the novel several times; then I abandoned it definitively.[6] In February I began composing a long comparative study about rituals connected with the construction of buildings, which I finished in a few months. It appeared at the end of the year under the title, *Comentarii la legenda Meșterului Manole* (Commentaries on the Legend of Master Manole).

                    /   /   /

The personnel at the legation was doubled. The former chargé d'affaires at Washington, Brutus Coste, had arrived some time earlier; from Helsinki came Dinu Cantemir, and from Bucharest Ticu Burileanu. The Faculty of Letters at Lisbon established a lectureship in the Romanian language; N. I. Herescu recommended a former student of his, Victor Buescu. The longer the war continued, the more important Portugal became: a neutral country, the age-old ally of England, but with a nationalist and anti-Communist government which long ago had severed diplomatic ties with the USSR. For us Romanians, Portugal was even more valued for its Latinity, to which we also laid

5. I read later in Jünger's *Journal* the impression made on him by my article, "Notes sur le symbolisme aquatique." [See entries for November 15, 1942 and May 5, 1944. Tr.]
6. I was to use this character, Vădastra, in the novel *Noaptea de Sânziene* (see chapter 22).

claim. I continued, therefore, the cultural propaganda through articles, interviews, receptions, and meetings with Portuguese journalists and writers.

At the end of April I accepted the invitation of our minister in Madrid to accompany him on a long automobile trip through Andalusia. I visited for the first time Cordoba, Seville, Granada, Malaga, and Cadiz. A few weeks prior to the trip, Nina had gone to Bucharest; I thought she had seemed sad, worried. From the letters I received via diplomatic mail, I understood that she had been confined to a hospital for a week, but she assured me that it was nothing serious. On the nineteenth of June when she returned, accompanied by Giza, I realized she hadn't told me the whole truth. She admitted then that she had undergone minor surgery for the removal of a cyst, and the operation had left her tired. The truth was she had been operated on—too late—for a malignant tumor, but she had requested everyone—family, friends, colleagues at the legation, doctors—not to tell me anything. I learned the truth only a few weeks before the end.

The first half of the month of November we spent at Paris. Nina had to consult a specialist. She assured me again that everything was going well, that I mustn't worry. Indeed, she returned in very good spirits from the Parisian clinic which the surgeon in Bucharest had recommended to her: the results of the tests were satisfactory. At Paris I met Georges Dumézil, René Grousset, Paul Morand (then ambassador to Bucharest), and Jean Cocteau. I spent almost the whole time with Emil Cioran. We made the rounds of the bookstores, and I bought more books then than I had purchased in two years at Lisbon.

That brief immersion in the cultural atmosphere of Paris reinvigorated me. I realized the cost of those years spent far from libraries, devoid of prolonged contact with Orientalists and historians of religions. Of course, I had been doing my duty, and in the most favorable conditions at that. I knew that because of my myopia and the pleurisy trouble I had suffered in 1938, I had become unfit for military service; but I might have been sent to the front as a correspondent, like many others. But now, I had to recoup the time spent on cultural propa-

7. Herescu was glad later, because less than a year after that he fled with his family to Lisbon.

ganda; in other words, I had to double the hours of work. When, at the end of November, I received a telegram from Herescu informing me that the competition for the new chair would be held on December 12, I replied emphatically that I would not be present.[7] I sensed that the era of creation in the context of contemporary Romanian culture was ended. I knew we were on the threshold of a new stage.

We celebrated New Year's Eve on avienda Elias Garcia very modestly, with just Brutus Coste, Leontin Constantinescu, and their wives. The year 1944 looked very dark for us Romanians. Toward the end of January I noted in the *Journal:* "I should like to write about the 'terror of history.'" But I was concentrating on *Prolegomena (Patterns)*; I had at my disposal a wealth of documentary material. (In addition to the books brought from Paris, I had bought whole series from Finland, Germany, and Italy.) The work on *Prolegomena* restored my spiritual equilibrium and helped me withstand the trials History had in store for us. After the Soviets had crossed the Dniester and during the time of the massive American aerial bombardment of Bucharest, our lives, Nina's and mine, were a nightmare. Now and then a meeting, a long conversation with a thinker or a notable artist, freed me from the oppression of the present. Such were the discussions with Carl Schmitt, who came to Portugal for a week at the end of May, and those with Ortega y Gasset.

,   ,   ,

In the summer, Nina's health worsened. Fortunately, N. I. Herescu came with his wife and daughter, and we invited them to stay with us. (They had lost their clothes and money in a German airplane on which they had been traveling: it had been bombed and burned in an airport.) In those very difficult days and nights, the presence of a friend from home helped me greatly.

The doctor advised us to put Nina in a sanatorium, the Casa de Saude e de Repouso in Lousa, a few kilometers from Lisbon. She stayed there two months, August and September, but the results were negligible. After the capitulation of Romania on August 23, 1944, almost all the staff members of the legation were recalled to Romania, but until means of transportation could be found, we were put on one-third salary. Obviously, the economizing we did could hardly cover the expenses of the two months at the sanatorium, the hospital, the medicine, and the doctor's visits. Brutus Coste, named chargé d'affaires after the recall of V. Cădere, succeeded in obtaining a sizeable supplement for me from the Foreign Ministry, and thus we were able to make ends meet.

In the last week, Nina survived on blood transfusions only. For a long time she couldn't read. The doctors marvelled at her endurance. She passed away in her sleep on the morning of November 20. For a good part of the night I had stayed by her bedside, reading from the Gospel of St. John. The thought that she would suffer no more, consoled me.

／ ／ ／

I sold a good part of the library and gave up the apartment on avienda Elias Garcia. Just before Christmas we moved—Maria (the old, devoted housekeeper), Giza, and I—to Cascaes. I had rented for six months an old but solid house owned by a family of impoverished gentry. The house was situated on a picturesque little street, rua de Saudade, number 13, and it had a small terrace extending out over the cliffs, a few meters from the ocean. In the largest room there were some empty shelves, adequate to hold the books I had kept.

For a long time I could read nothing but the Bible and a few authors: Kierkegaard, Leon Chestov, Dilthey, Heidegger—and I could write nothing except journal entries. And yet I followed with anxiety the course of the war. I was isolated from the homeland, and very little news pertaining to Romania could be obtained from the newspapers or radio. Then one evening, by chance, I picked up a broadcast in the Romanian language. It was the news bulletin sent daily from the Bucharest newspapers to the provinces. From then on, I listened to it regularly, sending Brutus Coste notes, which Giza delivered to him. In this way I kept informed about all the crises and difficulties encountered by the first "free government" of Romania during that winter and spring.

My attacks of insomnia had begun again, lasting until 3:00 or 4:00 A.M., but I did not resort to sleeping pills. Instead, I reread and meditated on the Gospels, trying to discover the direction to take to get out of the labyrinth. It had seemed to me for a long time that I had been wandering in a labyrinth, and as time passed I became more and more convinced that it was yet another initiatory ordeal, as many crises in the past several years had been. All the despair, depression, and suffering had a meaning: I must understand them as so many "initiatory tortures" preparing me for the symbolic death and spiritual resurrection toward which I was heading. I knew that I could not remain indefinitely in my present state: I was no longer the man I had been in the first year of the war, but still I had not attained another mode of being. I was in an obscure phase, a transition period.

Moreover, the whole world was in the process of being transformed, and at least one of the important transformations could only make me glad, because I had foreseen it and announced it in many writings between 1933 and 1940. India was on the threshold of inevitable independence; Asia was reentering history. For me, the event had more than a political significance. Soon there would become possible a new confrontation—on a footing of equality—between Oriental and Occidental spirituality. But the dialogue was possible only if the *true* Oriental spirituality—that is, its religious matrix—was correctly known and understood in the Occident. The phenomenology and history of religions, as I practiced it, seemed to me the most suitable preparation for this imminent dialogue. On the other hand, the archaic world—that of the "primitives" whom anthropologists had studied for a century—could not remain very long under its colonial guise. But for Occidentals, the understanding of archaic spirituality was even more difficult, because it presupposed a minimum comprehension of mythical thought.

That is why, when I began working again, I concentrated with a passion on *Prolegomena*. Since I had assembled and classified the essential documents already, the writing went forward rather quickly. I went to Lisbon less and less often. Instead, I stayed home all day, writing. In the evenings I would walk for half an hour along the shore of the ocean, listen to the news bulletins, and after dinner shut myself away in my room and work till 3:00 A.M. This schedule, which I called "Balzacian," was interrupted now and then by some exceptionally grave news (such as, for example, the brutal dismissal of General Rădescu by Molotov). At the end of March, together with Leontin Constantinescu, I walked several hundred kilometers in eight days, to Fatima. To give myself a "break," I would sometimes lay aside the manuscript of *Prolegomena* and resume work on *Cosmos and History* (*Le Mythe de l'eternel retour*), the little book in which

I was trying to clarify the origins of the phenomenon I called the "terror of history."

I was waiting, like everyone else, for the end of the war. Since I had decided not to return, for the time being, to the homeland, I hoped to be able to go as soon as possible to Paris, in order to be able to put the finishing touches to the two books and to try to publish them in French (I was writing then in Romanian). I considered them useful for the Orient-Occident dialogue. In any event, I had contributed to the transcending of the cultural provincialism from which some European countries still suffered. It seemed to me that contemporary history itself obliged us to open ourselves to universal values. I did not have the sentiment that by establishing myself for some time in Paris and publishing in French, I would cut myself off from Romanian culture. I knew that no culture is monolithic, dominated by a single spiritual tradition. At the roots of Romanian culture there are two traditions: that of the ploughmen and that of the pastoralists. The latter were more open to universal values than were the agriculturalists. The exemplary model seemed to me to be intertestamental Judaism, with its two creative sources: the Temple and the Diaspora. These ideas I was to take up again and discuss constantly in the first years I spent in Paris.

On May 29 I learned of the death of Mihail Sebastian, run down by a truck while going to open his course on French literature at the University of Bucharest. The news grieved me, and the memory of that absurd accident haunted me for a long while. Sometimes there came over me the sentiment of the irreparable: Mihail would never know the reasons why I avoided meeting with him in Bucharest in the summer of 1942. I was sure that he would have understood if we had met again, that we would have resumed our old friendship. But destiny decided otherwise.

I worked with something close to fury on *Prolegomena* until July 19, when we were obliged to move to another house, located directly across the street from a fish market, which the family of Consul Călin Botez had rented for the summer. And here, as soon as I had located a wooden table, I returned to the manuscript of *Prolegomena;* but I did not succeed in finishing the book.

Nicolae Herescu had left for Paris at the beginning of July. Spitzmüller, the former chargé d'affaires at Bucharest, who knew my book

Yoga and the review *Zalmoxis*, had promised me long before a French visa. Only at the end of August did I receive it. Then I sold almost all the books I had left (I knew the same books were readily accessible in Paris) and reserved places on a sleeping car. The last days spent in Cascaes were the hardest and, it seemed to me, the longest. The house in which we had resided for six weeks had to be torn down by the first of October. We lived surrounded by rubble, with a hand-kerchief in hand, ready to put it to our mouths whenever a breeze raised the dust on the street. To me it was like an image of Europe itself, at the end of the Second World War.

APPENDIX

From the *Lusitanian Journal*

NOWHERE, in any country, have I heard a cry more melancholy, more heartrending, than that of the grinder-man in Lisbon. This craftsman has the habit of announcing his passing on the streets by blowing notes of infinite sorrow on a short reed pipe: long, lingering notes, ending abruptly in a sharp, piercing plaint, like the cry of a wounded bird. The grinder pipes most despairingly on hot afternoons, when the sun puts the great trees to sleep and a glassy vapor hovers over the pavement. It is as though he were the last man alive, passing in sorrow through a deserted city.

And again I hear him toward sunset, when the air recovers its transparency and the trees begin to exude their fragrances. It is, undoubtedly, the most consumate expression of *saudade* (longing).

￼   ￼   ￼

I like to stand on these afternoons of late spring in the Plaço do Commercio on the embankment of the Tejo. I watch the many kingfishers that, untiringly, try their luck in the yellow, oily waters of the river; and after following their short, plunging flight from a cry to a rebound upward again, I come to my senses at length without a care, calm, detached from myself, wondering when the world around me became transfigured, when it became so beautiful.

￼   ￼   ￼

This is a sad people. A Portuguese friend told me that once, but I didn't want to believe it. The more I get to know them, the more convinced I become that *saudade* is not an invention of Coimbrei, the poets, and the romantic travelers. The Portuguese don't possess the expansiveness of the southerners; they have no vehemence of any kind, no cry that bursts forth from a surplus of emotion. I think of all my friends, all the Portuguese I have met, the people I've seen in trains, city squares, seated at tables in cafés, in theaters. All have a strange, awkward ponderousness about their movements, although they aren't apathetic either. They are melancholy, they smile absently all the time; they are affable, like all those who carry about a vague, groundless sorrow.

19. Paris

WE ARRIVED in Paris on Sunday, September 16, 1945. Waiting for us at the station were Emil Cioran and Lică Cracanera, a businessman, the friend and protector of intellectuals whom I had met on the visit to Paris two years before. Cioran had found us a room at Hôtel de l'Avenir, on rue Madame, very close to the Luxembourg Gardens. We had lunch at N. I. Herescu's place, an apartment loaned to him, temporarily, by a colleague. He was quite optimistic: "We have one more hard year to go, and after that the situation will be rectified." That evening, as he did many times that autumn, Cracanera invited us to an expensive restaurant (more precisely, a black market restaurant); I couldn't believe my eyes when I saw the bill.

The week passed quickly. There were formalities that had to be attended to the next day: we registered at the police station and the city hall, in order to obtain food cards and identification papers. We had now an ordinary passport, but the French visa was valid for an indefinite time, and this eased the situation. When we weren't invited out, we ate from the stores we had brought from Portugal (tins of sardines, canned meat, biscuits, sugar, coffee, tea). According to my calculations, the savings we had accumulated in the last year would allow us to live modestly, student-fashion, for eight or nine months. By then, I hoped I would have been able to obtain a study grant or a position at some American university. I knew, in any event, that I couldn't count on receiving honoraria for books in preparation before a year or two.

Very soon I met again Stéphane Lupasco, Georges Dumézil, and René Grousset, and for the first time I met several important Indologists: Louis Renou, Jean Filliozat, and Paul Masson-Oursel. Presented by Renou and Dumézil, I was elected a member of the Société Asiatique. Thereafter, for many years, I attended regularly the meetings of that venerable society. Accompanied by Emil Cioran, I went one afternoon to meet Elena Văcărescu, recently appointed cultural counselor of the Romanian Legation. I met again, after five years, Eugène Ionesco; I dined in his apartment on Claude-Terrasse, where Rodica, his wife, showed me with pride their daughter, Marie-France, who had recently celebrated her first birthday. I met again, also, my former students, Mariana and Mihai Şora, and I was delighted to learn that Gallimard had accepted Mihai's manuscript, *Du dialogue intérieur.* I met many Romanians with whom I would quickly become friends: among the first, the painter Lili Verea, in whose studio I was to spend many Sunday afternoons, and Lizica Codreanu, who was putting the finishing touches then to a "medical gymnastics" employing certain Hatha-Yoga exercises.

The discovery of Paris was a series of unexpected delights. Not only the art museums and the parks, but also the concerts (especially the ensemble Ars Rediviva, conducted by Claude Crussand), the plays (I've never forgotten *Meurtre dans la Cathédrale* at Vieux-Colombier), the cafés in Montparnasse and St. Germain-des-Prés. On the evening of October 29, crushed by the throng crowded into the auditorium, I listened to Jean-Paul Sartre lecture on "L'existentialisme est un humanisme." (Sartre spoke without notes and without touching the glass of water for more than an hour and a half.)

I tried to take full advantage of this new freedom of which I had dreamed for years. Many weeks I didn't read a newspaper (I knew I'd hear about any important events from my friends). But I read insatiably the new reviews and certain books that had recently appeared; I felt I had to familiarize myself with the current Parisian philosophical and literary scene. Soon, however, I found my time preempted by urgent tasks; with melancholy I realized that the freedom I enjoyed had been reduced to the two hours I stubbornly persisted in spending each morning in art museums, parks or just walking the streets.

When I went to see him in his old-fashioned bookstore on rue Jacob, the publisher Paul Guethner declared that if he had a larger quota of paper available he'd reprint *Yoga;* he was receiving requests for it all the time, and not just from France. He suggested that I publish in the meantime a small, less technical book on the subject. A few days later, Georges Dumézil introduced me to Brice Parain, who directed Gallimard's series *La Montagne Sainte-Geneviève*, and he told him about my project. I hadn't finished either *Prolegomena* or *Cosmos and History* (*Le mythe de l'éternel retour*), but because Parain appeared interested in an "Introduction to the Study of Yoga," I undertook the work. I thought that I'd be able to summarize my doctoral thesis, reproducing as many pages as possible and condensing others. But I soon abandoned that facile solution. After all those years, I plunged again into Sanskrit, Indian philosophy, and Yoga problematics. I purchased Renou's Sanskrit-French dictionary, I borrowed Orientalist texts and journals from the Societé Asiatique, and in a few months I had a better mastery of the subject than ever. (Of course, I took advantage of the recent critical bibliography.) In the spring of 1946, at the Institute of Indian Civilization, I gave a talk on Yoga vocabulary and, at the invitation of Jules Bloch and Jean Filliozat, two lectures on Yoga techniques. Later I would be asked to speak to various groups and at centers for spiritual studies. As I had foreseen long before, Yoga was becoming of interest to an increasingly larger and more varied public. Naturally, such an interest threatened to become—as it soon did, in fact—a fad. That is why Louis Renou and other Indologists looked favorably on my efforts to present Yoga philosophy and practices as scientifically as possible, at the same time situating them in the broader perspective of the history of religions. I finished the book at the beginning of summer, and Brice Parain promised me an advance as soon as it went to the typesetter. Due to a combination of circumstances at the press, *Techniques du Yoga* did not appear until the spring of 1948. Fortunately, I received the advance on schedule.

At the beginning of November, Georges Dumézil opened his course at l'Ecole des Hautes Études, Section des Sciences Religieuses—a course which I would follow with the liveliest interest until 1950. When he learned that I was working on a morphology of religious phenomena, Dumézil invited me to give a series of lectures in the context of his chair of comparative mythology. Needless to say, I was flattered immensely. I had already typed several lengthy chapters of *Prolegomena;* in the weeks that followed, several young people translated them, more or less felicitously.[1] However, I had to select pages that could be presented orally and, especially, to develop my commentaries. I launched the series of lectures on February 8, 1946, with an analysis of the divinities of a uranic structure in archaic religions. In addition to Georges Dumézil and the Tibetan scholar Marcelle Lalou, the audience consisted of a small group of Romanians. In the ten lectures that I gave, I succeeded in discussing only the subjects of the first four chapters of *Traité d'histoire des religions.* Dumézil insisted I continue the presentation in the winter and spring of 1947, but, caught up in other projects, I didn't do it. However, in the spring of 1948 I expounded the essence of the little book *Le mythe de l'éternal retour*—this time to a much larger audience.

Cracanera assured me he would find me a small apartment. In the fall of 1945 such a privilege seemed—and proved to be—almost unrealizable. Quite by chance I found out that a lady of Russian origin, Mme Chernass, was willing to sublet a part of the apartment she occupied on rue des Saints-Pères. We installed ourselves in February of 1946; we had three rooms, almost empty, and the use of the kitchen. Fortunately, I located a table on which I could arrange my files and manuscripts.

I had begun my lectures at Hautes Études and the table was a great help. (At the hotel, for four months, I had contented myself with a flimsy little stand.) Sanskrit whetted my appetite to take up again ancient Greek and even more so to study the Russian language seriously. During the war, at Oxford, Lisbon, and Cascaes, I had undertaken Russian several times, studying it twice a day, but each time I had broken off after a few weeks. This time I wanted at all costs to learn it. On the one hand, I would be able to read the works of Russian ethnologists on Siberian shamanism; on the other hand, because by learning the language (one I loved very much) I would prove I was not confusing the Russian people with the current regime, with Soviet

---

1. The entire text of the French version, *Traité d'histoire des religions,* would be corrected by Georges Dumézil.

imperialism. I kept repeating to myself that hatred for the occupation troops and for their puppets in Romania must not extend also to the Russian people.

Having now at our disposal a kitchen, a few pieces of silverware, and a dozen glasses, we could entertain guests! The rations brought from Portugal were almost exhausted, but we still had some tea, coffee, and a few tins of sardines. From time to time, N. I. Herescu or Emil Cioran would give us a bottle of wine. For a long time we dared not offer our guests anything but coffee and, sometimes, a glass of wine.

Gradually, the circle of acquaintances—and later, colleagues and friends—expanded. That spring I met Philippe Lavastine. I admired him for his wide reading and enormous library. Through Lavastine I met Dr. Henry Hunwald, an enthusiast for alchemy and hermeticism; he gave me a copy of *Alchimia asiatică* (my book of 1935), purchased at Cluj in the year of its publication. Soon I would become friends with Henry and Anne Hunwald. In their apartment on rue St. Jacques we were to meet many writers and hermeticists: old Paul Vuillaud (who was amazed that I possessed in Bucharest in 1926 the two volumes of his *La Kabbale Juive*), the critics Aimé Patri and Michel Carrouges, the alchemist Eugène Canseliet, and especially André Breton, who would later read with interest my *Techniques du Yoga*. Louis Renou did me the honor of inviting me to dinner once with E. Benveniste, who was curious to find out certain particulars about the ecstasy of Asiatic shamans; and on another occasion with Paul Mus, just back from Indochina (he was still wearing his officer's uniform). Mus recalled my long article about *Barabudur*; he had deciphered it, with the help of a Româno-French dictionary, at Saigon, on the eve of the war.

I spent the summer of 1946 working as in my youth, twelve to fourteen hours a day. In spite of the heat, I finished in July "Le problème du chamanisme," the study H. Ch. Puech had asked of me for *Revue de l'histoire des religions*. Immediately after that I concentrated on the chapters of *Prolegomena* not yet written. Shamanism had interested me for many years; the first documents I had collected at the British Museum in the summer of 1940; at Lisbon I read all the volumes of Folklore Fellows Communications (Helsinki) containing facts and exegeses concerning Asiatic and Siberian shamanism. The pretext for the study in *Revue de l'histoire des religions* was a book by Åke Ohlmark. Following an old, naively materialistic interpretation, the author assimilated shamanic ecstasy to trances provoked by "Arctic hysteria." I attempted to situate the "problem of shamanism" in the context of the history of religions, the only perspective which does not nullify its significance and function. Thus I analyzed the typology of shamanic initiation and the structure of the ecstatic journeys shamans take into celestial and subterranean regions, emphasizing analogies with the initiatory rites and mystical experiences of certain primitive and Oriental peoples. "Le probleme du chamanisme" was my first study to appear in print after my coming to Paris (it appeared in February 1947). The enthusiastic letters which I received then from many Orientalists and historians of religions encouraged me to pursue the problem further in a full-length monograph.

Of course, the twelve to fourteen hours per day work schedule was sometimes interrupted by the political situation. Recently the Peace Conference had begun and a number of Romanian intellectuals had come to Paris along with the official delegation from the country. At the beginning of August Professor Alexander Rosetti telephoned me, saying it was urgent he see me. We met the next day. He confirmed the rumor I had heard somewhat earlier: that the French minister of education, intending to give me a chair at L'Ecole des Hautes Études, had asked the advice of the Romanian Legation; our minister, the distinguished mathematician Stoilov, had asked Bucharest—and of course the reply was negative. Several days later. Rosetti went with me to Stoilov's office, to "see what we can do." Naturally, nothing could be done. I admitted to Rosetti my surprise and disappointment: I couldn't believe that a great savant would behave like a common informer. (A few years later such a procedure would seem natural.)

/   /   /

As one would expect, the official Romanian delegation to the peace conference, under the leadership of Ana Pauker, maintained the theses of the Communist party—that is, of Moscow. Grigore Gafencu and several other Romanian diplomats who had remained in the West established a news bureau for the purpose of informing political circles and European public opinion. Brutus Coste was among the most active in this work. Thus, he and I met again after a year, and we resumed the themes of some of our discussions in Portugal.[2] Among

2. Churchill's speech of September 20 in which he suggested a federation of European states and a definitive reconciliation between France and Germany provoked end-

the "technicians" of the commission attending the peace conference was a good friend of Coste, Anton Golopenția. I was glad to see him again. From him I learned that he had sent the three volumes of *Zalmoxis* to his erstwhile professor, Joachim Wach, and in a letter to him he had spoken about me, asking him to send me his latest works. Indeed, Wach, who was teaching the history of religions as the University of Chicago, had sent me his *Sociology of Religion* and had written me, saying that he would soon be coming to Europe. But he did not come until the summer of 1950, and when we met (at Ascona), Anton Golopenția had long since been arrested. (Several years later his wife was called to identify his corpse.)

The month of October promised to be, for us, rather difficult. Sometimes I thought I could see the specter of poverty facing us. I managed to sell part of the clothing I had brought from Portugal. Then I discovered the *mont-de-piété* where I pawned Nina's silverware and fur coat several times. Giza learned to make women's hats, but she had difficulty at first finding customers. Fortunately, from time to time, Brutus Coste and other friends would send me small sums of money. I was able to borrow from Cracanera the amounts needed for rent and the translations of chapters of *Prolegomena*. But there were days when this "temporary situation"—with no end in sight— depressed me.

I decided at that point to try my luck in the United States. Ananda Coomaraswamy had written me at the beginning of October, saying I must by all means come to see him in Boston in 1947, because in 1948 he would retire and move permanently to India. I asked him to find something for me to do in the United States. He replied that all the positions in Indian studies and the history of religions in universities and colleges were long since filled, but he assured me that he would try. Only in August of 1947 did he write that there would be a position available—in French—at a new college soon to be established (in addition to room and board, I would have an annual salary of $2,800). I accepted even this solution (telling myself it would be temporary), but in October Louis Renou informed me of Coomaraswamy's death. The news grieved me deeply. I had dreamed of a trip to the United States especially to meet Ananda Coomaraswamy, to talk with him at length about his latest exegeses based on the *philosophia perennis*.

---

less debates and polemics. Some naive persons wondered why Churchill had been so late in discovering this bold political solution.

Despite my financial straits, I continued to work on the last two chapters of *Prolegomena*. I was happy every time I was able to meet personally some of the authors recently discovered: for instance, Robert Dessoile and Gabriel Marcel. At the beginning of February, Theodore Besterman, recently appointed to an important post at UNESCO, called me on the telephone. I had met him in London in the spring of 1940 and we had met again the following winter at Oxford. I admired his erudition and his courage in switching specialties: from parapsychology to ethnology and folklore, then to regional bibliographies, culminating in a *Bibliography of Bibliographies*. I found him now excited about Voltaire, whose whole *oeuvre* he wanted at that time to translate into English. We spent several afternoons making the rounds of bookstores and antiquaries, Besterman asking always to see any book by or about Voltaire.[3]

                    *   *   *

On December 24 Madame Chesnass informed us that we must move in a month. Because we could no longer hope to find an apartment, we began looking for rooms in "residence" hotels. I found, for myself, a large, spacious room in Hôtel de Suède, on rue Vaneau. Since we were obliged to eat lunch and dinner at home, Giza sought a hotel which would allow her to prepare a few simple kinds of dishes on a Primus. At last, in a modest hotel on rue de Beaune, she found a little room with an alcove-like extension furnished with a sink; here she installed her valises and the Primus.

On Christmas Eve George Dumézil came to see me, bringing me the chapters of *Prolegomena*, the French version of which he had had the kindness to improve. What he told me that afternoon about the value and importance of the book made me forget my worries and poverty. He suggested I submit it to the Payot publishing firm, and he offered, if necessary, to write a preface for it. But since the last two chapters weren't finished, I didn't dare present the manuscript to a publisher. I ended the year in the studio of Lili Verea, bringing along Theodore Besterman; it was his first contact with the "amusements of the postwar French intellectual elite" (as he liked to say).

We moved on January 28, 1947, after two days of tension and fear. Our landlady was suffering from a strange attack of rage, and we slept at night fully clothed, ready for anything. We breathed easily

3. Later Besterman concentrated exclusively on Voltaire's correspondence, publishing a true critical edition in 110 volumes!

when we had loaded the suitcases and books into a little truck and had started for rue de Beaune and rue Vaneau. Soon we became adjusted to our new schedule: I worked all day and part of the night; Giza made hats and visited potential customers; at noon and in the evening we ate in the little room on rue Beaune, and sometimes we even invited friends for coffee.

The signing of the peace treaty did not elicit our enthusiasm. A few days previously I had been told the tragic details of the famine in Romania, and a few days after that I learned of the crash of the plane at Sintra in which Claude Crussard and eight members of the Ars Rediviva group had died. That winter and spring I had but two concerns: to pay the weekly hotel bill and to finish *Prolegomena*. I borrowed from all my friends and acquaintances. I borrowed even from a student, Alphonse Juilland, recently arrived from Bucharest with other holders of French government scholarships. Sometimes Giza wept in despair, having failed to sell any hats. (And yet that fall the situation changed suddenly: a fashionable shop bought her entire collection and ordered several dozen more. There were months when we lived exclusively on her earnings.)

In May I received 20,000 francs from Brutus Coste, out of a special fund he supervised, which allowed me to pay a good share of my debts and catch up on my hotel rent. That same month N. I. Herescu introduced me to General Rădescu, the president of the last free government of Romania. After the ultimatum of Vishinski to King Mihail in March 1945, General Rădescu had taken refuge in the British Legation. A few months later he and his secretary were transported by military plane to the island of Cyprus. He had come recently to Paris where other political figures had begun to arrive also, by various routes. Thus I met again in July the former foreign minister, Constantin Vişovianu. I had met him in Romania in 1938 when he was the director of the review *Viata românească*. He told me that during the war he had moved close to socialism, and he had believed then that we must at all costs obtain the trust and friendship of the Soviets. But recent experiences had shattered his illusions. I was troubled by the pessimism with which he viewed the immediate future. He was convinced (and rightly so) that we had been abandoned by "our Great Allies"; that Romania, as well as the rest of Central and Eastern Europe, had been surrendered to the Soviets.

All this news made me sad, but it didn't surprise me. After the

Teheran Conference, where Europe had been divided into two great "spheres of influence," I knew that our fate was sealed. The principal problem was, in Anton Golopenția's phrase, "how to hibernate," how to preserve our national identity during this new Dark Age which could last many generations. But we, those living in the West, had no right to let ourselves be paralyzed by despair. We must, at all costs, continue to work and create, according to our several vocations.

Therefore, I returned resolutely to my tasks. In June I wrote a study about the work of Dumézil, which Lucien Febvre had requested of me for *Annales,* and in August I finished *Prolegomena.* I still had to put the final touches to *Le mythe de l'éternel retour,* translated in part by my former student, Mihail Șora. But, as I feared, the effort of the past six or seven months had alienated me from theoretical works. In September I suddenly found myself engrossed in Balzac. Every time I had a free afternoon and every night until the small hours I read or reread the works of this idol of my adolescence and youth. Soon I discovered the correspondence and the monographs recently published about Balzac's youth and literary beginnings. Since 1950 would mark the hundredth anniversary of his death, I told myself that I would write—and publish under a pseudonym—a life of Balzac, which would be a biography composed by a writer familiar with the exegesis of various religious and para-religious symbolisms. When I finally abandoned the project, I had arrived at the year immediately prior to his first success with both the public and the critics, *Les Chouans.* But I didn't regret the time lost; the unplanned Balzacian intermezzo had helped me to recover my equilibrium.

That autumn I met Antoine Bibesco and had lunch for the first time at his splendid apartment on l'Île St. Louis. Also, I was invited by Maruca Cantacuzino and George Enesco to their house in Belvue. Thus I was enabled to know more closely that fabulous couple to whom—owing to the Nae Ionescu episode of 1931–32—so many memories were linked.

At the beginning of October, following the advice of H. Ch. Puech and Alphonse Dupront, former director of the French Institute whom I had met long ago in Bucharest, I submitted a request for a fellowship at the Centre de la Recherche Scientifique. The request was accompanied by letters of recommendation from Louis Renou, Georges Dumézil, and Paul Masson-Oursel, and by a number of publications (*Yoga, Zalmoxis* I–III, "Le probleme du chamanisme," etc.). I imagine that my dossier made a considerable impression, because a few days later I received from CNRS an "emergency grant" of 25,000 francs. But to forestall possible future opposition from the legation, Dupront considered it advisable to inform Stoilov. The minister, undoubtedly, did his duty. To my surprise—and the indignation of the French savants who had extolled my activity—I found out on December 3 that my request had been rejected. (In 1951, Louis Renou would reopen the dossier—this time, with complete success. But a month later I received the Bollingen grant and had to refuse the one from CNRS.)

A few days after the "unmerited catastrophe" (as a friend termed it), I went to see Gustave Payot. Georges Dumézil had spoken to him already about the book and had promised him a preface. I was greeted by a tall, thin, elderly man who, in spite of diabetes and other ailments, impressed me by his surprising energy. He frowned upon seeing the title: *Prolégomènes à l'histoire des religions*. He thumbed through the manuscript and frowned again: there were almost 700 typed pages.

"If for a Prologue you need seven hundred pages, a *History of Religions* would have to have ten volumes! . . . We've got to change the title."

I proposed *Morphologie du sacré*, but he shook his head.

"Too vague. The only title that could interest and attract buyers is *Traité d'histoire des religions*."

He added that, if I were agreeable, he would accept the book immediately. Otherwise, with the problem of obtaining paper, I would have to wait. I remembered the winter of 1940, in the house we had rented with Mrs. Sassoon, at Oxford, when I had begun to write the first pages. I remembered the nights of the past two years when, on rue des Sts.-Pères and at Hôtel de Suède, I had toiled to finish the final chapters. . . . Of course, I had never thought of myself as working on a *History of Religions*. But I agreed immediately. The essential thing was that the book would appear, even though with a title it didn't merit.

Gustave Payot asked me if the manuscript was complete and definitive; he called my attention to the fact that typesetters are expensive, and the simplest modifications cost tremendously. I assured him that the text was complete, but I said that in any event I should have to review it one more time before sending it to the printer. Three days

Mircea Eliade with father Gheorghe,
ca. 1938 in Romania

*BELOW Nina and Mircea Eliade in Lisbon, summer 1942
(Courtesy Giza Tataresco)*

*BOTTOM Nina Eliade, Mircea's first wife, ca. 1942
(Courtesy Giza Tataresco)*

RIGHT Eliade in Cascaes, Portugal, 1945

*BELOW RIGHT Christinel Eliade, Mircea's second wife,
and Mircea in Southern Italy, ca. 1952*

LEFT Eliade, 1952

RIGHT Eliade at Ascona, 1955

Christinel and Mircea Eliade in their
Chicago apartment, 1972

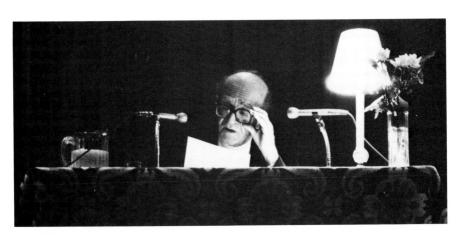

*Portrait of Mircea Eliade by
Nina Batalli, 1949*

Eliade, ca. 1982

later he telephoned to say that he had located a printer who, if I could present him with the manuscript in two weeks, would be able to have the book in print by the beginning of spring. He added that on delivery of the manuscript I would receive 60,000 francs.

I shall never forget the ordeal I underwent in those days and nights between December 13 and 18. I worked at night, especially, when rue Vaneau and Hôtel de Suède acquired an unnatural, almost eerie quiet. I went to bed toward morning and slept no more than three or four hours. Then I'd make myself a cup of coffee and return to my work. At a certain moment I realized I'd lost track of what day it was. I didn't dare go down to ask the porter; I was afraid of collapsing on the stairs. Again I suffered from those attacks of vertigo preceded by the terrible sensation of déja vu, which I had known in youth. At such times I would throw myself on the bed, fully clothed, and somehow manage to go to sleep. In spite of exhaustion, I completed the bibliography and put the final touches to the text before the deadline. (But since then I have never dared to repeat the ordeal of working twenty hours without stopping.) After handing over the manuscript to Payot, I tried to read a Balzac novella in an attempt to escape from the infernal circle within which I had been struggling for a week. Impossible; the overwork brought on an attack of vagatonia. For the next several days I slept like a larva from morning till evening.

A little while later, Gustave Payot telephoned to inform me that he, indignant over the financial arrangements the printer was offering, had withdrawn the manuscript. He did not know when another chance would arise. (It arose at the beginning of summer, but I didn't learn of this good news until somewhat later.)

For a long time we knew nothing concerning the whereabouts of Lică Cracanera. We had found out that, in hopes of making a "simply sensational deal," he had borrowed large sums of money and, some time before, had disappeared from Paris. Then, one glassy afternoon in January, Emil Cioran brought me the news of his suicide: his body had been found on a beach in Belgium. The rumor circulated that, realizing he had been swindled, Cracanera had gone to Brussels in an attempt to recover at least a part of the sums invested in the famous "deal"—and, apparently, he had failed. In this way the savings of several Romanian intellectuals were lost: they had entrusted them to him to "multiply" them. I don't doubt that Lică Cracanera fell victim to his own naïveté. That he was a man of good faith is proved by the very fact that he committed suicide: a swindler would have disappeared, taking refuge on another continent. In any case, I can't forget Cracanera's generosity in aiding a great many Romanian intellectuals during the time of the German occupation and immediately after the liberation.[4]

For Romanians, the year 1947 ended with the forced abdication of King Mihai, while the year just begun allowed us to foresee the aggravation of political tensions. The number of those who had left the country—politicians, intellectuals, students—had grown much in recent months, and it continued to grow. Also gathered in Paris were those who had been in camps in Germany and Austria, the majority of them Legionaries.

A communication from the legation announced that soon the repatriation would begin; those who did not return within six months would automatically lose their citizenship. With the exception of a few workers and a few old people, all decided to remain in France. The International Refugee Organization (IRO) had been established. Any exile could deposit his passport (if he had one) and sign a declaration renouncing his citizenship (of whatever country). He would receive then an identification card and, in principle, come under the protection of the country in which he had chosen to live. Even more importantly, IRO made available to the refugees the means of transportation to the states that had accepted them: that is, the republics of South America, Canada, and Australia.

Many Romanians—fugitives from the country or persons who had belonged to the diplomatic, consular, or economic services—decided to leave as soon as possible for Argentina. On the one hand, the Argentine regime was encouraging immigration; on the other hand, the tension between the U.S. and the Soviets was becoming more pronounced, and it was believed that war was inevitable. The risk of being caught by events in Central or Western Europe seemed imminent. In addition, many refugees believed that the possibilities for earning a living on other continents would diminish with the passage of time. These things explain why the majority of Romanians emigrated to Argentina in the course of the year 1948.

The same reason led Giza to sign her name that spring on the list at

4. The figure and fate of Lică Cracanera served as my model for a character in *Noaptea de Sânziene*, Mişu Weissmann.

the Argentine consulate. The fashionable stores continued to order her hats, and recently she had learned dressmaking. She said to herself that now was the best moment for her to try her luck in Buenos Aires. But the number of names on the list was considerable. She had to have patience and wait.

Personally, I gave no thought to emigration. I had made up my mind to stay in France, at whatever risk. I was waiting for my books and studies—at least those already accepted—to appear. In February I received the proofs of the book *Techniques du Yoga* and of a long study, "Le 'dieu lieur' et le symbolisme des noeux" (The "God who Binds" and the Symbolism of Knots), which was to appear in *Revue de l'Histoire des Religions*. In March I met Georges Bataille. He talked with me a long while in my room at Hôtel de Suède; he had read *Yoga* in 1936 and had been especially interested in the chapters on Tantrism. He invited me to contribute to *Critique*, and a few weeks later I sent him the first article. Also, I hadn't given up hope that Payot would publish *Traité* before the end of the year. In May, soon after the appearance of *Techniques du Yoga*, I summarized in a few lectures given at L'Ecole des Hautes Études my favorite work, *Le mythe de l'éternel retour.*[5]

But that spring is linked in my memory to the first efforts at a cultural organization of the exiles. Besides the holders of French government scholarships who had refused to return home, there were living in Paris older students from before the war, as well as many intellectuals (journalists, professors, scientists). General Rădescu asked me to make a plan for cultural activities of Romanians in exile. I suggested, for the time being, the establishment of a Mihail Eminescu Association, which would organize public lectures and publish a literary review (*Luceafărul*); in addition, it would provide a number of grants for needy students and certain intellectuals without means.

I shall not survey here the history of the Romanian diaspora of those years. Suffice it to recall that, following the abdication of King Mihail and the flight of many political persons and former members of the Foreign Ministry, it was possible to envision the founding of a national committee which would represent the whole resistance movement both outside and inside Romania. Certain funds on deposit mainly in Switzerland and Portugal could cover the expenses of

5. Begun as Cascaes in March 1945, this little book would be finished in November 1948, and would be published by Gallimard the following spring.

the organization and activities of the committee, at least at first. (After a few years, the American organization Free Europe would encourage and support committees of "captive nations.") As was natural, the last president of the council, General Rădescu, with the assistance of Grigore Gafencu and Brutus Coste, tried to form a national committee. But owing to the jealousies and conflicts inherent in any group of émigrés, he did not succeed, and eventually he had to give up the idea. Meanwhile, the industrialist N. Malaxa, who had recently left Romania, had put at General Rădescu's disposition a part of the sum realized from the sale of the famous Malaxa industries, then on deposit in Switzerland. Thus, from May 1948 to the winter of 1949, General Rădescu could assure stipends to students and intellectuals, and the publication of two numbers of *Luceafărul*.

Together with several friends and colleagues, I founded the Mihail Eminescu Cultural Association. The first public demonstration we held was the commemoration of the Tenth of May in a packed auditorium of the Sociétés Savantes. Also at the Sociétés Savantes I was later to deliver public lectures on the two spiritual traditions of Romania and on Mihail Eminescu. At the same time, I was preparing the first issue of *Luceafărul*, which contained contributions from many Romanian writers in the diaspora. The volume, consisting of 180 pages, opened with a poem, "Adio libertate!" (Farewell, freedom!), signed with a pseudonymn. It was, in fact, written by Vasile Voiculescu and was sent surreptitiously from Romania.

Of course, I realized that such demonstrations could create difficulties for my family in Romania. But this was true of all Romanians in exile. I had found out that for some two years my books had ceased to be reprinted; I had become a persona non grata. Correspondence with family and friends in the homeland had slackened gradually, and in 1948 it was interrupted for a long time. From my parents' last letters, I understood that the iron band had tightened beyond expectations, but they all were glad that I could live, work, and publish in Paris. Whenever I had a chance, I sent them packages of food and, later, small sums of money, but I wasn't sure these things reached their destination. A year later I found out that due to such a "transfer" of money, Corina had been questioned by the police. After that, I didn't try to help her financially. For a long time I received no more news from home except indirectly.

/   /   /

At the end of July the first International Congress of Orientalists was held in Paris. It was also the first Orientalist congress of any kind in which I had participated. (I presented a short paper on the symbolism of the Buddha's seven steps.) On this occasion I met many foreign Orientalists; with some of them (J. Duschesne-Guillemin, Geo. Widengren, Stig Wikander, etc.) I was to become friends. I was happy also to meet Etienne Lamotte and other Indianists who had written me enthusiastically about *Techniques du Yoga*.

A few months before the congress, Theodore Besterman proposed that I take the place of a UNESCO functionary who had been sent on an assignment to the Orient for three or four months. In this way I came to know the daily work schedule of the intellectual who is involved in an institution, and I met all sorts of technicians of education and functionaries of cultural planning. I was free to organize my work as I saw fit, so that there were several hours left every day for reading. One afternoon Payot called me; he wanted to know how soon I could finish *Le chamanisme*, about which I had spoken to him long ago. It was on this occasion that I learned that *Traité d'histoire des religions* was at the printer. (Indeed, I received the first proofs in September.)

On August 27, accompanied by our friend Martha, daughter of Dr. Vasile Voiculescu, I took Giza to Marseilles. She embarked on a ship leased by IRO, together with some two thousand other immigrants. As I learned from her first letters after arriving, her voyage had been made in miserable conditions. Fortunately friends and acquaintances already settled in Buenos Aires helped her to forget quickly that nightmare. Within a few months Giza succeeded in setting up a dressmaking establishment. In time she began earning enough to buy the little apartment where she lived. But it was to be five years before she could visit Paris.

At the end of October, I had the opportunity to spend a day at Sochoire, with Father de Menasce and the group Eau Vive. I returned fascinated by the majestic solitude of the place. I asked myself, on the way home, if my continuous working, and the books and articles I was writing, were not alienating me little by little from the sources of life and the soul.

New Year's Eve I spent with Herescu, Cioran, and other friends, at the house of Mme Foll on avenue Trudaine. Actually, I spent it with Christinel, as if we two were the only ones there.

20. Christinel

AMONG THE Romanians living in Paris with whom I became acquainted was the former correspondent for the newspaper *Universul*, Mihai Niculescu. At that time he was preparing a doctoral thesis on Jean Giraudoux. One afternoon in late autumn of 1947, when Giza had invited him for coffee, he arrived accompanied by a friend, Sibylle Cottescu, whom he very much wanted me to meet. She was a beautiful young woman, dark, with black tresses falling to her shoulders. I was impressed from the start by her slow gestures and her calm, sure manner of looking one straight in the eyes. She spoke contemporary Romanian, but with a decided French accent. Mihai Niculescu told me that she had lived in Paris since the age of six and had studied in a Catholic college, where she was now a professor of Latin. I found out also that Sibylle was the sister-in-law of Ionel Perlea, the conductor, who had an engagement at La Scala for the entire winter season.

We met several times and I came to know some of her friends who, like herself, taught at Collège Sainte Thérèse. Sibylle had a small apartment in Bois-Colombes which she had rented during the war. She invited a group of friends there for New Year's Eve, but being in the midst of an attack of vagatonia, I couldn't attend. I made my first visit to Bois-Colombes in the spring of 1948. I remember almost nothing about the lunch, but I do remember that it was then I met Christinel. In contrast to her sister, Christinel was blond and blue-eyed, but like Sibylle she let her hair fall to her shoulders. That first image has never been erased from my mind: she laughed like a child, yet with a troubling femininity, showing her teeth, inclining her head slightly.

I knew she had arrived recently from Italy where she had spent more than a year with Lisette and Ionel Perlea. I never suspected then, as I listened to her talking about Naples, Santa Margherita, and Rome, that our destinies were about to be fulfilled. I was just interested in the stories she was telling me about things that had happened to her. She had embarked from Constanța on the Romanian ship *Transylvania*, had arrived at Naples, and had left immediately for Milan to be with Ionel and Lisette. The three of them had spent a part of the winter at Santa Margherita and Milan, then had gone down to Rome and finally to Naples, where Ionel had directed a series of performances at the San Carlo Theater. At Naples she had been reunited with Nina Battali, a young painter with whom I had become acquainted in 1938. On learning later that Christinel was going to Paris, Nina Battali had spoken to her about me. But Christinel already knew about *Maitreyi* and other successful novels I had written; she considered me an established author and therefore of a "certain age." When I asked her about how old she had imagined me to be, she laughed, slightly self-conscious, and didn't answer. I laughed too, without knowing quite why.

Very probably the mother of the three sisters was present at that lunch also—Maria Șendrea, or "Mamy," as Sibylle's friends called her and as I too would soon be doing. I don't believe I've ever met another woman who had remained so youthful, so good-looking, and so seductive at the age of a grandmother. In my memory she has never changed: her hair has remained just as white and lustrous, her face as noble and gentle, with deep-set eyes that sometimes bore a melancholy shadow but were never darkened by sadness. For all who met her, Mamy evoked the beauty of princesses of other ages. (And twenty years later, Petru Comarnescu did not forget to remind us— several times inopportunely—that the Șendrești are descended from the family of Ștefan the Great.) I was unable to see my own mother again, who died in 1976 at the age of ninety; but as long as Mamy lived, she was like a mother to me.

A little after that I met Lisette (seemingly even more beautiful than her sisters) and Ionel Perlea, still wearing the Vandyke he had grown in the prison camp at Mariafahr, Austria. I shall have much to say about these two in the pages that follow. I soon became close to Lisette; from the start I liked her spontaneity and good-heartedness, her optimistic way of viewing the future. I was impressed, too, to see how devoted she was to her sisters, how she watched over them, spending as much time with them and Mamy as possible.

Ionel Perlea was, at least at first, more reserved. He liked to listen to the others talking, but he didn't get involved in conversations that did not concern him directly. We became friends later, and the better I grew to understand him (and I imagined his true life, isolated as he was in the universe of his musical genius), the greater my admiration for him became. For Easter, Ionel invited his family and a few friends to a Romanian restaurant recently opened on rue St. Jacques. After the intense work schedule of the past year and the successes won everywhere in Italy, he allowed himself a short vacation in Paris (but he didn't like to say, "in the bosom of my family").

On that Easter night, which lasted until 2:00 A.M., I discovered how fascinating and fresh, and how much fun Christinel could be when she let herself get caught up in the festive atmosphere. I hadn't suspected that this angelic blonde with eyes of blue and hair falling over her shoulders could laugh so gaily and sing with such good will and humor. I watched her and listened to her fascinated, but I didn't realize what was happening to me. I didn't know we were fated for each other. . . .

I met her again about two weeks later, at a party organized by the Mihail Eminescu Association at Sociétés Savantes. The hat Giza had made for her was brightened with a small bouquet of violets. I sensed that she would have liked me to stay and talk with her awhile, but other friends and colleagues were waiting. It was to be some time before I saw her again; my days were taken up with various visits and appointments. One afternoon she telephoned me to say that she had just read *Techniques du Yoga*. The book had interested her, but, she admitted shyly, the technical terms and the Sanskrit vocabulary had slowed the reading for her. I couldn't have imagined then that, a few years later, she would type the manuscripts of the monographs *Le chamanisme* and *Le Yoga* and would master perfectly the terminology of many Oriental languages.

That autumn was long and, in my memory, exceptionally beautiful. The position I was occupying temporarily at UNESCO was well remunerated; thus I was able to invite friends to restaurants and plays. I would finish my day's tasks in two or three hours; the rest of the time I would read manuscripts for *Luceafărul*, revise page proofs for *Traité*, and work on the index for that volume. Only in the evenings was I free to be myself. I sensed that I was beginning a new life; even Paris seemed new, as I discovered it on long walks with Christinel. At that time she was living with a friend in an apartment on rue de Ségur, not far from rue Vaneau. The owner of the apartment, the elderly and distinguished Mlle Blanche de la Rivière, sublet two rooms to them.

We met almost every evening and dined together; sometimes we invited Sibylle or Herescu too; and we discovered the cafés and shows in Montparnasse. But what we liked best was to wander the streets between Ecole Militaire and Sèvres-Babylone. We knew every bench, every *bureau de tabac*, every street lamp. And yet one night we lost our way; we didn't succeed in reaching rue Ségur until very late, toward morning.

Sometimes I wondered by what miracle I had regained the naiveté and enthusiasm of an adolescent without being crushed by the feeling of ridiculousness. Indeed I was acting like a teenager in love. But I sensed there was something more to it, that the lamentable banality of my behavior was concealing, very probably, a process of total renewal. Beside Christinel, I felt I was rediscovering a vitality and a spiritual dimension which the "history" of the past few years had obscured.

Sometimes, in my room at Hôtel de Suède, recalling certain apparently ridiculous gestures or expressions, I shrugged my shoulders and smiled. I had long since understood the mysterious and apparently ridiculous manifestations of the sacred in profane objects and actions. It seemed to me that this dialectics of hierophanies constituted—*though camouflaged*—the exemplary model of every human existence. It would have been both tragic and comic for me not to have guessed what was happening, not to have perceived that through Christinel I would be able to find myself again wholly.

She liked to have me tell her fragments of my life story. Once when she had asked me what I was working on, I had told her, somewhat glibly, about the initiations and ecstasies of shamans. She smiled, trying to hide her melancholy. I pretended to be surprised and asked her, "Don't you find that interesting?"

"Yes, of course," she replied. "All you do is interesting; all you've written about Indian philosophy, about the history of religions is fascinating. This is part of your vocation. . . . But," she added after a pause, "literature is part of your vocation too."

"For whom would I write?" I asked her. "Literature I can write only in Romanian, the language in which I dream."

"Write for those few Romanians who esteem you." She smiled, then added quickly, "Me, for example. Write for me."

We looked each other in the eyes, surprised at what had happened. (But a few moments later I was asking myself, what *did* happen?). However, I had to say something. "It's been three or four years since I wrote any literature, and the last things I wrote weren't very good."

"That doesn't mean anything," she interrupted me. "But if it's truly the language in which you dream, isn't it possible that later on. . . ."

"It's also the language in which I can tell a woman that I love her. . . ."

I'm sure she was blushing, but she gave me an ironic smile. "Perhaps you're exaggerating," she said softly. (She was thinking, of course, about my youth in India.)

We both knew that we were in love, but I made no confession then; it was as though I wanted to prolong an incomparable state of bliss, a magic spell from which I was reluctant to awaken. And yet one evening, after we had seated ourselves in a taxi that had stopped for us, I told her, "I'd like you to know that I was very happy when I was married."

Her whole face brightened, and she gazed at me for a long while, smiling. For a few moments I thought she was about to say something, but she remained silent, looking me with a curious expression I had never seen before. (I knew she had been married twice and was now separated from her second husband, although the divorce had not yet been finalized.) Then we talked of something else.

But the "signs" (as I later called them) were repeated. Once, invited to dine at rue Ségur, I very carefully selected a pear from a bowl of fruit, wiped it clean, and offered half to Christinel. Since no one else wanted the other half, I kept it for myself. Then Mlle de la Rivière, rather casually and with humor cited to us an old tradition to the effect that the man who shares with a woman a pear which he himself has wiped, is destined to share the rest of his life with her.

Because I felt I had to say something in response, I declared that I had always admired folk wisdom and traditions.

,   ,   ,

In the last weeks of the year we were together all the time. We didn't hesitate to walk with arms around each other's shoulders on the street, stopping now and then—even under street lamps—for long kisses, like very young couples do, who have just discovered the spontaneity and innocence of such pleasures. Actually, we were no longer aware of where we were, and we hadn't the sense to hide our feelings. We were certain that everyone—beginning with Mamy— had long since guessed the truth. For my part, I didn't consider it necessary to be more explicit, to try to clarify a situation which seemed to me transparent.

We had decided to celebrate New Year's Eve with the whole family at the house of Mme Foll, mother of Sibylle's best friend, Jacqueline Desjardin. In addition to two or three colleagues, Sibylle had invited Herescu, Emil Cioran, Lucian Bădescu, and Mihai Niculescu. I knew Christinel had a cold, but I couldn't believe she'd miss the party. When she appeared in a marvelous evening gown that left the shoulders bare, and I embraced her lightly, kissing her on both cheeks, I was alarmed: her body was much warmer than usual. She explained, laughing, that, when she had taken her temperature a few hours before, it had registered 40°C. (104°F.) and then she had hidden the thermometer. She begged me not to say anything about the fever or what she had done. "With you, I'm not afraid of anything! Nothing can happen to me when you're protecting me!"

I protected her by keeping her by my side all the time. Sometimes I forgot I was at a party, with a whole group of friends; I had eyes only for her, I talked only with her. Fortunately, in spite of the fever, Christinel succeeded in entertaining us all with her songs and laughter, with her jokes—claiming, for instance that she could empty a glass of champagne more quickly than anyone else. Eventually, she calmed the anxieties of Mamy and Lisette, making them believe her fever had fallen appreciably.

The party ended at 8:00 A.M.—but we remained together. When, on January 9, Christinel moved into an apartment of her own in a hotel beside Ecole Militaire, I stayed with her; it was our betrothal. We didn't think of anything but the present; we were happy that finally we could be together as much as we wanted. What the future might bring, we did not try to guess. (For various reasons, the finalization of the divorce was delayed, but eventually Christinel succeeded in obtaining it. And, as we had promised each other, we had a civil ceremony on January 9, 1950, one year to the day from our betrothal, and on that same evening we celebrated the religious rites also.)

Gradually, I began to realize how my life would be changed. I continued my work schedule (in the first place, studies in the history of religions, especially Asia), but I no longer let myself be absorbed completely by such exclusively scientific activities; I was attracted even more by the deep, enigmatic dimensions of my latest experiences; I sensed that in some mysterious way they had been predestined and were intended for some definite objective which I could not yet understand.

Therefore, I continued to follow my routine. On January 15, at the Musée Guimet, I gave a lecture on Tantrism. Present were Puech, Masson-Oursel, and the Tibetanist Jacques Bacot, among others. All three urged me to take up the subject in a special monograph.[1] A few days later I did press service for *Traité d'histoire des religions.* I was well aware of the importance and value of the book. The enthusiastic appreciation of Dumézil, plus the letters received later from the many savants who admired it, as well as the first reviews which were exceptionally favorable, confirmed my faith in the destiny of this book. The first edition of *Traité* quickly sold out and it was reprinted. A few months after its appearance the Einaudi Publishing House arranged for an Italian translation. (But neither I nor Gustav Payot suspected then the success the book would have with the public and critics, nor the number of languages into which it would be translated.) At the end of May there appeared *Le mythe de l'éternel retour.* It is, probably, my most discussed writing, especially by philosophers and, in the United States, by theologians. (I read with much excitement the postcard sent by Benedetto Croce; the venerable philosopher developed some of his observations on the book in a review published in *Quaderni della Critica.*)[2]

1. Georges Bataille had suggested the same idea to me some time before, assuring me that Editions de Minuit would publish the book as quickly as possible.
2. In a series of articles in his column Novisimo Glosario, in *Arriba,* Eugenio d'Ors discussed *Le mythe de l'éternel retour* with enthusiasm. The first article bore the title: "Se trata de un libro muy importante." D'Ors appreciated especially the fact that I had brought out the Platonic structure of traditional ("popular") archaic ontologies.

That spring I met Rafaelle Pettazzoni. He had stopped in Paris in order to meet me; he hoped also to persuade Gustav Payot to translate his work of 1924, *La religione greca*, revised and with an up-to-date bibliography. In Gare de Lyon, recognizing him at a distance—gray-haired, dressed with conservative elegance, smiling, also often frowning (because he was deaf and sometimes failed to understand what was said, he didn't know how to respond)—I remembered my attic on strada Melodiei where I had read *I misteri*, and the room on Ripon Street, rereading late at night *La religione greca*. It was one of my great satisfactions that I contributed to the appearance of that book in French. After that, I was to see Pettazzoni again several times: at Rome, invited to lecture on Shamanism, at the Congress of Amsterdam, and, the last time, at Tokyo, in the fall of 1958, a few months before his passing.

In February, Christinel moved to Sibylle's apartment in Bois-Colombes. We met as often as we could. She liked hearing me talk about the works I had in progress, and especially about plans for the future. Excitedly, she leafed through the copy of *Das Mädchen Maitreyi* which I had received from Nymphenbürger Verlag, and she clapped her hands like a child, much elated, when I told her that Brice Parain was fascinated by the novel and had contracted for it at Gallimard.

"I hope it will be as successful as it was at home. Then other novels can be translated, beginning with *Nuntă în Cer* . . . and ending with the novel you're *going* to write," she added quickly.

I interrupted her with some hesitation. "First I must finish *Le chamanisme*."

"That's all right," she encouraged me, smiling ironically. "I'll wait."

I returned from Bois-Colombes before noon, ordinarily, and if I didn't have any appointments I would shut myself away in my room at Hôtel de Suède and work until evening, when Christinel would come and we would dine in a neighborhood restaurant. Lisette and Ionel had rented a villa at Capri for the use of the whole family. We were all invited to spend a part of the summer there together. In the latter half of May Christinel left, leaving Sibylle and me to follow two months later. I hoped by then to have been able to complete the first chapters of *Le chamanisme*. Again I resumed the twelve or fourteen hours a day work schedule. I spent almost all my afternoons at Musée de l'Homme, rechecking and completing the ethnological documentation; nights, I wrote into the small hours. I had long since finished the chapter on the symbolism of the shamanic costume; the very favorable comments of Georges Dumézil—who had corrected it with his wonderful meticulousness—intensified my appetite for work tenfold. I wrote with enthusiasm, almost enchanted by the important meanings that I was discovering in what I called the "archaic techniques of ecstasy."

One afternoon at Abbaye de Royaumont—where I had been invited to hear the last concert in the series Semaines musicales internationales—I awoke from that euphoria. I noted in the *Journal* the thrill I experienced on that 26th day of June while looking from the window of the bus at the fields studded with poppies. I was reminded of landscapes from my childhood, of Romanian fields and skies. And suddenly I felt the magic of Midsummer take hold of me. The excellent concert by Poulenc failed to break that spell. Returning at night in the same bus, I began to visualize a new novel, seeing it unroll in my mind like a mental film. But I "saw" with precision only the beginning and the end. The very next day I began to write. I had found the title: *Noaptea de Sânziene,* and I knew already that the action would unfold over a twelve-year period. I tried to continue *Le chamanisme,* devoting afternoons and evenings to it and working nights on the novel. But I soon had to abandon that optimistic plan.

Rereading the 300 pages of *Apocalips,* the novel I had begun at Lisbon and broke off writing in 1944, I thought I could "save" one character, Vădastra, and a good share of the episodes in which he played the principal role. I don't know if this was a mistake or not, but integrating Vădastra into the framework of *Noaptea de Sânziene* gave me many headaches. Since the writing continued for almost five years (although I could devote only a few months per year to the work), I shall return several times in subsequent pages to this flowing novel. Naturally, the plot, scenes, and characters of *Noaptea de Sânziene* underwent many transformations in those five years. But the central theme remained the same, just as I had "seen" it in the bus on the way home from Royaumont: the certainty of the main character, Ştefan Viziru, that the cosmic rhythms and historical events camouflage deep meanings of a spiritual order; and above all his hope that love can break through the plane of existence, revealing a new existential dimension—that is, the experience of absolute freedom. I must add, however, that very soon Ştefan Viziru will find himself obsessed with a paradoxical hope: namely, the possibility of being in love, at the same time, with two women.[3] In Ştefan's conception, such an experience—apparently unattainable—would be equivalent, on another plane, to the experience of the saints.

As I had anticipated, Christinel was overjoyed on finding out about the novel. It had happened just as she had predicted. For my part, I felt that I would be able to write better once we were together again. The first hundred pages, penned in my hotel room, had not seemed to me entirely satisfactory—so I had interrupted work on the novel. Besides, I had to compose an article for *Critique* and several book reviews for *Revue d'histoire des religions*. Moreover, obtaining a *titre de voyage* from police headquarters and an Italian visa required much time.

On July 14 I left Paris, together with Sibylle, Jacqueline, and Oani, the little son of Lisette and Ionel, and three days later we arrived at Capri. From Genoa, where I found again the oleanders of my youth, I lived in a continuous euphoria. It seemed to me that I had recovered the true dimension of my existence, that from now on destiny would allow me to devote myself exclusively to the vocation I had perceived already in adolescence: to decipher, through vigorous analysis, the meanings of religious phenomena and, whenever the documents would permit, to attempt to reconstruct their history, but without repressing—as I had done for the past several years—the activity of my literary imagination.

For the first two weeks Christinel and I stayed in an annex of the Villa Monacone, directly opposite the famous Faraglione cliffs. Then, until September 1, when we left for Rome, we were the guests of Nina Batalli in Villa Ruggiero, which she had recently rented. I wrote furiously and whenever I could: in the shade of a pine or resting on a rock, and, after we moved into the Villa Ruggiero, in a corner of the terrace. But mostly we walked, Christinel and I, on the little paths we traced among the stones.

That summer, when everything seemed to have become possible for me again, has remained in our memory as a gift from another realm. We have returned to Capri for visits several times since then, but even after we had been freed from poverty we didn't dare spend our vacation again on what had been once "our island."

*   *   *

3. Pavel Anicet, one of the main characters in the novel *Întoarcerera din rai*, ends by committing suicide precisely because he does not dare choose between the two women he loves.

In the nine days we spent in Rome, I met Ernesto de Martino who, after translating *Techniques du Yoga,* had been engaged for the Italian translation of *Traité d'histoire des religions* also. De Martino had separated from his first wife, the daughter of V. Macchioro (whom I met at Naples in 1927) and had married a young woman he had met in southern Italy during his field researches. The favorite pupil of Macchioro, a disciple of Benedetto Croce (who had published his first book on history and ethnology), de Martino had been for several years a member of the Communist party and enjoyed a well-deserved prestige among intellectuals of the far left. In the series he directed at Einaudi he had published recently *Il pensiero magico* in which he had tried to carry Croce's "historicism" further, into the interpretation of the archaic mentality. In de Martino's view, "nature" itself, and not human existence only, is "culturally conditioned." In other words, phenomena of a magical or shamanistic type (bilocation, the evocation of spirits, possession, etc.)—unreal for a Westerner who lives in the universe of Newton and his successors, were "real" and "natural" for "primitives" living in a world governed by magical thought. "Nature," being "culturally conditioned," permitted archaic societies *really* to evoke the dead, whereas spiritualism practiced in Western societies is either an illusion of a farce. Benedetto Croce criticized this attempt to "historicize" nature, insisting that history is the creation exclusively of the spirit.[4]

From de Martino I learned that after the appearance of *Techniche dello Yoga,* Einaudi had received several denunciations—probably originating from the legation—concerning my alleged "fascist" activity before the war. But de Martino's response was clear and simple: with regard to the series under his direction, he allowed no objections of a nonscientific nature. The objections he himself raised several months later in his preface to the Italian translation of *Traité* concerned exclusively the method used in the investigation of religious data—which de Martino called "phenomenology" (for me, it was rather a morphology), and to which he opposed Crocian historicism. But the denunciations received by Einaudi, although they failed to have the result expected by those who had made them, were a timely reminder that my imprudent acts and errors committed in youth constituted a series of malentendus that would follow me all my life.

4. I sketched similar observations in an article in *Critique* no. 23 [1948]:315–23), "Science, idéalisme et phènoménes paranormaux."

Later I realized I had no right to complain. It was on account of those malentendus that I was living in the West, free to continue my work in the history of religions, Oriental studies, and the philosophy of culture. If it had not been for Nae Ionescu—or, more precisely, if the professor, in his radical opposition to King Carol, had not allied himself with Hitlerist Germany—I'd have stayed in Romania, probably as a professor at the university, until 1946–47. Then I'd have shared the fate of so many others of my generation. (But sometimes I told myself that this fate had only been postponed. Why, after so many years, was I still preoccupied with the enigma of collective death?)

/   /   /

On September 11 I returned alone to Paris, and between the 14th and the 19th of the month I participated in the Conference on Religious Psychology held at Royaumont. My talk (it had been suggested that I speak on "Images religieuses—images naturelles") was rather well received, and the discussion lasted more than two hours. Upon returning to Paris, I reread the 370 pages of the novel that I had written so far; aside from the numerous excerpts from *Apocalips*, the text disappointed me. I began immediately, with fury, to revise the manuscript, drastically reducing the episodes having to do with characters from the old novel and redoing several chapters—some in their entirety.

But, at times, news and meetings removed me from the horizon of *Noptea de Sânziene*. On October 3, R. P. Jean Bruno, director of the review *Études Carmélitaines*, came to invite me to participate in the conference on Chastity and Mystical Experience to be held the following year in September. Two days later I received a letter from Frau Olga Froebe-Kapteyin, requesting me to lecture at the Eranos Conference in August of 1950. The invitation delighted and flattered me. I had read the first *Eranos-bücher* while still living in Romania, and I had been fascinated by this type of multidisciplinary symposium in which, in addition to C. J. Jung, a number of savants I much admired had already participated: Paul Pelliot, Jean Przluski, Louis Massignon, H. Zimmer, H. Ch. Puech, Gershom Scholem, and others.

Henri Corbin, who had lectured for the first time that year at Eranos, invited me to his little apartment on rue de l'Odeon and he, his wife Stella, and I talked at length about the meetings and discussions at Ascona. Stella had succeeded, with discretion, in conveying to him all the nuances which the deaf miss, even when they wear a hearing aid. Henry spoke to me with understanding and admiration about *Traité* and *Le mythe de l'éternel retour*. He proposed that we revive, together, the journal *Zalmoxis*, publishing it under the auspices of the Institute of Iranology which he directed in Teheran. If I hadn't been engaged in so many projects, I would have accepted the proposition with joy. But I postponed the revival of the journal until later.

Toward the end of October it became so cold in my room that I could write only by warming my hands from time to time on a hotwater bottle. With a great effort I finished correcting the text of the novel. Christinel had returned recently from Italy, and I was eager for her to read it. When she finished the 370 typed pages, she threw her arms around me, thrilled. This reaction of my first reader (and Christinel has remained since then the first reader of all my literary writings) encouraged me. Finally, I said to myself, I've succeeded in "saving" the novel. (I didn't suspect then the difficulties I'd encounter later.) I continued to work on it at least two or three hours per day, although other projects were calling me.

Professor Stig Wikander, whose scholarship, intelligence, and originality I had admired from his first works, had arrived recently from Lund and had rented a room in Hôtel de Suède. Of course, we spent much time together, discussing especially the history of Indo-European religions whose study Georges Dumézil had so brilliantly revitalized in the past ten years. As might be expected, such discussions, to which were added other concerns, detached me from *Noptea de Sânziene*. In November I took up again the writing of *Le chamanisme*, interrupted four months earlier. I could tell that my abandonment of the novel disappointed Christinel. But, on the other hand, she realized that I was doing something important for me, and she tried to help me as best she could. She learned how to type, and then began typing the chapters of *Le chamanisme* as soon as I transcribed them.

Through Denis de Rougemont, Le Mouvement Européen invited me to a cultural conference taking place in Lausanne between the 8th and 13th of December. Having only a simple *titre de voyage*, at the Franco-Swiss border I was invited—the only one in my coach—to get off, carrying my suitcase, and enter an office of the station where I underwent a thorough search. Setting eyes on *Traité* and *Le mythe* and learning that I had been forced to become stateless, the inspector apologized. He added, however, that the fault had been largely my own. Why was it written on my *titre de voyage* "sans profession"?

Why hadn't I stated that I was a "homme de lettres"? Of course, I admitted he was right. (A few months later I became a member of the Association of French Writers.)

I saw Lausanne again after twenty-three years, and I spent the first hours walking around the lake. First I met Denis de Rougemont; then, the next morning, Salvador de Madariaga, Stephen Spender, and Etienne Gilson—almost the only persons there worth meeting. The majority of the participants were preoccupied with other things: above all, with obtaining places on the various committees that were being constituted. I had hoped fervently in Le Mouvement Européen, in the possibilities for "Europeanizing" the cultures of the Continent (if not, for the time being, also the political institutions), considering as evidence the solidarity of the various European spiritual traditions. But I did not believe in the virtues of bureaucracies or in the creativity of "committees." Nevertheless, I did my duty. In order to strengthen the trend toward transcending Romanian-Magyar frictions, I proposed to Professor Andreas Alföldi that I read, in the final session, the text he had written: a pathetic appeal for the safe-guarding of the intellectual elite beyond the Iron Curtain.

/ / /

On January 9, after our civil marriage ceremony, because the Romanian church was still closed, the religious service (celebrated by two priests, one Orthodox, the other Greek-Catholic) was conducted in the sumptuous, old-fashioned apartment of a friend of the family on rue Mignard. My witness was Nicolas Herescu, the sponsors Sibylle and Emil Cioran, and among the guests were Georges Dumézil and Henri Ch. Puech with their wives, and Stig Wikander. A few days before I had rented the little room connecting directly with mine— number 18; in which I had lived since 1946—at Hôtel de Suède. Thus we had now a little "apartment"; however, since we were not allowed to prepare anything except tea and coffee, we took our meals in a cheap but clean restaurant in the neighborhood. Apparently, nothing had changed. And yet, as I had sensed a year before, I had begun a new life.

21. The Tide Begins to Turn

THE YEAR 1950 was rich in events, and not for me alone. Turning the pages of my journal I was reminded of the disordered activity of those winter months, the exhausting labor, and the hopes I cherished, followed by the surprises and disappointments I experienced toward the end of spring.

But, above all, 1950 was the year of papers and conferences. At the invitation of Jean Wahl I spoke at Collège Philosophique about "Le structure des mythes" (January 13) and "Le mythe dans le monde moderne" (January 20). At the first lecture, the audience included Maurice Leenhardt and Claude Lévi-Strauss. As I expected, Lévi-Strauss did not seem at all in accord with my interpretation, but, significantly, he kept silent during the discussion period. The second lecture was more successful (I dispensed with a written text this time); there followed fervent (for me at least) discussions with Eric Weil, Abbot Morel, Michel Carrougès, and Aimé Patri.

The next day I gave the inaugural address at Centre Roumaine de Recherches, with Prince Nicolae, patron and supporter of the center, being present.[1] I spoke about "Romania and the Orient," developing

1. This Centre Roumaine des Recherches, the secretary of which was Octavian Vuia (at the insistence of Prince Nicolae, I accepted the presidency), had in the course of many years, a varied and stimulating program of activities. Among the French lecturers, I remember R. P. Jean de Menasce, R. P. Jean Daniélou, Gabriel Marcel, Marcel Brion, Henry Corbin, and Marcel Griaule.

one of my favorite themes. I emphasized especially the intermediary function—a true "bridge" connecting the East with Western Europe—which Romanian culture could fulfill. Indeed, down through the centuries this country realized a synthesis of several important spiritual traditions: of the neolithic and the Ancient East, of Thrace and Byzantium, to which was added, along with cultural contributions of Slavic origin and recently those of extreme Western Europe, familiarity with the beliefs, customs, and institutions peculiar to the Ottoman Empire.

At the end of January, R. P. Jean Daniélou—whom I had met the previous year and with whom I had become friends—invited me to lunch at the house of the Jesuit Fathers on rue Vaneau, where the office of the journal *Études* also was located. In this way I had the opportunity to meet Teilhard de Chardin. After lunch, together with Jean Daniélou, we withdrew to Teilhard's room, where we spent a long time in conversation. As soon as I returned to my hotel I set down in writing a part of our conversation. Unfortunately, I have lost those pages, but I have not forgotten the essence of what was said. At that time Teilhard could not publish any of his philosophical or theological works; still he was allowed to distribute certain short texts in mimeographed form. As I was leaving, he gave me several of these. I read them the same day, with great interest, but I did not realize the originality of Teilhard's thought until many years later, after the appearance of his book *Le phenomène humain*.

In February I began working hard again on *Le chamanisme*. I wrote as many as twelve hours a day, and Christinel began typing the finished chapters. But our financial situation worsened. In January General Rădescu had suspended the subventions given to students and certain Romanian intellectuals in Paris. The appearance of *La nuit bengali* (the title chosen by Gallimard for *Maitreyi*) had been postponed, and I didn't dare ask for another advance on royalties. Other than honoraria for articles published in *Critique*, we could count on nothing but the 20,000 francs Lisette sent us monthly. (She was living now in New York where Ionel Perlea, affiliated with the Metropolitan Opera, had achieved a great success directing *Tristan and Isolde*; a critic had written that such a perfect execution had not been heard in forty years, not since Gustav Mahler. I had begun to borrow funds anywhere I could. But still I could not decide to give up the second room, number 17, at Hôtel de Suède.

,   ,   ,

At the beginning of March I interrupted work again on *Le chama-nisme* in order to write the two lectures I was to give at Rome: "Le cha-manisme" at the university, invited by Pettazzoni, and "Le tantrisme et le chamanisme" at the Institute for Oriental Studies (ISMEO), invited by Giuseppe Tucci. We left Paris on March 20 in a third-class coach and arrived, exhausted, in the morning of the next day. ISMEO had reserved a room for us at Pensione Huber on via Paisiello, very close to Villa Borghese. But the twelve-hour general strike then in effect prevented me from seeing Tucci. I did succeed, however, in reaching Pettazzoni's place. From him I learned that I would be lecturing in the Aula Prima and that the rector of the university would be present. I was thrilled, but I regretted having chosen such a technical subject; I might have spoken, for instance, about the structure and function of myth, problems of general interest. Nevertheless, as I noted in my journal, the next morning that magnificent auditorium was al-most full. I met or renewed acquaintances with a number of scholars (among others, A. Grenier, director of the French Institute, Angelo Brelich, Karl Kerényi, L. Vancelli, and others). Pettazzoni introduced me in terms unusual for one of his standards and discretion.

After the lecture, Giuseppe Tucci invited us to his house, along with Pettazzoni, for coffee. With that Orientalist I had maintained a rather steady contact by mail, but this was the first time I had seen him in eighteen years. He seemed unchanged: the same presence and vivacity, the same boundless energy (he was editing Sanskrit and Ti-betan texts, publishing scholarly works, and directing ISMEO), the same unlimited curiosity. His gigantic library (he had built the house in which he lived in order to be able to have a place for his library) fascinated me as soon as I entered the first room of it. Tucci showed me all my books, bound, and he proposed that we begin publishing *Zalmoxis* again, under the auspices of ISMEO. I replied, as I had to Corbin, that I was grateful, but for the time being I had to finish the books I had begun. "I've been carrying them on my back for five or six years now!" I confessed, smiling. Two days later I gave my lecture— which was followed by a long, ardent discussion—in one of the halls of the institute. Thanks to Tucci's generosity, we remained at Rome for another two days, and thus I was able to revisit the Forum and other favorite places.

Back in Paris, I reopened the manuscript of *Le chamanisme*. Perhaps

I'd have succeeded in finishing the two additional chapters I'd begun if a series of unforeseen annoyances and obstacles had not arisen. Toward the end of April, the chambermaid asked me if she could take the wastepaper basket and empty it. From the next room, where I was working, I answered affirmatively. I had forgotten that on top of the wastebasket I had placed several files, so full that I had tied them with cord to prevent their contents from spilling. In this way several kilograms of manuscripts, notes, and letters were incinerated. I regretted most the loss of some sixty letters from colleagues, critics, and other readers of my books (among them, those of Benedetto Croce, G. Bachelard, and E. Bréhier).

I succeeded, nevertheless, in continuing to work at almost the same rhythm. But on May 27 I left for Venice in order to participate in the constitutive assembly of the European Society for Culture. All the guests were lodged in the famous Hotel Bauer-Grunwald (which I have never entered since). I noted in my *Journal* many particulars in connection with this improbable revisit to Venice, through which I had passed the last time en route to Berne, where Lucian Blaga was awaiting me.

On June 2 I returned to Paris, but I was unable to make much headway in my work. I wrote with difficulty, with much effort, and without enthusiasm. Moreover, my health was declining; I felt threatened with a new attack of vagotonia. Bad news came in an unbroken chain. The publication of *La nuit bengali*, printed several months earlier, had been postponed until June and eventually appeared only in September. Ionel Perlea, piqued that Berg, director at the Metropolitan, had demanded he open the fall season with *Die Fledermaus* rather than *Parsifal* as he had promised, broke his contract signed for three years and accepted other offers which proved in time less bright than he had believed them to be. Finally, at the end of June, the United States intervened in Korea and the Third World War seemed again imminent.

Fortunately, Sibylle rented a villa at Briançon where we installed ourselves, along with Mamy, on July 20. The next two weeks spent there in the Alps reminded me, with melancholy, of my excursions along the Carpathians in adolescence. Soon the vagotonia attack passed, and my health and appetite for work returned. But except for notations in the *Journal*, I wrote nothing. With Christinel I took long walks through the forest on the edge of Briançon and, as often as possible, climbed the mountains. Although I attempted to resist, my mind kept returning to the only book I really would have liked to be writing then, *L'Homme comme symbole*. Next to *Le mythe de l'éternel retour*, I considered it my most original work; erudition and historico-religious hermeneutics gave place there to philosophical reflection. It would have been a short book, without footnotes, accompanied by a summary bibliography at the end. But I knew I had no right to start it before finishing *Le chamanisme*. On the other hand, in a few weeks I had to present a two-hour lecture at Eranos and a short while after that a brief communication at the International Congress of the History of Religions.

At the beginning of August I returned, alone, to Paris, in order to compose and perfect these texts. I had given up Room 17, and now I could hear my neighbors through both walls. When I was working, I stuffed my ears with "Boules Quies" and succeeded in convincing myself I heard nothing. For Eranos I utilized excerpts from older works, some unpublished. Nevertheless, by the day I left, I still had not finished the second half of the lecture (after the first hour, there was a break of a half-hour before the second part). The last ten or twelve pages I wrote at night in my room at Casa Tomaro where I was housed at Ascona.

Ascona and the Eranos group fascinated me from the start. The pages of the *Journal* have preserved only a small part of my enthusiasm at discovering Ticino and Lago Maggiore, and the joy of my first meetings with Olga Froebe, C. G. Jung, G. Scholem, and the other participants. I could not suspect then the role Eranos would play in my life in the next five or six years nor that of Frau Olga Froebe-Kapteyin, a silver-haired lady, the founder and animating spirit of the group. The day after my arrival, in the morning, I discovered with delight the Villa Eranos, separated from the Villa Gabriella by a garden which descended on terraces to the shore of the lake.

The first lecturer was Karl Kerényi, the only one who spoke without notes, his eyes ranging over the audience, seemingly seeking a face upon which to rest his gaze. Frau Froebe detained me for lunch at her famous "round table" under the eucalyptus in the garden of the Villa Gabriella. The next day Professor Scholem lectured; he fascinated me from the moment I met him on the evening of my arrival. I had long admired his scholarship and perspicacity, but that evening what impressed me were his gifts as a storyteller and his genius for asking only essential questions. At the time of Scholem's lecture, I caught sight of Jung. He was listening while reclining on a chaise longue on the terrace, in front of an open window. I was struck by his physical vigor and the youthfulness of his eyes. But only the next day, when, after finding me on his left at lunch, he had spent two hours in conversaton with me, did I begin to admire his wisdom and candor. I noted in my *Journal* (cf. *Fragments d'un Journal*, I, p. 130) some of his bitter comments relative to "official science."

The lecture I delivered on August 25 was rather successful, and this fact led Olga Froebe to invite me to Eranos in 1951, and then to all the other conferences until her death in 1962. Like the other participants, I had hardly any time to rest. Long discussions with Jung, Louis Massignon, Henry Corbin, Raffael Pettazzoni (cf. *Fragments*, pp. 130ff.). Joachim Wach, who was spending his summer vacation at his sister's place in Locarno, invited me to lunch with him at a trattoria. He admired *Traité* and *Le mythe de l'éternel retour*, books which he discussed in his course on the history of religions at the University of Chicago. I noted in my *Journal:* "He wants to do something to invite me to the United States, but he doesn't know exactly what or how." (He did it, nonetheless, five years later.)

I had a long conversation also with John Barrett of the Bollingen Foundation; Henry Corbin had spoken to him about me, insisting especially on the difficulties under which I was laboring. John Barrett promised me he would intercede with the directors of the foundation with a view to granting me a fellowship for study (as was being done for other scholars—Karl Kerényi, for instance). I couldn't imagine, on that warm August afternoon, that I would obtain it so soon.

/ / /

As I wrote at the beginning of this chapter, 1950 was the year of lectures, meetings, and conferences. No sooner had I returned from Switzerland than I was off again (on September 3) for Amsterdam, where the International Congress on the History of Religions was being held. Professor Gerardus van der Leeuw, president of the congress, had named me a member of the committee to initiate the creation of an international association of historico-religious studies, so that I was obliged to participate in all the preliminary discussions. (I had the satisfaction along with all the others of seeing the association solemnly proclaimed to exist on the final day of the congress. Professor Bleeker was named secretary general and Raffael Pettazzoni vice president and director of the new journal, *Numen*.) Because I had no money to pay for a hotel, I stayed in a private residence: a governess's room, with an army cot, no writing table, and no bath. That week, several colleagues, under the pretext that they had discovered an "exotic restaurant" or a "true Dutch tavern," invited me to dinner numerous times.

As at any international congress, the most important part consisted not so much in the lectures and "communications" as in the discussions with masters and colleagues from other countries or other continents. Some of them I met for the first time then, at Amsterdam. I presented a short paper, "Mythes cosmogoniques et guérisons magiques," which I was to develop later in *Aspects du mythe* (*Myth and Reality*). I remember even now conversations with Stig Wikander and Maurice Leenhardt, the stroll with Puech and Filliozat and their wives at the zoo, the reception at the Rijkmuseum. . . .

La nuit bengali appeared, finally, in September, but it was not the success—either with the public or with the critics—that Brice Parain and I had thought it would be. On the other hand, Gustav Payot seemed upset that less than two years after the appearance of *Traité d'histoire des religions* I had published a *novel*. Your name, he told me, evokes in the minds of readers an Orientalist and historian of religions. You must not disorient them! He was right, of course. But I had thought that the tradition of strict compartmentalization, imposed by positivism (the objectivity of scientific researchers and philosophical thinkers on the one hand, the subjectivity of artistic creators on the other) had become passé. I couldn't forget that nearly all the German philosophers at the beginning of the nineteenth century wrote novels, while the success of authors like Gabriel Marcel, Albert Camus, or Jean-Paul Sartre demonstrated the solidarity of philosophical thought and literary creativity. I was wrong, however, in choosing *Maitreyi* for my literary debut in France. How many readers would have been able, like Bachelard, to decipher a "mythology of voluptousness" in that novel of my youth?

Fortunately, in that autumn of 1950, I believed that *La nuit bengali* would be successful, at least with the public, and I ventured to ask for another advance against royalties. Our financial situation was worsening from day to day. We were obliged to borrow money from friends and Sibylle in order to have rent for the room and one good meal at the restaurant (cheap as it was) on rue Sèvres.

At the end of September I participated in the Conference on Religious Psychology organized by R. P. Bruno and *Études Carmélitaines.* I was housed in the Carmelite monastery at Fontainbleau. I improvised a lecture on "Chasteté et états mystiques chez les primitifs," but more importantly I spent some time in conversation with several psychologists and psychoanalysts, especially Dr. René Laforgue, whose book on Baudelaire (*La psychologie de l'échec*) I had read not long before. Two weeks later, René and Délia Laforgue invited us to lunch at their apartment at 62½ rue de la Tour, and because they were leaving soon for Casablanca, they proposed that we stay in it for the four or five months they would be gone. We couldn't believe it: to live in a five-room apartment, with a living room that seemed gigantic; to be able to work without noisy neighbors, in a perfectly isolated room (the office where Dr. Laforgue received his patients)!

We moved a few days later, but I could not immediately resume work on *Le chamanisme.* I had to write the "communication" for *Études Carmélitaines,* an article for *Critique,* and several other texts. The only nuisance concerned Anna, the housekeeper Dr. Laforgue had left us. Every morning we had to give her money for the marketing. Several times we gave her only half the usual amount, pretending we were invited out for lunch. In fact, we went to the Luxembourg Gardens and contented ourselves with a sandwich.

In the first weeks of December the world situation as well as our personal one seemed desperate. The Chinese had launched their offensive in Korea, and the panic of war spread again. When I changed the last banknote of 500 francs, Christinel decided to try to obtain another loan from a friend of hers who had rescued us from poverty several times before. She returned with 5,000 francs, which assured us of meals for a few more days. The next morning I received a letter from the Bollingen Foundation notifying me that I had been accorded a grant for three years, and that beginning January 1 I would receive a monthly stipend of $200. That same week the Centre National de la Recherche Scientifique informed me that I had been named "research attaché" at 35,000 francs per month. But since I could not benefit from both grants simultaneously, I had to choose; and because I could receive it in any country, not France only, I chose the Bollingen grant.

From that morning of December 9, I felt delivered from the nightmare of poverty. We could allow ourselves to take lunch at home every day. We could also invite friends, as we hadn't dared to do for a long time. Finally, I was free to devote myself to the writing of the last chapters of *Le chamanisme*. I promised myself, at all costs, to finish that book in the course of the winter.

,   ,   ,

I shut myself away in Dr. Laforgue's office and worked as much as twelve hours a day. Fortunately, we lived very close to the Musée d'Homme and right beside the Metro station for Musée Guimet. I could consult their rich libraries without wasting too much time. On the other hand, my good friend, Jean Gouillard, had moved recently to the same neighborhood. Learning that Georges Dumézil, burdened with courses and his own writings, did not dare take time to read and correct the last chapters, Jean Gouillard offered to take his place. Once a week I climbed the stairs to his attic room and brought him a certain number of pages. Jean would correct them that very night, and a few days later Christinel, having typed them, would file them in their proper folders.

Sometimes we invited guests for dinner; they could hardly believe (even as we ourselves) that we ate in such an elegant dining room. For many years they, like us, had been accustomed to eat their meals on a little table in a hotel room or a servant's quarters, or, at best, in a cheap neighborhood restaurant. (I believe at that time only Rodica and Eugène Ionesco enjoyed what we exiles called a "true" dining room table.)

N. I. Herescu, who had been called to the chair of Latin at the University of Lisbon, remained as optimistic as ever; he continued to believe in the indestructible justice of history. A year before, Emil Cioran had published his first book written in French, *Précis de décomposition*, amazing us all, and especially the literary critics, with its stylistic perfection. In the spring of 1950, at the Noctambule Theater, Eugène Ionesco's play, *La cantatrice chauve*, had been performed, thus inaugurating that exceptional career which continues still, in all parts of the world.

Recently we had become friends with Monica Lovinescu, a lover of literature and the theater (she had contributed to the success of Ionesco's play), and with Virgil Ierunca, enthusiastic and indefatigable where any cultural initiative of the exiles was concerned. To our delight—but to the surprise of all—Monica and Virgil were married the following spring.

Another who came to see us was Albert Samuel, who wrote under the pen name of Alexandru Vona. We had known each other for several years, and I had admired a novel he had written; I even hoped it would be published by Gallimard.[2]

At the end of the winter Délia and René returned from Casablanca and we returned to Room 18 in Hôtel de Suède. The last chapter of *Le chamanisme* was written with great effort; I had begun to feel the consequences of overwork. In March Christinel finished the typing: over 700 pages, which I hastened to deliver to Payot. I told him, offhandedly, that I would add a conclusion of a few pages. "I'm too tired to write it now," I admitted. "I'll do it in a week or two, at Rome." To my surprise and delight, Payot handed me on the spot a rather considerable sum, which allowed us to spend a full month in Italy.

On the 25th of March we arrived in Rome, and the first person I went to see was Pettazzoni. He congratulated me, with surprise and admiration, on learning that *Le chamanisme* was at the printer. We left then for Naples, where Nina Battali and the engineer Giacomo Nardone were expecting us. Our friends took us for a drive along the Amalfitane Coast, and we saw again the lakes and Pozzuoli. A few days later we went by train down to Taormina. Thus I set foot for the first time on the soil of Sicily, and since then I have never forgotten that fabulous island. After spending ten days at Taormina, Catania, and Palermo, I regained my health and appetite for work. The botanical gardens at Palermo reminded me of Goethe and his famous theory of the "Urpflanze." I would have liked to devote two or three months to reading Goethe, but I realized that such an excursion into the spiritual universes discovered in adolescence and youth were, for the time being, forbidden. Thus, I contented myself with reading works about Asia and the history of religions given me recently by my Italian masters and colleagues. We embarked at nightfall on a little vessel going to Naples, arriving there in the morning. As usual, the rhythm of the waves, the starry sky, and those mysterious sounds which are transformed somehow into whispers, projected me into a past hard to identify: a trip on the Danube or the Black Sea? Evenings spent on the bridge of the ship that took me from Naples to Athens in 1928? Or the

2. Indeed, although translated (badly) into French, it had been read with interest by Brice Parain and others at Gallimard. It might have been published, if the author had presented it in a new translation. But after losing his wife, Mira, in an absurd accident, Vona lost all interest in the fate of his novel.

voyage from Constanţa to Alexandria, or from Port Said to Columbo? I did not try to be more specific. I was fascinated by this sudden, blissful regaining of the past.

After spending three days at Naples, we took a room for a week at Rome. I believe[3] that it was then that I saw J. Evola for the second time. He had written to me at Hôtel de Suède, and I had learned that having been wounded in in the spine by a shell fragment during the siege of Vienna by Soviet troops, he was condemned to spend the rest of his life in a wheelchair. When I was ushered into his room, however, Evola greeted me on his feet; he had been raised to a standing position by his aged father and the nurse. After we had shaken hands, the two reseated him in the chair and left the room. I had read books by Evola as early as my student days, but I had met him for the first and only other time in the spring of 1937 at a luncheon given by Nae Ionescu. I admired his intelligence and, even more, the density and clarity of his prose. Like René Guénon, Evola presumed a "primordial tradition," in the existence of which I could not believe; I was suspicious of its artificial, ahistorical character.

On that afternoon we spoke of many things, but in particular about the decadence—or, as Evola termed it, the "putrefaction"—of contemporary Western culture. From a certain point of view—that of an exemplary, ahistorical "tradition"—he was right. But the problem that concerned me was a different one: to the extent that I believe in the creativity of the human spirit, I cannot despair; culture, even in a crepuscular era, is the only means of conveying certain values and of transmitting a certain spiritual message. In a new Noah's Ark, by means of which the spiritual creations of the West could be saved, it is not enough for René Guénon's *L'esotérisme de Dante* to be included; there must be also the poetic, historical, and philosophical understanding of *The Divine Comedy*. The limiting of the hermeneutics of European spiritual creations exclusively to their "esoteric meanings" repeats, in reverse, the reductionsim of a materialistic type illustrated so successfully by Marx or Freud.

On the other hand, I added, the reentry of Asia into history and the discovery of the spirituality of archaic societies cannot be without consequence. J. Evola believed that, in any event, it was too late, that

3. I hesitate over the date because I have lost my appointment calendar for the years 1949–54.

we are witnessing in fact, a general acculturation. At first glance, he was right. But the acculturation represents only the first phase of a more complex process. The camouflage or even occultation of the sacred and of spiritual meanings in general characterizes all crepuscular eras. It is a matter of the larval survival of the original meaning, which in this way becomes *unrecognizable*. Hence the importance I ascribe to images, symbols, and narratives, or more precisely to the hermeneutical analysis which describes their meanings and identifies their original functions.

But, of course, in the hour spent conversing with Evola, I only touched on these problems.

￼ ￼ ￼

After our return to Paris, my time was confiscated again by *Le chamanisme:* corrections of page proofs, preparation of the index, and composition of the "Conclusions" took me two weeks. But only now could I appreciate the merits and shortcomings of the book. I was dissatisfied, especially, with the "Conclusions"—written too succinctly, in great haste, under pressure of the press.[4] But of the novelty and value of this book I had no doubt. For the first time, all varieties of shamanism—not only the "classical" ones, characteristic of Siberia and Central Asia—were presented and interpreted from the perspective of the history of religions. In addition, I had analyzed the structure and function of certain shamanic mythologies and techniques surviving, more or less camouflaged, in "historical religions" (of India, ancient Greece, China, Japan, etc.). Moreover, I had not accepted, as was usually done, any physiological arguments (lack of vitamins!) or psychological ones (the irruption of certain elements from the unconscious) by which the shamanic type of ecstasy has been explained. The analysis of the experiences and the presentation of the ceremonies by which the neophyte is consecrated bring to light their solidarity with the exemplary model of initiation. No less useful and pertinent, it seemed to me, was the examination of the varoius meanings accorded to ecstatic trance in both primitive and historical religions. The distance between the shamanic techniques and Yoga practice, the qualitative difference between ecstasy and enstasis, and their great importance for understanding the universal history of spiritualities became evident.

4. I elaborated them later in preparing the English version, which constitutes, in fact, a second edition, revised and augmented.

When I returned the proofs and the rest as "ready to print," I was
sure that *Le chamanisme* would interest not only ethnologists and historians of religions but also nonspecialists. Indeed, the book, which
appeared in September, was very well received; soon it would be reprinted and translated into several languages.

          /   /   /

At the beginning of summer I became free again. The lecture for
Eranos, "Le Temps et l'Éternité dans la pensée indienne," I had decided to write in August. I had succeeded too in convincing Georges
Bataille that I had to postpone the writing of *Le tantrisme*. At Rome I
had learned from Giuseppe Tucci that he was about to publish, with
an English translation, the commentary of Candrakirti on the *Guhya-
samāja Tantra*, together with the glosses by Tson K'a-pa—heretofore
accessible only in Tibetan.[5] I told Georges Bataille that I didn't dare
begin my little monograph on tantrism before knowing these texts.

I was, therefore, free to devote myself wholly to the novel. I told
myself that I would write very productively in the villa Sibylle had
rented at Guétary. But because the rent had been raised again, we decided to leave the room in Hôtel de Suède and move to the small
apartment of Jacqueline Desjardin on rue Duhesme. I packed with
melancholy the books and papers that had accumulated in the four
and a half years I had lived on rue Vaneau. Fortunately, at the beginning of July we left for Guétary. I was impatient to read again, with
pencil in hand, the manuscript of *Noaptea de Sânziene*. And this time
too the text disappointed me. I couldn't forgive myself for the fact that
in the summer of 1949, instead of attempting a sequel to *Huliganii*, I
had let myself be drawn into a labyrinth. Indeed, I realized now that
the scenario of the novel, so far as the main characters were concerned, resembled a wandering in a labyrinth—a long and depressing
wandering, because they still had not perceived its initiatory significance. Their difficulties increased from chapter to chapter. Although
the action extended over twelve years, and although the number of
characters was large, *Noaptea de Sânziene* could not be allowed to resemble a miniature *War and Peace*. On the other hand, certain obses-
sions of the leading character, Ştefan Viziru, and the happenings—
sometimes enigmatic—in which he found himself involved could not
be allowed to evoke the "atmosphere" of a fantastic tale. All trans-

5. Unfortunately, the work appeared only fragmentarily and much later.

historical meanings must be perfectly camouflaged in the concrete of historical events.

After several days of hesitation, I set to work. I wrote every day, stubbornly, sometimes with enthusiasm, correcting and sometimes rewriting whole episodes. In this fashion, by August 1, when we returned to Paris, I had reworked some 150 pages which seemed to me now "definitive."

We felt strange, of course, in our new neighborhood, but in that time of late summer I had scarcely any leisure to explore it. I stayed home all day, working on my lecture for Eranos. This time, Christinel went with me to Ascona. She was fascinated, as I had been the previous year, by the beauty of the place and delighted by the presence of so many colleagues and friends (Corbin, Puech, Dr. Godel) all gathered together at Casa Tamaro. She was delighted also by the appearance and manner of Frau Froebe. It is very probable that Olga was impressed by Christinel's modesty and charm, because she invited us both to spend the month of June, in 1952, at Casa Gabriella.

I delivered my lecture with considerable gusto, although I had feared that after the first hour I would be exhausted. The night before I had suffered the most prolonged and tenacious insomnia I could remember. I tried to rest in the afternoon, but I did not succeed. I had then, for a half an hour, an intense, mysterious "waking dream," provoked, probably, by my reimmersion in Indian spirituality and in the memory of my experiences in India. (See *Fragments d'un Journal*, I, pp. 153–55.)

After the Eranos Conference had ended, Alice and Roger Godel invited us to spend a few days with them at Hergisville, on the shore of the lake, ten kilometers from Lucerne, and at Geneva. We had met them in the fall of 1949. A cardiologist of world renown, Dr. Roger Godel was the director of the hospital of the Suez Canal Company at Ismailia, but he was also interested in ancient Greece and Indian spirituality. He had visited India several times and knew Ramana Maharishi personally. He told me about a book on which he was working, boldly titled *L'expérience libératrice* (the book was to be publsihed, with a preface by myself, by Gallimard in 1954). After that journey with the Godels in Switzerland in 1951, we became good friends. Several years later Alice and Roger invited us to stay in the superb apartment they had just purchased at Val d'Or.

/   /   /

We returned to Paris at the beginning of September. I was resolved to concentrate exclusively on the novel. This time, I felt I had found the solution: a plurality of temporal rhythms, different from one chapter to another, which allowed me to strengthen the narrative and, at the same time, pursue the destinies of the main characters without disclosing their deep meanings. I wrote every afternoon, sometimes in the mornings also, in what formerly had been Sibylle's studio, at 47 rue Saint-Ouen. It was in an old, abandoned hotel, half in ruins. Several Italian families had moved in amongst the rubble, but in back, where the workshop was located, it was quiet, and I could work undisturbed until nightfall.

However, on October 15 I had to interrupt work on the novel again, in order to prepare the volume *Images et symboles*, for which Brice Parain was waiting. I had planned this book in the summer, in Switzerland, stimulated by conversations with many scholars. I had decided to republish (corrected and augmented) two older studies concerning religious symbolism,[6] together with the texts of the Eranos lectures, accompanied by an introduction on images and the imagination and a chapter of conclusions: "Symbolism and History." In a few weeks' time I had drafted the conclusion and was ready to write the introduction. Unfortunately, I failed to set to work on it immediately, and after getting started I was interrupted repeatedly. Thus, I wrote the last and most important part in much haste, and I did not dwell enough on certain observations which seemed important to me. In particular, that the imagination is not an arbitrary invention; etymologically, it is cognate with *imago*, "representation, imitation," and with *imitor*, "to imitate, to reproduce." The imagination *imitates* exemplary models—"images"—reactualizes them, repeats them over and over. In those years, the interpretation of images and the imagination helped me to understand folkloric creations better, and sometimes even my own literary works.

On November 17 I received a postcard from Corina. She had written to inform me that on October 30, after three months of suffering, our father had died, and a week before that, Uncle Mitache, following a cardiac attack. For days afterward I lived in another world, a world long forgotten, consoled only by sorrow. I sensed that I had lost an-

6. "Notes sur le symbolisme aquatique" (from *Zalmoxis*, II, 1939) and "Le 'dieu lieur' et le symbolisme des noeuds" (*Revue de l'histoire des religions*, 1947–48).

other part—the largest part—of my past. Alone, I walked the streets around Sacré-Coeur, remembering scenes from childhood, adolescence, and early youth. In recent years I had succeeded in controlling my longing for the homeland; it came upon me only in sleep, in certain dreams. Now it overwhelmed me again. If I had been free to do so, I would have begun to write my memories from childhood.

With a great effort, I succeeded in resuming my work. Christinel had typed almost all the new chapters of *Images et symboles*. She was waiting now for the last pages of the Introduction. These I wrote wherever it was convenient, wherever I could find a quiet spot: in Sibylle's old ceramics studio or in the office I shared with Jacqueline on rue Duhesme.

On December 17 I bundled up the whole manuscript and took it to Brice Parain. And a few days later we left Paris, to be gone for three months. It was necessary for me, at all costs, to regain the world in which I had been born and had lived until the spring of 1940. Very soon that world would disappear, condemned by history. I knew that I numbered among the few survivors, and I wanted to do my duty as a witness. But I knew also that back of the catastrophes and sufferings of all sorts lay other meanings, perfectly camouflaged. And I thought that I was beginning to understand them.

22. *The Forbidden Forest*

So THAT I would be able to work in peace, we took lodgings at Monte Carlo. A friend of ours had found us a convenient room at Hôtel Excelsior and, because we were renting for at least two months, it was unusually cheap. When we got off the train we were struck again by the fragrance of the mimosa trees in bloom. The discovery I made the very next morning, however, depressed me. The walls of the room were even thinner than those at Hôtel de Suède. The manager allowed me to work in the lobby area, in a room adjacent to his office. But there the noise was unbearable: telephone conversations, shouting from the kitchen, voices and laughter in the lobby. The manager proposed then a little room, perfectly isolated, but with no windows, illuminated only by a bare bulb hanging from the ceiling. I noted morosely in my *Journal:* "To come to the Côte d'Azur in order to write by the light of a dusty bulb in semi-darkness, as if I were in the tower of a medieval prison. . . ." Ten days after our arrival I found, and rented, a cheap little room without neighbors; there I worked until we returned to Paris.

I was unable to give my full attention to the novel until I had written a short preface for a posthumous book of Paul Vulliard which I had promised Payot, and the article "Examen leprosorum," for *Preuves.* To conserve time, I left the room only at mealtimes and, occasionally, at night, when Christinel and I strolled on the boulevards. We visited briefly and in passing Nice and Menton. My correspondence I reduced drastically (but later I was obliged to write ten or twelve letters per day). I read very little and only at night, in order to escape from the world and atmosphere of the novel. Nevertheless, the correcting and extensive modification of the episodes in the new chapters of Part I took me several weeks. In the meantime, Alice Godel had come to see us and had brought the manuscript of the book *L'expérience libératrice*. Gallimard had consented to publish it, but I had to write a preface—and as soon as possible.

I began the first chapter of Part II with considerable confidence; I had learned how to avoid the temptation of facile solutions and picturesque dialogue. Probably I would have succeeded in finishing the book if a new attack of vagotonia had not struck me following a case of food poisoning. We returned to rue Duhesme earlier than planned. It was necessary, in any event, that I prepare the lectures I had agreed to give at the University of Lund. Fortunately, the rector asked me to postpone them until the end of April. But I couldn't seem to get well. Dr. Hunwald was afraid of a gastric ulcer and he prescribed a strict diet. Nevertheless, when I took the plane for Malmö I was very pale and I felt weaker than ever. To my amazement, the vagotonia and gastritis vanished as if by magic after the first meals taken in the student canteen at Lund: fried fish (judging from the grease, it was certainly sturgeon), fried potatoes, and milk.

I changed planes at Copenhagen and after a few minutes' flight in an aircraft with only six seats, I arrived in Malmö. This was my first visit to Sweden, and I was not disappointed either by the people or by the picturesque university town—although I was housed in a modest hotel located between two funeral parlors.

The professor of history of religions, Ehnmark, had invited me to give two lectures on shamanism. In addition, I conducted three seminars for Alf Lombard's course in Romanian. Among the scholars I met, I was impressed most by M. P. Nilsson, the learned and prolific historian of Greek religion. He was past eighty then, but he seemed indefatigable; he had not given up one of the academic responsibilities and honors accumulated in his long life. He still defended vigorously—sometimes aggressively—the methodological concepts he had adopted in youth. But, unfortunately, Stig Wikander had been hospitalized a short time before; therefore, although we saw each other daily, we couldn't have the long conversations we had promised each other. However, I met his wife and three daughters, whom I would see several times again over the next twenty years.

       /   /   /

I returned more rested than when I left. The week spent among Orientalists and historians of religions had stimulated me. I wrote wih mounting interest, almost with enthusiasm, the lecture Tucci was expecting of me, "Langages secrets et techniques mystiques." I promised myself to return later (after the novel was finished!) to a certain type of mystical experience: I saw already the chapter it would constitute in the volume *La nostalgie du Paradis*. At the beginning of May I was again in Rome, with Christinel. I read the lecture in the largest hall of the Oriental Institute and three days later, in the same place, an ardent discussion of methodology in the history of religions occurred. Thus I met again R. Pettazzoni, E. de Martino, and other, younger colleagues. But most of all, on that unexpected vacation, we enjoyed the Roman springtime that greeted us every morning.

With a friend, Horia Roman, former editor of *Cuvântul liber*, we drove around the outskirts of the city, all the way to Viterbo, and I was thrilled when we arrived at the Etruscan tombs. I wanted at all costs to visit Papini again, not having seen him since 1927. So I wrote to him in Florence, and he replied instantly, with enthusiasm. In my *Journal*, and in the lengthy interview which I published subsequently in *Les nouvelles littéraires* (6 March 1953), I have related in some detail this reunion with one of the idols of my adolescence. I had found out some time before that he was nearly blind—and indeed, writing dedications on several recent books, he took off his glasses and put his face down close to the page, almost touching it with his forehead. I was much impressed by his youthful attitude, his passion to keep abreast of literary and philosophical developments in many countries, and his courage in continuing to work. I had no way of knowing, that afternoon in May, that a year later Papini would lose the use of his hands and legs, and that in 1954 he would no longer be able to speak.

       /   /   /

When we entered the room Olga Froebe had reserved for us at Casa Gabriella, we could scarcely believe that we would be living there for the whole month of June. It was a spacious room, on the second floor, with a terrace as large as the room itself, just a few meters from Lake Maggiore. It would be impossible to imagine a place more suitable for rest and meditation—and, above all, for writing. There was no sound to be heard, save the occasional auto horn from Italian cars on the highway back of the garden. From the terrace one could distinguish the backs of the fish which swim near the Villa Gabriella in anticipation of the crumbs and crusts of bread which the cook, Maria, would toss from the kitchen window from time to time. At night the lights glimmered on the opposite shore of the lake. Now and then we could hear the sound of motorboats late at night— fishermen hurrying to put down their nets as far away as possible, right on the Italian border.

Listening to Olga reminiscing about the first guests to have slept in our room and the rooms on either side of us, I let myself be caught up in the charm and mysteries of Casa Gabriella. In this way also we learned the story, evening by evening, of her friendships (sometimes rather complex) with Rudolf Otto, the Sinologist Richard Wilhelm, and many other lesser-known savants—but above all, Carl Jung. Unfortunately, I was unable to set down in the *Journal* everything about the meetings and surprising discoveries that preceded the founding and first phase of the Eranos circle.

In those incomparable weeks of vacation, in which I rediscovered the delight of swimming and the joy of hiking in the mountains, I worked with considerable success. We were happy when Olga invited us to spend at least one month each summer from then on at Casa Gabriella. I had the impression that, without our being aware of it, a new, more fortunate phase of our life was beginning.

En route home, we stopped at Bâle to meet Karl Meuli; I was interested in his highly original observations concerning *Le mythe de l'éternel retour*. Upon arriving at rue Duhesme, I realized that I had left my reading glasses on the train. For several days I was obliged to read like Papini, with my face close to the page. Still, I was glad there was a space of two or three centimeters. . . . Toward the middle of the summer G. Racoveanu arrived in Paris. I hadn't seen him since the spring of 1940, at Nae Ionescu's funeral, but we had been in correspondence for the past five or six years. He was living in a little town outside Munich, painting icons and managing somehow to sell them. He had finished a monograph on the monk Paisie, and in conjunction with Monsignor Octavian Bârlea he was publishing in an ecumenical spirit the review *Indreptar,* to which the majority of Romanian writers and scholars in exile had contributed. He wrote as brilliantly, and with as

much effort, as ever.[1] We were both glad that we would be seeing each
other soon again in Germany.

*   *   *

At the end of August I returned alone to Ascona to present the lecture "Puissance et sacralité dans l'histoire des religions." This time I
was bold enough to ask Jung for an interview for *Combat*. His book
Antwort auf Job had recently appeared, provoking endless debates and
controversies. The theme which (after a long hesitation) he had decided to treat, troubled, baffled, and angered both psychologists and
theologians. Professor Scholem, somewhat in jest, said that Jung had
tried to psychoanalyze Yahweh!

After reading *Le chamanisme*, Jung had written me several weighty
and enthusiastic pages. In the oneiric and psychopathological experience of shamanic initiation rites, Jung had found confirmation for
some of his hypotheses. We talked for two hours, and I immediately
recorded a great many invaluable details. In that interview Jung related—probably for the first time—the crisis which had brought an
end to his collaboration with Freud, as well as the highly dramatic vi-
sions which had forced him to postulate the collective unconscious.
Not until several years later, in his *Memoirs*, destined to be published
posthumously, did he return (in greater detail) to these decisive experiences and events.

Not being a psychologist, and knowing only from books the theory
and practice of depth psychology, I could not be a "Jungian," but I
was interested in his hypothesis of the collective unconscious and archetypes. As I admitted to Jung, and as I wrote in the preface to the
English translation of *Le mythe de l'éternel retour*, the subtitle of that
book, "Archétypes et répétition," could give rise to confusions. I was
using the term "archetype" in its original, Neoplatonic sense of "para-
digm, exemplary model." But for Jung, archetypes were "structures
of the collective unconscious." I made a mistake in using—albeit in a
very different sense—a term which had become familiar and even
popular, owing to Jung, in the sense *he* had given it. I should have
used the expression "exemplary model" as I have, in fact, since then.

1. He had announced a volume of memoirs about Nae Ionescu and a novel (concerning which he had spoken to Mihail Sebastian and me as early as 1933), but I don't
know whether or not they were found among his papers. On the other hand, in *Indreptar* and *Cuvântul in exil*, which he founded and directed until the eve of his death in
1967, he was able to publish a series of excellent articles on Eastern theology.

Christinel came at the end of the conference and we left together for Alpbach where the seminars organized by the Europäische College were being held. En route, we stopped for a day and a night at Innsbruck; I hadn't seen it for a quarter of a century and the old city and the River Inn charmed me again. We ascended then to Alpbach, at an altitude of 1,000 meters. Although it rained nearly the whole time we were there, I was happy to rediscover a landscape and mountain air like that of the Bucegis of my youth. Karl Kerényi and I conducted a seminar on the history of religions, he speaking in German (the language of most of the group), I in English or French. Methodologically we found ourselves in different positions, and often our discussions threatened to turn into polemics. But since I admired his work, I didn't lose my temper.[2]

After a week, we went down to Kupfstein, on the German frontier, where G. Racoveanu and Father Popan were waiting for us. Passing by auto through Munich, I no longer recognized the city. The central part had been destroyed, and the buildings which had been erected on the site made it resemble any other "modern" city. After we had visited Garmisch and Oberammergau, we spent the night at Rudesheim, and the following day Father Popan let us out of the car in front of the house of Günther Spaltmann, at Bonn. Spaltmann had translated several of my books, and he was following with great interest my "work in progress," as he liked to call *Noaptea de Sânziene*. In the two days we spent together, we talked much of the time. He had reread recently the first part of the novel and he liked it, but he urged me insistently to finish the book as soon as possible. Among other arguments, he invoked this one: according to indications he had deciphered in the lines of my palm, my literary creativity would dry up soon, or else it would be transformed so radically that my future works would seem written by another author. Therefore, I must hurry!

/ / /

Without sharing the certainties of a chiromantic order, I was in accord with Spaltmann: I must indeed hurry. I had published a good

2. After I met him in 1950, Kerényi asked me to speak to Gustave Payot about publishing the French translation of his latest book—the one he believed his best: *Griechische Mythologie*. I convinced Payot, and the book appeared. But for the past two years Olga had not invited him to lecture at Eranos, and Kerényi suspected that I had influenced her.

share of my works in the history of religions and the philosophy of culture developed in the past ten years, and in November *Images et symboles* would appear. I could allow myself a rest of four or five months, the time needed, I calculated, for writing Part II. But as usual, I was solicited by unforeseen and urgent obligations. It was necessary for me to devote a large part of that fall to the preparation of new, corrected, and augmented editions of *Le mythe de l'éternel retour* and *Traité d'histoire des religions* for German, English, and Spanish translations.

Fortunately, at the end of November René and Délia Laforgue again placed their apartment at our disposal, until April. In order to recover the world of literary imagination, I wrote, in a few days' time, the sketch, "12,000 capete de vită" (Twelve thousand head of cattle). Then I reread and corrected once again (how many times did that make?) Part I, and as Christmas approached, I found myself completely involved in the story of all those characters struggling to survive "the events of History." Shut away in Dr. Laforgue's office, I wrote in a state of exaltation, almost with fury, though sometimes sadness overwhelmed me: one by one, the majority of the leading characters of my novel were preparing to meet their destiny, approaching death. Never have I sensed more precisely than in that winter of 1953 the analogy between initiatory (i.e., symbolic-ritual) death and the sufferings or the unexpected and enigmatic events which, in the universe of literary imagination, lead to the death of an important character.

Seldom did I allow myself an interruption from work for even a few hours or, exceptionally, for a few days, as I did at the end of January 1953, when Alice and Roger Godel came to Paris. That winter Allain Guillermou began the translation of the first part and Christinel was typing the manuscript as fast as I corrected it. Sometimes we both felt the need to escape the world of *Noptea de Sânziene*. For example, there was that unforgettable evening spent in the new apartment of Monica Lovinescu and Virgil Ierunca, on rue Cassini, listening to the first records from a collection which, in years to follow, would become gigantic.

After three months of intense labor, in the middle of March, I interrupted work on the novel in order to classify materials collected in the last several years and to begin the preparation of a new edition— corrected and considerably enlarged—of my thesis on Yoga. But once

I began to write, I realized it would be a matter of a total transformation of the text of 1936. I returned to this new book whenever I had a few days absolutely free, that is, when I could devote to it ten or twelve hours without interruption.

, , ,

I took up the novel again toward the end of April 1953, at Meilen, near Zurich. I had agreed to deliver five lectures of two hours each, in the course of a month, at the Jung-Institut, Zurich. Housing was provided for me in the villa of Dr. Riklin, a recently constructed building situated on a hill at the edge of a forest. The first three weeks I was alone: Christinel had gone to Rome at the invitation of Nina Batalli. Apart from the days of lecturing at the Institute and a few meetings with Jung and other psychologists, I was free to work, undisturbed by anyone, from early morning till late at night. In a few weeks I had written two more chapters of the novel. And since, after the month at Meilen, I had another five or six weeks' vacation at Casa Gabriella, I told myself that I could finish *Noptea de Sânziene* in the course of the year. But, as usual, unforeseen events kept intruding. *La nouvelle NFR* had reappeared, and Jean Paulhan had asked me for a contribution. I had promised him an article on "Le mythe du monde moderne," and since he hadn't yet received it, he reminded me of it in two letters. In addition, a "Romanian Week" was to be held in Madrid and I had to write an inaugural lecture for that. Finally, I had been invited—and had agreed—to lecture in September at the "Recontres Internationales de Genève," along with François Mauriac, Robert Schumann, and Paul Ricoeur. In that era of savage Stalinism, Romanian culture was completely absent in the West, since men of culture were either in prison or, at best, condemned to silence. I could not refuse an opportunity to speak on behalf of Romanian culture just because I hoped to finish my novel.

I noted in the *Journal* the luncheon I had with C. G. Jung and Mme Jung at their famous residence at Küsnacht, and a few of his recollections about S. N. Dasgupta and R. Eisler. Also, I recorded meetings and discussions with Dr. Schoppe and Dr. Boss (cf. *Fragments*, I, pp. 207ff.), but I regret that I didn't record in more detail what Dr. Boss told me about his trip to Italy in company with Martin Heidegger.

From May 20 to June 29 we lived at Casa Gabriella. Despite all the temptations—especially the books that Olga placed on my work table every morning: volumes about alchemy and mysticism, publications of Heinrich Zimmer, plus novels of the occult, detective, and spy type—despite all these temptations, I was able to write rather well. I interrupted work on the novel only to prepare a lecture for the Psychology Club of Zurich and to compose the article promised Jean Paulhan.

On July 1 we returned to the apartment on rue de la Tour. The day before, a storm had knocked down the wall of the Passy Cemetery, "our venerable neighbor," as N. I. Herescu called it. It became so cold that for a few days I had to wear a thick wool sweater underneath my jacket. I worked in Dr. Laforgue's office, now crammed with books and files transported from rue Duhesme; I needed as many sources as possible for writing my Eranos lecture on "La Terre-Mère et les hiérogamies cosmiques." The text which I was to read at Rencontres Internationales de Genève, of course, required less work.

On August 17 I returned to Ascona, this time without Christinel. Among the new lecturers that year were Dr. D. T. Suzuki, R. P. Jean Daniélou, Giuseppe Tucci, and Ernst Benz. On the morning of the opening session of Eranos I learned from Tucci the news of the death of Surendanath Dasgupta. He had died unexpectedly at Allahabad. I remembered all that Jung had told me about the visit (of a week!) my former master had made to Küsnacht in 1939. In that same year I received at Bucharest a telegram from Dasgupta proposing I come to Rome where he was staying as a guest of Tucci—"so we can meet again." I remembered also all I had learned from Louis Renou in the autumn of 1945 (see *Fragments*, I, p. 16).

Inasmuch as the central theme of the Eranos conference that year was the symbolism and religious meanings of the Earth in various cultures—from Tibet (Tucci) to Christian theologies and customs (Daniélou, Benz), I had decided to analyze a series of examples from archaic and Oriental civilizations, integrating them into the general perspective of the history of religions. As in preceding lectures, I tried to show the necessity, or rather the *obligation*, to study and understand the spiritual creations of "primitives" with the same zeal and hermeneutical rigor used by Western elites with respect to their own cultural traditions. I was convinced that the documents and method of the history of religions lead, more surely than any other historical discipline, to the deprovincialization of Western cultures. On the other hand, I was well aware of the privileges afforded by Eranos. The colleagues assembled at Ascona, the audience which hears the lectures, and especially the readers of the volumes of the *Eranos-Jahrbücher* constitute an exceptional instrument for the diffusion of any new hermeneutical advance.

The same conviction inspired the text prepared for the Rencontres Internationales de Genève. The central theme was "The Anxiety of the Present Time and the Duties of the Spirit." I considered that I could contribute to the understanding of the anxiety of contemporary man by analyzing it from the perspective of the history of religions. The title of my lecture, "Symbolisme religieux et valorisation de l'angoisse," indicated precisely the advantages of this course. The anxiety provoked by the precarious nature of the human condition and by the terror of an imminent catastrophe illustrates in an exemplary way the desacralization of death, so characteristic of contemporary civilization. In all traditional societies death was not considered the absolute end of human existence, but only a rite of passage to a new mode of being; one could say that death constitutes the last initiatory ordeal, thanks to which man obtains a new, purely spiritual existence.

At Geneva, the "international encounters" were presented in a more complex scenario than the Eranos colloquiums. The large number of foreign journalists, the Swiss and French radio broadcasting systems, the members of the diplomatic corps, the personalities invited to discuss the five or six lectures, the famous guests (among others, the former queen of Italy) combined to create a festive yet academically elevated atmosphere. I met again many members of the Société Européenne de Culture and I met for the first time several authors in whom I had long been interested. The discussion of my lecture took place in the library of the villa at Coppet, which we reached by means of a little boat. There, in that famous library, and elsewhere as well, I was obliged to respond to many questions. Fortunately, Christinel and I found time for a stroll around the lake by ourselves, once, late at night.

/   /   /

After our return to Paris toward the middle of September, an unsettled period ensued, which lasted until spring. We were obliged to live first at the apartment on rue de la Tour, then with friends on rue de Boulainvillers, then on rue Duhesme. I worked with much difficulty when and where I could. (That autumn I tried, for the first time in Paris, to write in a neighborhood café.) I remembered ruefully what Georges Dumézil had said to me regarding the last chapters of

Traité—that he admired my ability to write them in a hotel room. I thought, if only I had that room in Hôtel de Suède now! I had all my books, files, and manuscripts there; I knew where to find the quotation or bibliographic reference I needed. Now, every article or book review I had to write constituted a problem; first I had to discover where, in which apartment, the notes and necessary bibliography were located. Fortunately, I had collected all the manuscripts and documentation concerning Yoga in three cardboard boxes which I always moved with me from one residence to another. The book on Yoga, moreover, was the only one on which I could make any headway during this time.

I defended myself from fatigue and discouragement by repeating over and over that this unexpected agitation and wandering could constitute a new series of initiatory ordeals. I was "wandering in a labyrinth" in a period which I contemplated more serenely, however, than many others in the past. No longer did I live under the terror of poverty and insecurity, as in 1946–49. And yet, obstacles and annoyances kept arising on my path. One might have said that all the crises and difficulties had the same purpose: to delay the concluding of the novel. According to my calculations, I had about sixty pages yet to write, but I found it impossible to start work on them. I was obliged to understand that this repeated and prolonged postponement had a *meaning. Noaptea de Sânziene* meant for me more than just another book, a new title to add to my literary bibliography; I considered it the boundary stone between past and future. On no other novel had I worked with more persistence and attention. I was waiting for its conclusion in order to be able to judge, or to realize, whether or not I had *succeeded.* On the other hand, through the translation being made by Alain Guillermou, I should be able to confirm the extent of interest in my writing on the part of the French and foreign public. Of course, the failure of *Noaptea de Sânziene* would not have meant the end of my literary efforts, but I would have given up the idea of translating them.

For the time being, it was impossible for me to return to the novel. Now, I was very much excited over the new version of the monograph on Yoga. From November until April, when I finished it, I was caught up in this book; that is, I lived exclusively in the world of Indian spirituality. The letter that a Romanian naval captain brought me that fall seemed, therefore, all the more significant. I wrote in the *Journal:* "In a certain hotel here in Paris there is an Indian couple, who, not understanding French, asked him [the captain] to help them in their predicament. On learning that he was a Romanian, the woman became excited and asked him if he knew anything about me. She told him that I had lived at her house in Calcutta many years ago. Then she asked him to give me a letter. It was signed: 'Maitreyi Devi, daughter of S. N. Dasgupta.' Among other things, she wrote: 'I do not know whether you want to meet us or will consider it a waste of time—and I am also afraid whether you are the same Eliade who was with us in Calcutta or not [. . .]. I really want to see you very much.— 23 years have passed. I have two children, my husband is a Doctor in Chemistry [. . .].'"

I noted in my journal the coincidence: I had received this sign of life after twenty-three years, exactly half my age at that time. For many years I had believed Maitreyi was no longer living. How fortunate, I said to myself, that *La nuit bengali* was not a success. If it had been, I'd have risked having it translated into English. . . .

At the end of spring, 1954, a little while after I had handed over to Payot the typed text of *Le Yoga: Immortalité et liberté*, we left for two months at Ascona. With joy we rediscovered the garden of Casa Gabriella and our room with the terrace overlooking the lake. The very next day I returned to the manuscript of *Noaptea de Sânziene*. The last chapter I had begun long ago, but I progressed with it slowly, hesitantly. As I recalled in the *Journal*, I had imagined that Ştefan and Ileana would meet again at Royaumont, twelve years after their first meeting in the forest on the outskirts of Bucharest. I had believed, further, that for each of them the reunion would mean the beginning of a *vita nova*. Ştefan's "search" I had homologized to an initiatory "quest." The finding of Ileana was equivalent to the end of an initiation. "Now, today," I noted on June 26, "I have understood that it is a matter of something else." Ştefan's search was, in fact, the search for Death. I realized with despair that "the symbolism of death *is imposing itself upon me as I write the last chapter.*" But I did not doubt that "the symbolism of death allows *anything:* an extinction [i.e., in the perspective of modern societies, of course], or a regeneration, a true *incipit vita nova.*"

Then, a few days later, I added: "Today, 7 July, at 11:35 A.M., I finished writing and transcribing the last page. The novel is finished! I wrote in the last few days struggling not only with sadness but also with an almost physical oppression. It was impossible for me to understand the implacable destiny which had been decided long ago, and without my knowledge, that Ştefan and Ileana would perish on that Night of St. John, 1948, somewhere on a road to Lausanne. I wrote in a constant tension—and seemingly the weather reflected my inner tempest, because all the time there were storms on the lake, and lightning falling a few meters away, followed by a cold, autumn-like rain. [. . .] I can't seem to enjoy the fact that I've finished the book."

The curious state of sadness, fatigue, and despair persisted for several days. Going to Locarno to cash my Bollingen check, I forgot my passport (or rather my *titre de voyage*) at the bank. It was the first time such an accident had happened—an action which, for a stateless man like myself could have had serious consequences.[3] I wondered how a psychologist would interpret this forgetting (=*loss*) of my "identity." Could it be the presentiment that I had left behind an "identity," that I wanted to escape from a past in which I no longer recognized myself?

That fall we installed ourselves at Val d'Or in the apartment that Alice and Roger Godel had put at our disposal. It was located on the eleventh floor of a splendid and recently constructed building. The owners had just had time to furnish the apartment before returning to Ismailia. Since they spent only a part of the summer in Europe, we could live here from October till June, when Olga was expecting us at Ascona. I kept repeating to myself that we didn't deserve such a place: we had a huge living-dining room and a study, which was easily converted into a sleeping room for guests. From the windows we could see the Seine and the Bois de Boulogne, and in the distance the roofs and towers of Paris. I brought a part of my library stored at rue Duhesme, and prepared to work.

After I had reread the novel once again—sometimes excited, sometimes melancholic, struggling with sadness—I awoke to find myself another man. For the first time in five years I felt "free." I could travel without hurrying, and in any country in Western Europe. I could write anything my heart might desire. Still, I was concerned to know how *Fôret interdite* (the French title of *Noaptea de Sânziene*) would be

3. In the summer of 1970 I was to forget my United States passport at the Stockholm airport. I had become an American citizen only a few months before and was traveling for the first time with an American passport instead of the famous *titre de voyage* of stateless persons.

received. I knew there was nothing I could do to promote its success with critics or the public. I knew also that the book could not appear before a year or two. Brice Parain had read Part I with interest, but Alain Guillermou had not yet finished translating Part II.

Although we were only fifteen or twenty minutes by train from the Saint-Lazare station, I seldom went into Paris. I enjoyed working in front of the window that faced Bois de Boulogne, occupying almost the whole outside wall of the study. At night, I would sit for a long while in the dark, fascinated by the lights sparkling far away in the city, following the trains gliding like tiny reptiles of diamond along the Seine. For the first time since the winter of 1945, which was spent at Cascaes (excepting, of course, vacation times at Casa Gabriella), I had a view from my window of something other than streets, walls, and trees.

Soon I began writing the volume *Forgerons et alchimistes* (*The Forge and the Crucible*); I had promised it to Flammarion for the series Homo Sapiens which Marie-Madeleine David directed. I utilized much material from *Alchimia asiatică* I and II (1935–37) and "Metallurgy, Magic and Alchemy" (*Zalmoxis*, I, 1938), considerably augmented from my readings of the past fifteen years. With great interest and energy I wrote the several new chapters on the magico-religious origins of Oriental metallurgy and alchemy. I believe I succeeded in introducing a new perspective, broader and more adequate, into the interpretation of the magico-religious values of metallurgy: minerals, considered as the "embryos" of metals, have their "growth" accelerated and therefore reach their "maturity" due to the metallurgical operations. Further, I insisted upon the initiatory valences of alchemy. I finished the manuscript in December and the book appeared a few months later.[4]

In a sense, *Forgerons et alchimistes*, like *Yoga*, constituted a "liquidation of the past." My first articles on Alexandrian alchemy were published while I was still in lycée; and my first researches into Indian and Chinese alchemy I began at Calcutta and continued at the Stadt-Bibliothek at Berlin (where, in 1934–36, I discovered the mythology and magic of metallurgy), then in 1940 at the British Museum, and beginning in 1946 at the Musée de l'Homme. I did not believe, after finishing *Forgerons et alchimistes*, that I would ever return to these

4. A few years later I had the satisfaction of reading or hearing the favorable opinions of many historians of science, such as Joseph Needham, R. Multhauf, A. G. Debus, N. Siven, and others.

problems which I had discovered in adolescence. And yet I continued to collect new materials and to follow with considerable attention the immense critical and external bibliography.[5]

/   /   /

With the exception of lectures and seminars organized by the Centre Roumain de Recherches, I refused invitations to lecture or participate in colloquiums. Nevertheless, I agreed to speak at Strasbourg. I was surprised by the large crowd and embarrassed by the microphone in front of which I had to read my text. But the next day Professor George Gusdorf, who had invited me, organized a seminar on a smaller scale, which was the occasion for some lively discussions.

I had told myself repeatedly that once I had finished *Forgerons et alchimistes* I would be able to concentrate on the book *Mort et initiation*. I had been interested in the subject for a long time, and already in Portugal I had begun collecting materials of all sorts for it. The past summer at Eranos I had presented a long analysis of several types of initiation ("Mystères et régénération spirituelle"). In fact, *Mort et initiation* was to have constituted only a section of a larger monograph, in two volumes: *Mythologies de la mort*. But in rereading and classifying the documentation, I realized that such a work would require at least three or four years. That was when I decided to limit myself for the time being to a book of more modest proportions and of a more general interest: *Mort et initiation*.

Linked to that winter of 1955 in my memory is a significant incident. One night, toward the end of February, I was awakened from sleep by a sinister corpse-like odor; the mole, the size of an almond, which I had had for many years on my right armpit, had become infected and was oozing blood mixed with pus. It should have been removed surgically long before, but I had put off having it done. That night I was unable to go back to sleep until almost morning, and then only after I felt I had understood the "spiritual meaning of the corpse." I noted in my journal: "I imagined my right arm amputated, I saw myself writing with my left hand, greeting people with my left hand raised. It was no use. The image of the 'shedding' of that part of my

---

5. I was greatly surprised when preparing a new edition in 1977 to realize that I had filled a whole shelf with recent monographs and articles, to which were added several files of notes and extracts. (I haven't yet dared to burn them, as I did with the files and notes of many works, from the second edition of *Shamanism* to the third volume of *Histoire des croyances et des idées religieux*.)

body which had begun to decay did not calm me. All at once I thought about *Mort et intitiation*. I had seen it up till now 'from the outside,' as a work of scholarship and philosophy. I was mistaken; I had not understood the essential thing. Initiation is a death, and any death, intelligently assumed, can equal an initiation. But 'symbolic (ritual, initiatory) death' is not only suffering, torture, illness, etc.; it is also the experience of your own corpse, the reconciliation with this simple fact, which we all forget, that we are not only *transients*, but we are also in a state of decomposition, and that we must *accept* this corpse which is our flesh, that we must reconcile ourselves with the idea that *we are this also*. We must not think *only of the soul*. That would be too simple[. . .] . I became reconciled only by accepting myself as such, assuming my own corpse-like odor, saying that *this too* belongs to me" (*Fragments*, I, pp. 224ff.).

The next morning, accompanied by Dr. Henri Hunwald, I went to the Curie Hospital. The surgeon, a colleague and friend of Dr. Hunwald, operated on me the next day. But I didn't learn the results of the biopsy until a week later. Although the surgeon assured me that he was "ninety percent certain it was a benign tumor," I calmed myself only by repeating that the regeneration which I was anticipating— and which, moreover, I had known several times in my life—would begin from *this point*, from the experience of death.[6]

In April 1955, at Rome, the Seventh International Congress on the History of Religions was held, with Raffaele Pettazzoni presiding (Van der Leeuw had died soon after the congress at Amsterdam). I presented a short communication—"Le vol magic"—which very much interested Joachim Wach and several other philosophers but annoyed certain "historicists."[7] Wach spoke to me about the Haskell Lectures

6. After learning the results of the biopsy, I had a long and curious "waking dream" which I related later: see *Fragments*, I, pp. 234–36 (*No Souvenirs*, pp. 4–6).

7. Wach asked to see the last two or three pages of the conclusions and, reading them over, declared that I had succeeded in demonstrating in a concrete way, with documents, that freedom and transcendence are constitutive dimensions of human existence. He underscored several sentences: "If we consider in their totality 'flight' and all the parallel symbolisms, their meaning is revealed immediately: all betray a rupture effected in the Universe of everyday experience. The double intentionality of that rupture is evident: it is at the same time *transcendence* and *freedom* which are obtained by 'flight.'" (Cf. "Symbolisms of Ascension," in *Myths, Dreams, and Mysteries*, especially pp. 106–10. Unfortunately, Joachim Wach died at Locarno a few months later, in the summer of 1955.)

at the University of Chicago (made famous by Rudolf Otto's "West-Östkiche Mystik"); for 1956–57 he had proposed my name. In addition to giving the six Haskell Lectures, I would function as visiting professor from October until June. Naturally, I was flattered by this honor, but, as I confessed to Wach, I wasn't sure I'd be able to obtain an American visa. The quota for immigrants of Romanian origin was filled until 1990.

Among the scholars and philosophers I met at Rome was E. Grassi, professor of philosophy at Munich. He spoke to me about the series *Rowohlt Deutsche Encyklopadie* which he directed; its first little volumes were scheduled for fall, and he wanted me, by all means, to give him a work of synthesis: *Das Heilige und das Profane,* an introduction to the history and phenomenology of religions. In it I could use the documentation of *Traité,* but I would concentrate on a few essential problems: sacred space and time, the structure and function of myth, and the morphology of divine figures. All this in 160 typed pages, and no later that the spring of 1956. . . . I agreed.

As honorarium for the lecture given at ISMEO, "Centre du monde, temple, maison," Tucci assured us of two weeks at a hotel. Thus I had the leisure to visit again, unhurriedly, the city of Rome and several of the towns of Latium. Having been invited by Professor Carlo Diano, we went then to Padua, where I repeated the lecture on "The Center of the World."

For the first time since 1950, I was not on the program of Eranos. Therefore, I had the whole summer free: I could write anything I liked. In June, at Paris, I found A. Guillermou proofreading *Forêt interdite;* the novel was scheduled to appear at the beginning of autumn. The month of July we spent at Casa Gabriella. I felt as though I were really on vacation. I wondered what kind of literature I should find to write if *Forêt interdite* were not a success. One morning I was tempted by a novella: "Fata Căpitanului" (The Captain's Daughter). It was very short, and I finished it that same day, in the evening. The principal characters were two adolescents, a girl and a boy, both exceptionally enigmatic.

Almost the whole month of August we spent at Täsch, a little village near Zermatt, where Alice and Roger Godel were staying. We took a room in a modest inn, almost without neighbors. Then, suddenly, I "saw" the beginning of a novella and started to write. I wrote with such impetus and ardor that I filled twelve to fifteen pages per day—many of them almost illegible, so that I had to decipher and transcribe them the same night. When, at the end of the month, we returned to Ascona to attend the Eranos lectures, the manuscript exceeded one hundred pages. I had begun *Pe strada Mântuleasa* (*The Old Man and the Bureaucrats*) as a long novella, but as I wrote I discovered new episodes and unsuspected implications. Christinel read the manuscript with interest, but also with impatience; I promised her I'd finish it as soon as we returned to Val d'Or. I tried to do it—several times, in fact—but it "wouldn't go." I took it up again the following summer, without success. For twelve years I carried the unfinished manuscript around with me. During that time I wrote other prose works but I couldn't finish *Pe strada Mântuleasa* . . . until one especially busy week (courses, visits, lectures) in November 1967.[8]

Forêt interdite was released at the beginning of the autumn, but aside for a column by R. Lalou in *Les nouvelles littéraires* and a few other brief reviews, the novel passed unnoticed. It soon disappeared from the bookstores and was not reprinted until fifteen years later. Friends and some of the readers tried to explain the failure: too many pages (640) and too small type ("Why didn't you publish it in two volumes" an "admirer" wrote to me sadly, almost indignantly); too many characters with hard-to-remember names; the beginning, especially, too difficult to follow. On the other hand, several literary critics told me in conversation, with disappointment: "It's a *roman-roman* [traditional novel], and today, you see. . . ."[9]

As I have stated several times, this failure did not depress me. I had enjoyed success and popularity in youth with my first novels, and in a sense that was enough for me. But this second "verification" reconciled me to the decision I had made: from here on I would write for Christinel and myself and for a few Romanian friends.

On the other hand, 1956 promised to be more fruitful and rich in

8. Published in 1968, it was translated into German by Edith Silbermann and published by Suhrkamp Verlag in 1972. *Auf der Mantuleasa Strasse* had considerable success, which led the editor, Siegfried Unseld, to decide to translate a large part of my literary writings. A significant detail: after Marcel Brion spoke highly of the French version, *La vieil homme et l'officier* (Gallimard, 1977), on television, the book sold out in a few days and was reprinted several times after that. It was, moreover, my first "literary success" in France—and, so far, my only one.

9. I noted extensively some of my observations made later concerning *Forêt interdite* (cf. *Fragments*, I, pp. 243ff. and 353; *No Souvenirs*, pp. 12–15, 119–20).

surprises than ever. In January I presented lectures at the University of Munich and at E. Grassi's Institute of Philology; at the University of Frankfort on the invitation of Adolf E. Jensen; and at the University of Marburg, invited by Ernst Benz. I met on these occasions many German writers and philosophers, including Adorno, who was intrigued by my interest in mythical thought.

Immediately after my return to Val d'Or, I began work on *Das Heilige und das Profane*. Following Grassi's suggestion, I utilized many examples from *Traité d'histoire des religions* and succeeded in finishing the manuscript by May. Never did I suspect that his little book, translated into twelve languages eventually, would become a "best-seller" in Europe, the United States, and Japan, much less that it would be used as a textbook in colleges, universities, and theological seminaries.

Meanwhile, the University of Chicago informed me that I would certainly obtain a visa inasmuch as I had been named visiting professor for the academic year 1956–57. After the death of Joachim Wach, the chair of History of Religions remained vacant. I was asked for the title of my Haskell Lectures and the subjects I would present in the winter and spring quarters of 1957. For the former I chose "Patterns of Initiation." As for the courses, I suggested "The Philosophy and Techniques of Yoga" and, for the last quarter, "Shamanism in Asia and America." The subjects were rather broad and complex, but I said to myself that I'd develop them according to the interests and preparation of the students.

Because Olga insisted that I participate in Eranos that summer, I chose a theme with which I was well acquainted: "La vertu créatrice du mythe." I knew that the preparation of the text would not require too much time. I had to concentrate all my energy on the drafting of those six lectures on initiation. I started to write them at the beginning of the summer; then we went to Ascona for a two-month's stay. Casa Gabriella was again a great help to me, as were also our friends, Christian and Marie Louise Dehollain. For several years they had spent their vacations in a neighboring villa. Toward evening we would go swimming together in the lake, then climb up to their terrace and talk.

After Christinel finished typing the first four lectures, I sent them to the excellent translator, Willard Trask, who had already translated *Le mythe de l'éternel retour* and *Le Yoga* into English, and who was to translate—up until his death in 1980—almost all my books in the history of religions. I was still working on the fifth lecture when we returned to Val d'Or. But I didn't succeed in finishing it before our departure.

,   ,   ,

Together with Mamy, Christinel and I embarked on September 17 1956, on the transatlantic liner *L'Ile de France*. After a week spent in New York in the apartment of Ionel and Lisette Perlea, we traveled by the then still famous Pullman sleeper to Chicago, arriving at the station on the morning of October 1.

We had enjoyed greatly our discovery of New York, but neither Christinel nor I dared admit our apprehension in Chicago as we looked around the platform in an almost deserted station. We could feel already that we were in a different kind of city. Without friends, without relatives, without acquaintances. . . . We were consoled by the thought that in seven or eight months at the most we would be back in Paris, with relatives and friends. We could not imagine that, after my being named titular professor and head of the Department of History of Religions at the University of Chicago, we would remain for twenty-seven years in this famous, enigmatic, and fascinating "Windy City."

23. I Begin to Discover America

CHICAGO, December 10, 1984. For a quarter of an hour I have been standing in front of the window, staring into space, not knowing why. I got up from my desk, thinking that it was beginning to snow. Then I couldn't tear myself away from the window, even though I hadn't seen a snowflake for a long time.

Last night at the Palmer House, in a large conference room converted into a banquet hall, full to capacity (over 800 persons, I was told), the American Academy of Religion celebrated its seventy-fifth anniversary. Speeches, reminiscences, applause. And at the end, the festivities in my honor: a short talk by Charles Long (Joe Kitagawa was supposed to have spoken but he is still ill); an excellent musical composition by Frank Burch Brown, "Ritual Compass": a quartet for piano, oboe, violin, and cello, performed by four young university faculty members; and the award of the academy, a sculpture, "Eliade," created and presented by Isamu Noguchi. It was the first time the AAR had ever given such an award: for the "most illustrious" (and probably the *oldest* I pointed out) specialist in religious studies.

A little while ago, gazing vacantly out the window, I was remembering a great many things—meetings, people, unrelated events. But every few minutes I returned to the same question: will I succeed in writing the *Autobiography* up to the point of last night's celebration? I broke off work on it last summer in Paris, at the point of our arrival in Chicago. Since then, I haven't had the time—or the inclination—to resume the task: fatigue, aggravated by the effects of the weekly injections of colloidal gold. I write with great difficulty because the joints of my right hand, inflamed again, scarcely permit me to hold the pen. Also, for several months I have been suffering from tendonitis in the right ankle, and when I walk, I lean on a cane. And I have so much to do! In the first place, the classification of the documentary materials (manuscripts, the *Journal*, books of notes, correspondence), selecting what I want to give to the Special Collections at the university library, deciding what I shall send to Paris. . . .

I think I'm beginning to understand why I was staring out the window just now with so much emotion. Directly in front of me, a few meters away, I can see the wooden stairs at the back of the house where we lived that first year, from October 1956 untill May 1957; and next door to it, my gaze stops on the back porch of our apartment, on the top floor (the third), which we have rented for the past twenty years or so. Yes, that's it—I realize now why I was so fascinated by those two old adjacent buildings, with their wooden stairs painted bright red, descending into a common yard which, until a few years ago, was almost completely shaded by the branches of old trees: in a sense, they represent the beginning and end of our residence in Chicago. Because, in five or six months, we shall leave the apartment at 5711 Woodlawn Avenue and move back (after twenty-seven years!) to Paris permanently.[1]

I heard a knock at the door. Ordinarily I answer only when I'm expecting someone, but today I hurried to open it. Because of the AAR Meeting (attended, this time, I was told, by some 7,000 members), many of my former students have returned to Chicago, the majority of them history of religions teachers in universities of the United States and Canada. About a dozen of them have come to the office to see me, in fact. As usual, before sitting down, they look around the room, moved, at the shelves of my library and the chairs, piled with file folders, journals, and books. They remember their youth, their afternoons of work some ten, fifteen, or twenty years

1. Translator's note: Eliade changed his mind about remaining in Paris after June of 1985, and he returned to the Woodlawn Avenue apartment as usual that fall. It was there he was stricken on April 14, 1986, and it is there that Mrs. Eliade continues to reside.

ago, when they came to consult me or to discuss problems related to the doctoral dissertations they were writing. I just found out from one of them that he has recently become a grandfather.

But this time I find in the hallway my neighbor and colleague. His office is right across the hall and, as usual, he has left his door open. He has come to congratulate me on my "great honor." Listening to him, I look out through the window that opens on 57th Street, and I catch myself smiling: on the other side of the street I can see the "Coach House," the small and picturesque building in which we lived in 1959–61. Suddenly I realize that in the past twenty-seven years we have spent a good part of our life in Chicago within a perimeter of no more than 100 square yards.

/ / /

On that morning of October 1, 1956, the taxi deposited us at the Quadrangle Club, the faculty club and guest house, where two large adjoining rooms had been reserved for us. After lunch, Joseph Kitagawa, whom we had met already at Ascona, and his wife, Evelyn, came to take us for an automobile ride downtown to visit "The Loop." We were impressed by the wild grandeur of Lake Michigan, on the shore of which the thoroughfare was built. Its size (we could not see the farther side), its purplish color, and its waves reminded us of the Black Sea. From the campus to the center of the city was nearly ten miles. But, as we found out, Chicago extends both to the south, where the university is located, and also to the north. Fortunately, the train passes close by the campus and the terminal is near the Loop. In the evening, the Kitagawas invited us to a Chinese restaurant. I found again the "style" I had known twenty-five years before in Chinatown in Calcutta, so different from the Chinese restaurants in Paris.

That night, although tired, we had difficulty falling asleep. We heard the howling of the wind; sometimes the gusts were so strong we thought they would blow the windows off their hinges. Later we learned that Chicago had been nicknamed "The Windy City."

The next day, accompanied by Joseph Kitagawa, I made my first visit to the Divinity School. We walked along University Avenue under tall, stately trees whose leaves had just begun to turn color. Joe pointed out to me the building of the famous Oriental Institute; we passed between two tennis courts and came to other trees, seemingly even more beautiful, beyond which rose various classroom and laboratory buildings. Then we entered Swift Hall (named for the millionaire who had given the money for it to be built). In the well-lighted office the dean, Jerald Brauer, was waiting, smiling cordially. Unexpectedly young, he seemed no more than thirty-two or thirty-three. After introducing me to William Weaver, the dean of students, he escorted Joe Kitagawa and me into the large room where I would be holding the Haskell Lectures. Finally, we went by elevator to the third floor, where we visited the reading room of the library, then to the office of the secretaries. There the dean introduced me to the whole staff and to several faculty members, among others the historian of Christian theology, Jaroslav Pelikan, and Robert Grant, specialist in Gnosticism and Patristics.[2]

As guests of the dean, Christinel and I had lunch at the Quadrangle Club. Then we retreated to our rooms. We were both tired and Christinel was a little depressed. Although she had studied English and read it fluently, she did not always understand what was said to her, and when she spoke, others didn't always understand the few sentences she dared to pronounce, because (as it was explained to me later) she had a "Franco-British accent." We encouraged each other: the eight months of teaching would pass quickly. The salary ($1,000 per month) would allow us to pay back the money Ionel Perlea had loaned us for travel expenses and the costs of getting settled. We hoped, also, that we would be able to save enough to live for a year at Val d'Or.

In a few days a small apartment was found for us in one of the houses belonging to the Federated Faculty—or more precisely, to the Unitarian Meadville Theological Seminary.[3] It was a rather modest place: a small workroom, one bedroom, a bath, and a kitchen. The windows opened onto the yard back of the house, and from the little wooden porch steps led directly down to the shady lawn. The writing table was small and unsteady; fortunately, I used it only at nights. In the daytime I worked in a spacious office the Federated Faculty had found for me at Meadville.

*   *   *

I gave the six lectures in Swift Commons. A good share of my colleagues attended, but also several professors from other divisions of the university who knew *The Myth of the Eternal Return* and even some

2. With Christinel, I met all the professors and their wives at the traditional faculty banquet which took place a few days later.
3. The recently established Federated Theological Faculty included the Divinity School of the University of Chicago and three theological schools; Meadville (Unitarian), the Chicago Theological Seminary, and the Disciples Divinity House.

of my books not translated into English. I didn't realize that my pro-
nunciation (which the months spent at London and Oxford in 1940–
41 had not succeeded in correcting) hindered the comprehension of a
text difficult enough in itself.[4] The room, crowded to capacity in
the beginning, was only three-fourths full at the last two lectures. I
understood later that among the obstacles was the French accent with
which I pronounced the names of familiar gods and goddesses (Isis
and Osiris, for example, and, with rare exceptions, the whole Greco-
Roman pantheon). When I asked one of my best students to what extent she could follow my lectures, she replied, "About fifty percent."
I should have realized from the outset the importance of these "phonetic trifles"; above all, I should have asked a student to read the text
of my lectures out loud to me beforehand, while I noted on my manuscript the correct pronunciations.

What troubled me even more was the variety and complexity of
the American languages. I did not succeed in learning the pronuncia-
tion peculiar to this vast "melting pot" of the Middle West. I had the
impression sometimes that there were phonetic nuances which escaped my ears; certain words which my students and colleagues
understood seemed unintelligible when I spoke them to a taxi driver
or even to clerks in various stores. Fortunately, several of my American colleagues assured me that the same thing often happened to
them too!

The seminar, which I began soon after inaugurating the Haskell
Lectures, gave me less work. There were just fifteen students enrolled, plus Charles ("Chuck") Long, my voluntary assistant, an intelligent young black man. Chuck, one of Joachim Wach's last pupils and
an ordained Baptist minister, was preparing then his doctoral dissertation in the history of religions on the subject of the concept of the
"demonic" in Paul Tillich's theology. In spite of our difference in age,
we quickly became friends. Soon Chuck would be named dean of students. And even before he obtained his doctorate, he was entrusted
with teaching an introductory course in the history and methodology
of the discipline.

I had decided to discuss in my seminars for the three academic
quarters a part of the documentation and problems presented in *Traité*

4. I read, for example, dozens of exotic names from Australian, African, and South
American tribes and from the pantheon and terminology specific to Oriental and
Hellenistic religions.

d'histoire des religions. I had a copy of the manuscript of the English translation (which would appear the following year under the title *Patterns in Comparative Religion*), and sometimes I would read a passage from it, taking care to write on the blackboard all the names and technical terms used. I have remembered for a long time, with melancholy, this seminar which I believed then was the first of a series that would be concluded at the end of the spring quarter. But destiny decided otherwise.

Soon Nasser occupied the Suez Canal Zone. In a letter from Roger Godel I learned that the hospital of the Suez Canal Company where he had worked for many years had been nationalized. It would be necessary, then, for him and Alice to return to France permanently and live in their apartment in Val d'Or. Again, we found ourselves without a residence. We hoped, however, that savings from our salary at Chicago would allow us to rent a small apartment in Paris. We were counting on Sibylle's initiative and connections. Meanwhile, Alice Godel had asked her to remove the books and manuscripts we had left at Val d'Or, and Sibylle had set to work.

*   ,   ,   ,*

At first we hardly had time to set foot off the campus. But toward the middle of October we learned that we could refuse, politely, some invitations to dinner. That autumn was an exceptionally beautiful one. We would leave for our walks in the late afternoon. Sometimes we would head toward the lake about a mile away. We would rest on a bench and, fascinated, watch the waves rolling in menacingly, only to break at last and disperse among the rocks. Or we would set off walking under the gigantic beeches and elms that lined Woodlawn Avenue, pass beside the strange Rockefeller Chapel (a Gothic cathedral built by Aztecs, I called it), cross the famous Midway, and stroll until late in the evening. Sometimes we would walk along the Midway beyond the university hospital and clinics and stroll through Washington Park.

But once when we were describing to the Grants the "geography" of our walks—from twilight until well after nightfall—they surprised us by expressing astonishment; they couldn't believe we'd traversed the Midway so many times without being "attacked." They urged us not to repeat this imprudent behavior, and with regret we heeded their advice. But in a few years' time, the whole Midway complex, although brightly lighted, became a truly dangerous place. We no longer dared to walk there at night except in a group.

In the first weeks we discovered the Field Museum and the Art Institute, and we visited them as often as we could (more precisely, as often as one of my colleagues offered to take us downtown in his car). The Field Museum, especially, intrigued me. I had been familiar with its publications for a long time. In Calcutta, at the library of the Asiatic Society, I had read almost all the contributions of the famous Orientalist and ethnologist, Berthold Laufer, one of the directors of the Field Museum. As for the Art Institute, it took me several years to discover all its treasures.

For a long time I did not venture to judge the American university instructional system. It seemed to me simpler, and at the same time more complex, than the tradition of European universities as I knew it in my youth in Romania and Italy, and immediately after the war in France. I was bothered a little by the number of hours spent in classes and seminars, to which were added discussions with students and the written work they had to present at the end of every quarter. These "term papers" of 15–20 pages, typed, were read by the instructor with red pencil in hand, and then commented on, at least orally, with their authors. For the preparation and writing of their own works, professors had only their months of summer vacation. To the extent that the famous formula, "Publish or perish!" was still valid, the large number of hours devoted to purely didactic activities seemed to me, if not a calamity, at least a great burden.[5]

On the other hand, the American university tradition puts the accent on the intrinsic value of the instructor, not on the "originality" of each lecture he has to give. The scientific importance and "creativity" of a new member of the faculty has been evaluated by the faculty council before it engages him. For the young, the evaluation is repeated after five years, and again after ten, on the occasion of his advance in rank from assistant professor to associate, and finally to full professor. In distinction from the classical system of European universities in former times—when the professor was obliged, at least morally, to "bring something new" to every course he taught—the American professor is free to repeat certain courses. He is allowed, likewise, to present and discuss certain problems without pretending to be "original." He is required only to master the material and *l'état*

5. For that reason, a great many scholars count on grants from various foundations which allow them to take a leave, unpaid, of from one to three quarters—the time necessary for the research and writing of their personal works.

des questions, and to present them competently and clearly. Thus, in the last analysis, the professor is free to present information gathered by other scholars and summarize their interpretations without this lack of "originality" being detrimental to his scientific prestige. His "originality" is verified, primarily, through his publications.

Taking all these things into account, the two or three lectures per week, and the seminars and meetings with students do not constitute a fatal obstacle to any attempt at "original creation" as it seemed to me at first sight, especially since the tradition of private universities (for example, Harvard and Chicago) allows the professors to choose their subjects and organize their courses according to the needs of the department but taking account also of their own concerns. Many books of my colleagues were written owing to the fact that they had taught certain courses repeatedly over a number of years.

/   /   /

Toward the end of the winter, Jerry Brauer, dean of the Federated Faculty, invited me to have lunch with him privately at the Quadrangle Club. He asked me how Christinel felt about Chicago, if she liked the "American academic environment." I didn't dare tell him the whole truth—that at present Christinel felt somewhat in exile—but I admitted that what discouraged her most was the "American language."

"But she speaks well enough," Jerry interrupted me. "In a few months she won't be having any difficulties."

Then he asked me my opinion of our university, and I replied, very sincerely, "Only good."

The Dean became exuberant.

"Then let me ask you one more question: Will you accept the position of full professor? To begin with, for ten years. The whole faculty is in accord."

"Of course," I replied, "I must talk this over with Christinel."

Jerry agreed immediately. He knew from others and from personal experience that if the wife was not fully satisfied, the professor would not stay very long at the university.

"But in any event," I continued, "I wouldn't dare commit myself for ten years; I have a number of works to finish. Let's begin with an agreement for four years."

Christinel didn't seem too excited, but she soon became reconciled to the thought of returning to Chicago, especially after I assured her that if we couldn't stand it, I could resign after two years (obviously, after notifying the administration in sufficient time for it to procure a replacement). A few days afterward I informed Jerry Brauer of my decision. I accepted the position of professor and chairman of the Department of History of Religions, agreeing to hold one course (three lectures per week) and one seminar of two hours during each of the first two quarters; but during the spring quarter I would hold no courses or seminars, making myself available, however, to students—above all, to those who were doctoral candidates in the history of religions. The dean consented, and I maintained this privileged schedule until 1983, when I became *emeritus*.

                    /   /   /

In the winter quarter I taught a course on Yoga. As I expected, every seat in the room was filled. I had received from Willard Trask the proofs of the book *Yoga: Immortality and Freedom* and in the first classes I read certain selections from it, taking care to add oral commentary whenever I sensed the text was too condensed. Soon, however, I abandoned that method, and, reducing the exposition of doctrine to a minimum, I emphasized the various yogic practices. The majority of the class were students from the college of the university or from graduate schools other than those in the Federated Theological Faculty. To my surprise, most of them stayed with the course until the end of the quarter. It is true that for several years in America the young people in universities were quite fascinated by India and, above all, by Yoga.

On the other hand, the course on shamanism which I offered in the spring quarter attracted only a small group of students. Very few were interested in that subject, then familiar only to anthropologists. (Shamanism would enjoy considerable popularity only in 1970–75.) Moreover, students in the Department of History of Religions were preparing now for examinations and they scarcely had any time (or curiosity) to follow the presentation of shamanic initiations and practices. I myself felt tired: in addition to my academic obligations, I was working as much as seven or eight hours per day preparing the text of the Haskell Lectures for publication.

Only in the spring of 1957 did I begin to know well the strengths and weaknesses of American students. On the one hand, with rare exceptions, the very young students—those in the college and in the first year of graduate studies—seemed to me less well prepared than their counterparts of the same age in France. They lacked the baccalaureate experience and above all the basic elements of a humanistic education. On the other hand—although often in an unsystematic way—they had a knowledge of certain cultural creations that would have surprised a European at that time (1955–60). For example, already in high school they had studied Faulkner or Camus (although they had not read Balzac, Stendhal, or Tolstoy), they knew *Waiting for Godot* or O'Neill's *Mourning Becomes Electra* (but no play by Shakespeare). In college they had taken courses on Freud and Sartre, or on modern art. Later I realized the significance and utility of this program: the majority of students would not continue their studies after high school or after college. (University education in the United States is expensive, and not everyone succeeds in obtaining a scholarship.) Thus it was preferable for the student to be initiated into at least a few problems and creations belonging to modern culture, such as psychoanalysis, existentialism, and the contemporary novel and theater.

But in the university, pursuing the courses necessary for the master of arts degree, the student was obliged to complete, at least in part, his "basic education." Nevertheless, in preparing for the doctorate in a humanistic discipline and being forced to master two European or classical languages, and one—if not several—Oriental ones, the American student could be compared with the European, at least as he was up until 1960. Of course, I was best acquainted with the limited group in my seminars in the history of religions. Some students were rather well prepared; others less so. But they all had the same preoccupation: how to familiarize themselves as quickly as possible with the methodology and problems of the history of religions. In time, I would realize that their passion for "methodology" constituted a part of the "American tradition." Often a student would ask me, solemnly and yet with strong feeling: "What's the best method to study and understand the history of religions?" It seemed to me I recognized the descendants of the first waves of pioneers, embarked on the conquest and cultivation of the enormous space that lay beyond the frontier. It was the same fundamental conviction: if we have the best tools possible, we can make a paradise of this land; if we have the best method available, we will understand the history of religions in all its complexity, and we will be in a position to make discoveries unsuspected by anyone before.

,   ,   ,

At the beginning of June all the instructors and students of the department, together with their wives and children, gathered for a traditional picnic held each year at the Dunes, on the shore of Lake

Michigan. Harriet Platt, wife of the professor of geography and an enthusiast for the "mystique of the Orient," had a house there to which
we could, if necessary, retreat. At that time I became aware of the
spontaneity of these festive meetings with the families of students
and professors. The university constituted a true community, and
each school and each department a family.

More than a quarter of a century has passed since that picnic of
June 1957. Almost all the students from then have long since become
professors, and the children we watched playing on the lakeshore are
preparing for master's or doctoral degrees, or are scattered on three
continents, doing research or working for various business concerns.
In the many years since they left Chicago, our former students have
continued to keep us informed—at least through long circular letters
at New Year's—about the latest academic news (publications, promo-
tions, etc.) and family affairs (we are told, for example, about the
name of the fiancée of the youngest son. . .).

                    /   /   /

A few days later we took the train for New York where Lisette and
Ionel Perlea were waiting for us. But Ionel had to leave shortly afterward; he had accepted, among others, the offer to direct several concerts at the festival at Aix-en-Provence. We remained until July 13,
when we embarked, with Lisette, on the *Liberty*.

I had to write the two Eranos lectures and prepare the paper for
the congress of Orientalists at Munich. I knew that we wouldn't find
the necessary peace and quiet at Paris, nor even a good table to write
on. Here at New York I had at my disposal Ionel's well-lighted room,
with windows looking out upon the little flower gardens of the neighboring houses. We didn't feel the heat, and the silence was unbroken
save for the occasional screams and curses of a demented old lady
living nearby.

I had brought with me several books and almost all the file folders
with notes and off-prints of articles relative to the experience of the
"inner light." These materials I had collected in the last few years,
since having decided to analyze this type of experience from the perspective of the history of religions. I had known for a long time the
Indian, Iranian, and Chinese materials, but recently I had discovered
a great many examples relative to "spontaneous experiences" of inner
light—that is, those occurring without preliminary ascetic-religious
instruction. I was interested in the fact that in the various religious

traditions as well as in the "spontaneous experiences," the inner light expresses always an epiphany of the Spirit. Such experiences project the subject into another universe from that of the everyday existence, radically altering his ontological status, opening him to the values of the Spirit. The meaning of the inner light was revealed directly to the one who experienced it. But on the other hand the meaning became intelligible only within the framework of the religious ideology familiar to the subject. Although the *experience* of the "mystic light" seemed to be the same in many cultures—from "primitives" to Vedic Indians, in Buddhism and Christian monasticism—its spiritual *meaning and value* varied from one religious tradition to another. Such comparative analyses interested me because they brought out the basic unity of certain religious experiences, as well as the variety of meanings which they acquired in different traditions and which prove, once again, the creativity of the Spirit.[6]

In those weeks of early summer I began to know the charm of this "last European city in America," as the immigrants call New York. At that time also I had the opportunity to visit the Metropolitan Museum several times a week and to have some leisurely talks with friends: Brutus and Tanzi Coste, Ion Vardala, N. Caramfil, and others.

We stayed only a few days in Paris. We were impatient to be back as quickly as possible at Ascona and Lago Maggiore. Olga Froebe had invited Stella and Henry Corbin, and Casa Gabriella was animated by our long conversations, prolonged sometimes until late in the night. Henry, like other French friends and colleagues, regretted that I had accepted the invitation of the University of Chicago for another four years, but they acknowledged that, for the time being, there was no other solution. On the contrary, our friends from the Bollingen Foundation, John Barrett and Vaun Gillmor, were delighted. The thing we need, they said, is not European professors who settle in the United States and return once in five or six years to see their homeland, but intellectuals who agree to make annually the voyage between the two continents. It is, certainly, fatiguing, and from the financial point of

---

6. "Significations de la lumière intérieure" appeared in the *Eranos-Jahrbuch,* XXVI (Zurich: 1958) and was reprinted in *Méphistophélès et l'androgyne* (Gallimard, 1962: in English in *Mephistopheles and the Androgyne* [1965]). Many years later I took up the problem again in the study "Spirit, Light, Seed" (in *Occultism, Witchcraft, and Cultural Fashions,* 1976).

view extravagant (You won't be able to save anything! they told us). But such a cultural activity carried on simultaneously on both sides of the Atlantic can contribute to a more authentic, deeper reciprocal knowledge of the traditions and creations of the two continents.

That summer the thunderstorms came in close succession, and we seldom had a chance to bathe in the lake or go hiking in the surrounding hills. I succeeded in finishing the text of the Eranos lectures and I wrote the paper for the congress of Orientalists to be held at Munich from August 28 untill September 4. The examples cited and discussed in "Experiences de la lumière intérieure" were followed with great interest. I remembered for a long time the passionate discussions with Gershom Scholem, Ernst Benz, Henry Corbin, and others.

We arrived at Munich just as the congress was opening, and in addition to the many Orientalist colleagues and friends whom I saw again, I had the opportunity to meet Joseph Needham (who professed admiration for *Forgerons et alchimistes*), Walter Reuben, Dominik Schröder, A. L. Basham, Franz Babinger, and others. On September 2 I presented a short paper, "Remarques sur le miracle de la corde." The problem had interested me for a long time: not only the fabulous "rope trick" of the fakirs, but also all the experiences, mythologies, and metaphysical speculations related to threads or ropes, which illustrate both the human condition and the structure of the universe.[7]

From Munich we left for Florence and from there, by bus, to Siena, Assisi, and Rome (cf. *No Souvenirs*, pp. 16–25). Christinel and I both felt the need to see Italy again at the beginning of autumn. I realized the risks I was taking in visiting cathedrals and art museums, and in making the rounds of bookstores and antiquaries, but I knew what was waiting for me: a hotel room in Paris. From July I had become a "wandering scholar," living and working—except for the time at Casa Gabriella—in hotel rooms.

At the beginning of October we returned to Paris and took up lodging, for two months, at Hôtel Pas de Calais. Our great joy, of course, was our reunion with friends (the family—Mamy, Sibylle, Lisette, Ionel, and Oani—we had seen in July in Paris, and then again at Ascona). But in the latter half of November I left by myself for Uppsala.

---

7. Considerably developed, the study appeared under the title "Mythes et symboles de la corde" in the *Eranos-Jahrbuch*, XXIX (1961) and it was reprinted in *Méphistophélès et l'androgyne*.

Geo Widengren had invited me long before for a series of lectures and seminars. It was a thrill to discover Uppsala. And after I had visited the library, I understood why Georges Dumézil had returned here several times in the past two or three years in order to complete his latest books: you could find *everything*, and you could obtain the book you needed *immediately*, even when someone else was consulting it.

I met now for the first time the young Orientalist and historian of religions H. H. Ringren, and I saw again Stig Wikander, who had left the University of Lund. I repeated the two lectures about "Experiences of Mystic Light" and, at the seminar, I discussed various problems of "methodology." But what most excited me were the conversations with Wikander, Widengren, and other colleagues. I am reminded also of the young man who had learned well all the Semitic languages and had just taken his doctorate—and was now preparing to return to the family farm near the Arctic Circle. That herd of cows his parents tended supplied the milk on which the whole region depended. The young man had studied Semitic languages—in order to be able to continue working on the farm in those six months of darkness.

We returned to Hôtel Pas de Calais at the beginning of December. On the fifteenth of the month we embarked on the *United States* in order to be able to spend Christmas in New York with Ionel and Lisette. On January 1, 1958, we were back in Chicago. A friend, Peggy Grant, had found us an apartment on Kimbark Avenue. Whatever may happen, we told ourselves, we'll have a place of our own for at least six months.

The apartment was rather dark, with furniture aged before its time, with walls covered with reproductions in gray and black, faded posters, and many photographs—probably family mementos. But Mrs. Sibley, the landlady, allowed us to arrange the place to suit our tastes and needs. The very next day Christinel set to work. Fortunately, I spent most of that day at the university and in my office at Meadville. Returning home that evening, I looked around in delight: the apartment had begun to become *ours*. Soon we dared to invite a few colleagues and their wives for dinner. It was the dead of winter now, but we both felt better than we had the first year: on the one hand, we knew we would not be living here more than five or six months this time; on the other hand, we kept remembering that at the end of August we would be going to Japan for the International Congress of the History of Religions Association, and that we would be staying there as long as possible (as long as our "savings" would allow) after the conference was over.

In that winter of 1958 I became acquainted with John Nef, the founder and chairman of that surprising department bearing the rather enigmatic name of Committee on Social Thought. Inaugurated in the time of the famous president of the university, Robert Hutchins, and with his assistance, the committee had distinguished itself not only by its bold and original program, but also by the professors it recruited and the personalities it had invited to hold lecture series or seminars (among others, T. S. Eliot, Jacques Maritain, and Marc Chagall).

I was attracted immediately by the "cultural project" the Committee on Social Thought had tried to achieve: a limited number of students (no more than thirty), very few courses properly speaking, but several seminars, conducted sometimes by two or three professors. A fundamental innovation was the system of instruction preliminary to "specialization": no matter to what area of research the student felt himself attracted, in the first two years his activity was concentrated in other directions. From a list of basic books the student selected between twelve and fifteen texts which he pondered and analyzed for a long time, with the assistance of a professor.[8] After two or three years, the student was allowed to take an examination. The examination consisted of a series of questions concerning some of these basic books. The student had a whole day in which to write his responses. On the basis of what he wrote, the professors decided if he had assimilated the basic elements of the Western cultural tradition; if so, he could enroll for the doctorate in the speciality that interested him. He began to work then with professors in other departments, but he continued to take part in the seminars of the committee. Obviously, the student who was doing research now on, say, Islam, the Pre-Socratic philosophers, or the history of science in the eighteenth century, had a broader experience and a more coherent vision of the whole than his fellow students in the same speciality.

I had been co-opted as a member of the committee, and twice each

8. The books selected had to include a Greek tragedy, a Platonic dialogue, a text by Aristotle, the work of a major historian, a famous novelist, an outstanding moralist, and a great political thinker.

month we dined at John Nef's home. Nearly always one or two foreign guests were present (thus I met Julian Huxley, Charles Darwin's grandson, Jean Hippolite, and many others). After dinner there ensued a general discussion, or else one of the guests was invited to talk about his recent interests or those of the institution to which he belonged. In a sense it could be said that the effort to "broaden and deepen the cultural horizon" to which students were urged continued to be practiced also by the committee members themselves.

In the winter and spring of that year I worked intensely, almost without interruption. For my courses I selected subjects which I knew well and which interested me: "The Structure of Religious Symbolism" and "Aspects of Myth," but as usual I reread and updated the files sent from Paris. At the seminar "Recent Trends in Religious Science" I discussed a number of authors representing different orientations, from William James and Rudolph Otto to van der Leeuw and Pettazzoni. The students, as well as many of my colleagues, were impressed by my "productivity": in 1958 three of my books appeared in English translation, including *Patterns in Comparative Religions* (*Traité*). But this editorial "productivity" was the result, of course, of coincidences.

Because I sensed we had begun to know one another better, I enjoyed having conversations with my students, in groups and individually. And whenever I had the chance, I urged them to read fundamental texts—from the *Rig Veda* and Egyptian and Mesopotamian documents to the *Qur'an*—and at least two or three monographs on primitive religions. I kept reminding them that now, in these few years which separated them from the master's degree, they must familiarize themselves with the central problems of the discipline: for example, the structure and function of myth, the morphology of supernatural figures (gods, goddesses, mythical heroes, etc.), the typology of rituals, certain religious institutions (e.g., initiation). After the master's degree, their time would be in good part preempted either by their academic activity (teaching in a college or theological institute) or by their preparation for a doctorate.

Indeed, the doctorate in the history of religions—which could be obtained then in only a few universities—entailed specialization in one of the great religious traditions: Hinduism, Buddhism, Islam, or religions of the Far East. In other words, the student was required to master the basic language of the religion he had chosen as the principal object of his research: Sanskrit or Pali, Arabic, Chinese, or Japanese. But in view of the growing importance of the Orient in the foreign policy of the United States, the student hoped, on the one hand, to obtain a study grant for two years in India, Japan, Taiwan, or one of the Arab countries: on the other hand, he knew that such a preparation (in distinction, for example, from specialization in classical religions), increased his chances for obtaining a teaching position in the history of religions. (In time, the study of the "primitive" religious traditions of Africa and South America began to be encouraged by universities.)

In later years I observed that many students enrolled for courses in Sanskrit, Chinese, or Japanese before obtaining a master's degree, as soon as they felt attracted to one of the Asian traditions. I encouraged them in this with all sincerity. No matter what you decide to do later, I told them, the learning of an Oriental language will be of great utility.

*   *   *

In the spring I began to write the text for Eranos: "Méphistophélès et l'androgyne, au le mystère de totalité." I reworked, after fifteen years, some of the documents and interpretations presented in the book *Mitul reintegrării* (Bucharest: 1942). But the problem of the unification of opposites had continued—and continues today—to engross me. I did not undertake to write more than the first part in Chicago; the rest I wrote at Ascona. I was forced to interrupt work on the lecture because it was the middle of June, and before leaving I had to give Jóe Kitagawa an article on religious symbolism. We had decided to prepare, in memory of Joachim Wach, a collection of studies, *The History of Religions: Essays in Methodology*. Among the contributors were R. Pettazzoni, Louis Massignon, Fredrich Heiler, and Jean Daniélou. As soon as Christinel had finished typing the article, we left for New York, and from there, by plane, for Paris.

*   *   *

We stayed there only a few days because Olga was expecting us at Ascona. This year I hardly had time to enjoy a vacation; I spent a good part of each day at my writing table. I succeeded, nevertheless, in finishing the text before the opening of the Eranos Conference. Thus, I was able to take advantage of the presence of many friends and colleagues. As usual, our discussions on the lakeshore continued until nearly midnight. For a whole evening we listened to Ernst Benz telling me excitedly and with enthusiasm about Japan, where he had recently spent several months. He was quite captivated by the religious and artistic genius of this people.

On August 22 we returned to Paris, and three days later we took the plane for Tokyo. We were still in the "pre-jet age" then. The flight over the polar ice cap, from Stockholm to Anchorage alone, took seventeen hours.

24. *Indispensable to the Security of the United States*

WAITING for us at the airport in Tokyo were Joseph Kitagawa and Professor Ishiro Hori, whom I knew well from Chicago, where he had presented the Haskell Lectures that year. A room had been reserved for us at the Dai-ichi Hotel. Although exhausted from our long trip, we dined that evening at a Japanese restaurant as guests of Hori and Kitagawa. We ate around a low table, seated on pillows and served by *geishi*. The ritual fascinated us.

Since our congress was the first international convention to take place in Japan since the war, the authorities accorded it special attention. The honorary president of the congress, moreover, was the brother of the emperor, Prince Mikasa, himself a scholar, a specialist in the history of the Ancient Orient and a student of the history of religions. In addition to several gala receptions (I remember especially the last, at the Ghengis Khan Restaurant, situated in a park on a little hill), the participants had at their disposal elegant motor coaches and special trains for excursions to Nara, Isi, Kyoto, and Yokohama.

A large number of scholar had come from Europe and the United States, including H. Ch. Puech, Paul Demieville, Jean Filliozat, F. Heiler, and E. Goodenough. But there were present also numerous specialists from India and Australia. Raffaele Pettazzoni, president of the International Association for the History of Religions, had the right to be proud of the prestige our discipline had obtained in the last several years. But shortly before the close of the congress, Pettazzoni fell ill and was admitted to a hospital, from which he returned directly to Rome. No one suspected then that this trip to Japan would be his last journey abroad.

The working sessions were held at the University of Tokyo. I did not attend very many of the lectures; I preferred to talk with colleagues from India and Japan. I read my paper on religious symbolism, but I did not encourage discussion; the problem was too complex, and in the twenty minutes allowed for each speaker I contented myself with presenting just a few aspects of the problem.

On the other hand, I had the surprise several times of being drawn into discussions I had not anticipated. I remember especially a very interesting paper on Mahayana Buddhism to which I listened seated beside a Japanese professor of philosophy. I had met him a few days before, and had learned that he was well versed in German philosophy, especially that of Heidegger. Walking with me to the cafeteria, he astonished me by saying that he hadn't understood the paper on Buddhism at all. Somewhat chagrined, he added that, with the exception of the life of the Buddha, he was ignorant of the whole history and philosophy of Buddhism. After we had seated ourselves at a little table with bottles of Coca-Cola in front of us, my companion, smiling politely, justified his ignorance by saying that the majority of Japanese philosophers today, not just he, had no desire to waste their time with problems that pertain to the prehistory of philosophy, such as those of Buddhism.

I tried to convince him that he was wrong, but the professor continued to smile, shaking his head skeptically. At length, that polite smile made me lose my patience. "I'm sorry," I said, raising my voice involuntarily, "but I'm afraid that contemporary Japanese philosophy is in danger of becoming provincialized. You make yourselves think the way people think today in Germany or France. You have available the boldest logic known to the world before Hegel—Buddhist logic, as it was elaborated by Nagarjuna, Vasubandhu, Dignaga, Dharmakirti—and you leave it exclusively in the hands of historians and orientalists. Your own philosophy you don't know, or at any rate, you don't utilize it. To you, perhaps, it seems 'old-fashioned.' But this proves you don't know it. Because, the problem of Nagarjuna and his successors was this: to demonstrate logically that *Samsāra* is identical with *Nirvāna*, that becoming (cosmic "unreality") is one with being (i.e., ontological bliss). On another plane, pursuing another objective, and using other means—Madhyamika philosophy was confronted with the same mystery of *coincidentia oppositorum* that confronted Cusanus. Now, *coincidentia oppositorum* confronts us today in certain principles of nuclear physics (for example, in Oppenheimer's principle of complementarity), but it is posed more and more insistently in the entire historical moment in which we live: for instance, how is freedom possible in a conditioned universe? How can one live in history without betraying it, without denying it, and nevertheless participating in a transhistorical reality? At bottom, the problem is this: how to recognize the *real* camouflaged in *appearances?* I am waiting for a Buddhist philosopher to present us with a *total* vision of the Real."[1]

The longer we stayed in Japan, the more enchanted Christinel and I felt. We were conquered from the start by the beauty and variety of the landscapes, and in the long excursions by train we discovered not only many legendary cities and religious centers—Kyoto, Nara, Isi— but also certain features characteristic of Japanese behavior and sensibility: for example, their passion for all the creations of nature, from animals and flowers to rocks, lakes, and springs. The Japanese artistic genius seemed stimulated by the predilection for an infinity of epiphanies of cosmic creativity. The same aesthetics can be recognized not only in paintings, architecture, and stage settings, but also in the art of arranging flowers and in the miniature universes which are the Japanese gardens. As I would understand after I had visited many temples and witnessed Shinto rituals (especially the ceremonies at Ise and Fuji), nature is susceptible of being sanctified by the "visitations" of the gods and spirits. The sanctification is celebrated most especially through ritual dances and gestures and through artistic creations.

At Ise I became better acquainted with Hirai, a young Shinto priest who had studied the history of religions at Chicago under Joachim Wach. He took us to a famous temple where we admired the grace and spontaneity of the ten young female dancers attached to the sanc-

---

1. Compare *No Souvenirs*, p. 31. [This and other passages taken from the *Journal* are not rendered exactly as in *No Souvenirs*, because the latter is a translation made from the French translation in *Fragments d'un Journal*, whereas the translation here is made directly from the Romanian. Tr.]

tuary. Turning to Hirai, an American philosopher in our group said, "I look at the temples, I watch the ceremonies and the dancers, I admire the costumes and the politeness of the priests, but I don't see the theology implied in Shintoism." After a few moments' reflection Hirai replied, smiling, "We don't have theology. We . . . dance!"

It was, apparently, a quip. But Hirai did not dare to remind the American philosopher that Shinto theology is expressed directly and as *explicitly* as possible not in verbal formulas but in ceremonials, and especially in dance.

In our two free evenings, along with Evelyn and Joe Kitagawa, Zwi Werblowski, and Joseph Campbell, we visited the Ginza, the most picturesque quarter of Tokyo, lighted like a fairyland with innumerable lanterns of many colors. Sometimes we would enter a shop and even before we could ask the price of an object—a doll, a kimono, a toy—the shopkeeper would offer us a gift. We were happy whenever, using English, we were able to make ourselves understood. The politeness and the general conduct of the Japanese h̲ inly, a ritual origin. That is why I felt so awkward (so "bar vhen, in the absence of Joe Kitagawa, I didn't know how to c̲ self.

I recall our trip to Kyoto. By evening Christinel ver-whelmed by all we had seen: not only the temples an ut also the streets and illuminated gardens of this prodigio night we slept in a Japanese hotel. The room seemed n apartment, divided by movable screens beautifully painted ous designs. For the first time, we slept Japanese style, spread on the floor. We were happy enough. But we were alo is, Joe and Evelyn Kitagawa weren't with us. That evening next morning, whenever the young maids came to ask us if we anything, we could only shrug our shoulders and smile.

After the congress was over, we went with the Kitagawas Joseph Campbell to Kobe, Fukuoka, Nagasaki, and Unzen. We spe one night at Beppu, and in this way we had the opportunity to bat according to Japanese tradition. In the morning, Professor Furu came to escort us to Fukuoka. En route, we stopped to visit the fa mous hill with the forest full of monkeys. As soon as we reached Nagasaki, we went directly to the immense vacant area where, thirteen years before, the second atomic bomb was exploded. A short text, written in several languages, explained why this section of the city had not been rebuilt: it was left to be a reminder to the whole world of the apocalypse of thermonuclear war.

At Kyushu University in Fukuoka, Professor Furuna had organized a symposium with the anthropologist Wilhelm Koppers, Joseph Campbell, Kitagawa, and me. The theme was "Contemporary Methods in the Study of the History of Religions." The almost pathetic interest of the Japanese savants for "methodology" reminded me of my students at Chicago. The discussion was lively. Wilhelm Koppers, although by training a theologian, maintained that, in our discipline, the accent must fall on *history*. For my part, I affirmed precisely the contrary: that the history of religions is the only discipline which allows the investigator to know and understand the innumerable expressions of *religious* experiences and ideologies.

That evening, Furuna took us to visit the ruins of the former capital in Fukuoka. Nothing now remained but a few stones and a floor plan, reconstructed by archeologists. We went next to a Buddhist temple, an unusually shabby one. Finally, after another ten kilometers, we stopped in front of a Shinto sanctuary. I remembered vividly for a long time that miniature lake and those bridges hung with lanterns, where groups of children were playing.

I need not evoke our impressions of Kobe, Hakata, and Unzen, or the names of persons we met there. After a week we returned to Tokyo. Christinel was suffering with a case of the flu, so I left alone for Sendai, where Hori had invited me. Destroyed by American aerial bombardment, the city had recently been rebuilt—too fast and quite unattractively. Many of the thoroughfares and side streets were still under construction. Hori took me to a park, a forest with gigantic trees, centuries old. We ascended a slope and suddenly we came upon a narrow bridge, spanning a deep ravine. To this bridge, Hori told me, residents of Sendai come to commit suicide. But people come re also from many other places, he added. An inscription on a etal plaque attempts to save them *in extremis:* "Take care," it says, let you be tempted to rash actions." [2]

Hori lived in one of the houses built by the Americans and ceded that year to the university. But for me he had reserved a room at the Park Hotel in Matsushima, some ten kilometers from Sendai. The

2. Cf. *No Souvenirs*, p. 29.

hotel was erected right on the shore of the ocean. It had an immense
flower garden and a wharf from which motor boats departed for tours
among the nearby islands. There were perhaps a hundred islands,
some no larger than a rock on which there was scarcely room to lie
down. Others were a few meters across, some several dozen meters
or even larger, with little grass but with numerous trees.[3]

I have never forgotten those days at Sendai, nor the evenings and
nights I spent relaxing on the terrace of the hotel in Matsushima, contemplating those rocky islets. In addition to giving the lecture and
seminar organized by Hori (about methodology, naturally!), I had the
opportunity to converse with many professors and students. I enjoyed especially my visit to a blind female pseudo-shaman (*miko*)
which Hori had arranged.[4]

But in the evenings, left to myself on the terrace of the hotel at Matsushima, I tried to organize my impressions. In the past few weeks it
seemed to me that I was beginning to understand certain aspects of
the Japanese religious genius. I noted in the *Journal* its principal char-
acteristics: "The need to communicate with and be instructed by a divinity or by a spirit temporarily embodied in a human being; the
tendency to confront the divine or the sacred *in concreto*, especially as
it is manifested in a living creature; a horror of the abstract and the
'transcendent.' . . . The Japanese soul yearns for concrete epiphanies
of the divine. . . . I should say that it is inclined toward a theology of
temporary, momentary incarnations of the Spirit—of any mode of
being of the Spirit: gods, god-men, souls of the dead, souls of animals, etc. The gods are par excellence travelers, *visitors*. Everything in
the Cosmos can be transfigured; nothing is unworthy of receiving the
'visit' of a god: a flower, a stone, a wooden post. The universe is constantly being sanctified by means of an infinity of instantaneous epiphanies. . . . The gods do not *take up residence* anywhere in the world.
The Spirit descends at any time and anywhere, but it does not remain,
it does not let itself be caught in temporal duration. The epiphany is par
excellence momentary. Every divine presence is provisional."[5]

I had known, of course, the mythology of religious traditions of
Japan, as well as certain creations specific to Japanese Buddhism,

3. Cf. ibid., p. 27.
4. Cf. ibid., pp. 31–32.
5. Cf. ibid., p. 35.

above all the doctrines and techniques of the Zen schools. But the experience of those four weeks spent in Japan allowed me to deepen and integrate the facts learned from books. After the India of my youth, I had had the opportunity to discover another Oriental civilization, quite different and yet somehow at one with the spiritual creations of India and, in general, of Asia.

, , ,

On our return flight, we stopped for a week in Honolulu. Our hotel, situated, like many others, right on the beach, was located in the new part of the city constructed for tourists. But the artificiality and calculated exotic exuberance of the quarter were so obvious that after a few hours you no longer were aware of them. You could not resist that unnatural transparency of the Pacific light. Soon you ceased to gaze at anything but the long, endless waves of the ocean (with or without the inevitable surfers).

One day we crossed the island to find the house in a forest where Joseph Campbell's sister and mother had been living for a long time. I recall this detail because of its fabulous character. Some twenty years earlier Campbell's sister, then very young, had visited Hawaii with a tour group. She was so fascinated by it that when she returned to New York she quit her job, sold all her belongings, and moved permamently to the island. Since then she had never returned to the mainland. She had succeeded, however, in persuading her mother to join her.

Another day we visited the house built by Jean Charlot outside the city, on the shore of the Pacific. I had admired his paintings and sketches, but I had never met him. That fall I recalled a number of times, with Christinel, Charlot's spontaneity and the beauty of his wife and children—but especially the strange and fascinating architecture of that house, mysterious and at the same time functional.

, , ,

After a nine-hour flight, we arrived in San Francisco. The city won our hearts as soon as the fog lifted and we dared to venture forth on the streets. We dined in Chinatown, and the next day an enterprising taxi driver possessed of a good imagination took us for a ride of almost three hours through all the neighborhoods and into the surrounding area, as far as Berkeley. In later years we returned several times to San Francisco, but in my memory there lingers still the image of the city as we discovered it on that October day of 1958.

Joseph Kitagawa had received a grant for research in Japan, so he put his apartment on Woodlawn Avenue at our disposal. A few days after we were settled, the so-called "Faculty Retreat" was held at Lake Geneva, Wisconsin. Each fall, at the start of the academic year, the professors gathered in a little hotel on the shore of the lake. We spent two or three days together, far from family and students. Except for two lectures—followed by long discussions—we were free. In this way we had the opportunity to get to know one another better. This was my first experience of this sort. It was all the more interesting and instructive inasmuch as I had not had a theological education. I was impressed from the beginning by the friendliness and, especially, the interdenominational tolerance of my colleagues. The majority belonged to various Protestant traditions, but there were two Unitarians, one Jew, one agnostic (atheist?) and one Buddhist (Myamoto, visiting professor in 1958–59). In time there would be added to the faculty another Jewish professor and several Catholics. Such a religious pluralism, hard to imagine in a European faculty of theology, aroused interminable dialogues and assured the authenticity of the collaboration among the various departments.

The dean had suggested to me that I present a lecture which would bring out the "specificity" of the history of religions and the potential contribution of this discipline to the problematics of contemporary theologies. I spoke on "The Prestige of the Cosmogonic Myth." It seemed to me that the examples and interpretations I presented to them constituted an excellent opportunity for them to reevaluate their understanding of Creation in the context of nonbiblical religions. The discussion was rather interesting. My colleagues discovered, to their amazement, the sacrality and conceptual coherence of archaic and Oriental religions.[6]

I have never forgotten those glorious days of October, the copper-colored woods, and the somber lake on whose shore I enjoyed walking with my new friends: Jaroslav Pelikan, Robert Grant, and Nathan Scott. The feeling that we were "free," without a schedule, that we could sit up talking until after midnight, were for us all surprisingly invigorating. We returned to Chicago refreshed, as after a long vacation.

*   *   *

6. Some years later, when we conducted together an interdisciplinary seminar on systematic theology and the history of religions, Paul Tillich was fascinated by the thoughts and discussions provoked by such comparisons between cosmic religions and biblical tradition. [Two joint seminars were taught, titled "Christian and Non-Christian Religions," in the winter and fall quarters of 1964. Tr.]

We were happy during those seven months we lived in the apartment of our friends, Evelyn and Joe Kitagawa. That autumn and the winter of 1959 passed more quickly than we had expected. In addition to the courses and the seminars, my time was confiscated by numerous obligations: lectures, articles I had promised, the preparation of a new edition (corrected and considerably augmented) of the book *Le Chamanisme*, which Willard Trask had recently translated into English. A little earlier that year *Yoga: Immortality and Freedom* had appeared, also translated by Trask. It was my fourth work published in English and, owing to the subject, probably, it enjoyed unusually good sales.

Toward the end of the winter I realized I would have to interrupt my works in progress. My mind was on the god Zalmoxis and the Geto-Dacian religions. For several weeks I reread and completed the documentation which I had brought with me. Then, in one night, I composed the article, "Les Daces et les loups." It was my first article for the book *De Zalmoxis à Genghis Khan*. In succeeding years I wrote studies about cosmogonic myths in Romania and Eastern Europe, about the legend of Dragos, Voda, about the ballad *Miorița* and Romanian religious folklore; the book was published by Payot in 1970. Although I didn't realize it, the periodical return to the study of Romanian spiritual traditions was, in a sense, a means of preserving my identity in the "melting pot" of the United States.

Then, suddenly, the desire for literature came over me. I hadn't written anything in Romanian since four years before, when I had broken off work on *Pe strada Mântuleasa*. In March and April I composed, quickly, two short stories.[7] But I didn't dare begin *La țigănci*, a novella whose subject had obsessed me for a long time. I had to prepare the course I had promised to teach at the Jung Institut in Zurich, and also the Eranos lecture.

On May 13 we were in Paris. Sibylle had found us a little apartment on rue de l'Yvette. We barely had time for reunions with friends. A few days later we were in Meilen; the director of the institute, Dr. Franz Rilkin, had invited us to stay at his house. The subject of the course was "Mythologies and Rituals of Initiation." I emphasized the traditions of archaic and Oriental societies. Obviously, I was re-

7. [The stories were: "Ghicitor în pietre" (The Man Who Could Read Stones), in March, and "O fotografie veche de 14 ani" (A Fourteen-Year-Old Photograph), in April. Tr.]

turning to problems discussed in *Birth and Rebirth,* but because I was addressing an audience composed primarily of Jungians I stressed elements they could use in their professional practice.

I had the opportunity to meet a number of the pupils of the institute and to renew acquaintances with Jolanda Jacobi, Anielle Jaffé, and Marie-Louise von Franz. From Anielle Jaffé I learned that Jung was dictating his autobiography, or more precisely, telling it to her and she was writing it; then he would review the text, correct it, reword it, and amplify it.

On the afternoon of June 6 I conversed with Jung for almost an hour and a half, in the garden of his residence at Küsnacht. It had been some five years since I had seen him, and, as I noted in the *Journal,*[8] he seemed to me almost unchanged. He was, however, weaker and used a cane for walking. A few days before that, Paul Mus had visited him, and had explained to him the origin and history of the Chinese character for *tao*. These technical details had so excited him that he repeated them to me, with great satisfaction. At certain moment he began talking about the meaning of numbers among "primitives." Evoking memories of his trip to Africa, he pronounced several Swahili words, each with a different intonation, signifying "five," "many," and "very many."

But now and then it seemed to me I detected a trace of bitterness. Speaking about the structure of mystical experiences, he declared that medical doctors and psychologists are "too stupid or too uncultivated" to understand such phenomena. I found again the verve which had impressed me in our first conversations in the summer of 1950. Nevertheless, Aniella Jaffé and others told me that Jung tired easily and could not receive many visitors on the same day. I found out also that he was no longer interested in therapies and case studies and no longer read contemporary theologians, but was still as enthusiastic as ever about Patristic theology.

I never saw him again after that. Jung died, serene and reconciled, on June 6, 1961.

’ ’ ’

At Meilen I received the first issue of the journal *Antaios*, and I was surprised and, of course, flattered to see listed on the cover my name as well as Ernst Jünger's as directors. The day after my visit with Jung

8. Cf. *No Souvenirs*, pp. 41–42.

at Küsnach, Jünger came from Germany, and Phillippe Wolfe, secretary of the journal, came from Berne, and the three of us ate lunch together at a picturesque restaurant on a hill overlooking the lake. It was necessary for us to discuss, in general, the future issues and for me to suggest names of possible contributors, both in Europe and the United States. As usual, I was impressed with Jünger's youthfulness and learning.

On June 9 we returned to Paris, happy to be back again in our little apartment on rue de l'Yvette. Into a cramped room with windows opening on a grayish-yellow wall, I brought a little table—a rather rickety one, at that—in order to be able to write. (Only after we had moved elsewhere did we learn that just a week before our arrival, a student had committed suicide with gas in that apartment.) On the fifteenth of June I began writing the novella, La țigănci. Working eight or nine hours a day, I succeeded in finishing it and transcribing it on July 5. Christinel read it that same evening. Her excitement and enthusiasm confirmed me in my conviction that La țigănci marked the beginning of a new phase in my literary creation.[9]

/ / /

Toward the middle of July we set out in Sibylle's automobile, and three days later we arrived at Ascona. When we caught sight of Lago Maggiore between the trees and the houses, we had the impression that a very happy period of our lives was coming to an end. I noted in the Journal: "Christinel, speaking this morning by telephone with Olga, was impressed by the weakness and fatigue she detected in her voice. Indeed, when Olga greeted us in the doorway of Casa Gabriella, we could hardly conceal our surprise. She has lost 30–35 pounds and her hands shake. For six months she had been bedridden with jaundice, after having suffered for two years from the aftereffects of the Asian flu. We were saddened that, for the first time since 1952, we didn't find the flowers in our room that Olga customarily placed there a few hours before the arrival of our train."[10] In the three weeks we spent at Villa Gabriella, we became convinced that Olga's health was truly undermined; only with great effort did she succeed some-

9. [Translated into English by the late William Ames Coates as "With the Gypsy Girls," it may be read in Eliade, *Tales of the Sacred and the Supernatural* (Philadelphia: Westminster Press, 1981), pp. 63–108. Tr.]

10. Cf. *No Souvenirs*, p. 48.

times in remaining with us at the table, and even then she ate almost nothing.

I had written only a part of my lecture for the Eranos Conference (on messianic movements in contemporary primitive societies). In order to complete my data, we spent a week at Fribourg, where the famous Anthropos-Institut is located. Working (as I liked to say) "as in the time of my youth," I succeeded in writing the last pages a few hours before I delivered the lecture. As usual, the Eranos hall was filled. And also as usual, the discussions begun in the afternoon continued until close to midnight.

Our true "vacation" came afterward, in Italy. This time we allowed ourselves to stay four days in Florence. Then we took the CIAT bus to Assisi, Perugia, Siena, and Rome. In the week spent at Rome, I saw friends and a good share of my Italian colleagues again. The visit to Pettazzoni impressed me profoundly. I knew he had been gravely ill, almost to the point of death. Now, he told me, he was "convalescing": pale, weak, his face lighted with a gentle melancholy I had never known. He confided that, for him, Japan had meant more than a discovery: it had been a revelation of the authenticity and nobility of Asian religious life.

When, as I was leaving, he shook my hand, gripping it with emotion, I knew that we would never meet again.

'   '   '

After spending three weeks in Paris, we returned to Chicago. An apartment had been promised us on the second floor of a house of sober beauty, at 5711 Woodlawn Avenue. But the young couple who were living there had decided to remain longer in Chicago, the husband wishing to take his doctorate. Meadville Theological School made available for us, temporarily, the attic of that lovely little building known as the "Coach House" because, half a century before, it had sheltered the numerous elegant carriages and cabriolets of the owner. ("Temporarily" stretched to almost four years. The young man did not succeed in finishing his dissertation, and we were determined at all costs to live in that apartment on Woodlawn Avenue.)

When we first moved into the Coach House, we had a bed, a sofa, a kitchen table, some dressers, and a part of the indispensable things: chairs, dishes, and shelves. But soon Christinel would complete the furnishings, even succeeding in buying some rugs. By the time we left for Paris at the beginning of summer, we had accumulated enough to be able to set up housekeeping in the Woodlawn Avenue apartment.

My office was just across the street from the Coach House, at Meadville Seminary. I had received from Paris several boxes of books and manuscripts. Now I had available all the documentation necessary for my courses and seminars.[11] The rest of the books and journals could be found in the libraries of the university, one of which was in Meadville. In November I put the finishing touches to the Eranos lectures of the past summer. Then there followed the colloquium sponsored by the Roger Williams Fellowship; I spoke on "The Sacred and the History of Religions," provoking diverse and heated reactions.[12] Indeed, addressing a group consisting almost entirely of theologians, I tried to show the importance of the history of religions in culture and even in contemporary American foreign policy. I insisted also on the fact that today, when Asia has reentered history and when "primitive" societies are on the way to achieving independence, the study and correct understanding of the religious concepts that structure these exotic civilizations constitute a necessity in the political realm. Diplomats, economists, and technologists sent on missions in Asian countries, especially former European colonies, must be initiated beforehand, and not only by missionaries and anthropologists.

But in those years, there existed only a few chairs of history of religions in American universities. Fifteen years later, their number had risen to twenty-five, almost all occupied by our former students who had obtained their doctorates at the University of Chicago. An organization of professors interested in the history of religions was soon constituted, but there did not exist a specialized journal in that field, even though many journals—some excellent—devoted to theological and sociological problems of religion appeared regularly. And so my colleagues Joseph Kitagawa and Charles H. Long, and I decided to inaugurate the journal *History of Religions*, and the University of Chicago Press agreed to publish it. Consequently, in the winter of 1960, we began to write to a number of European colleagues, asking them

11. That fall I conducted a seminar on new methods in the psychology of religions and a course on Indian religion from the *Rig Veda* to the *Bhagavad Gita*. The spring seminar was on "Sacred Time and Historical Consciousness" and the course was on Mediterranean religions.

12. [But cf. *No Souvenirs*, p. 71 (November 3, 1959) where Eliade states that he spoke on "The Sacred and Reality." Tr.]

to contribute. Since the international congress was to be held at Marburg in September of 1960, we proposed to present then, if not the first issue, at least a mock-up and prospectus of the review.[13]

I devoted the winter and spring of 1960 to articles for *History of Religions* and to the revision of the English translations of the books *Images et symboles* and *Rêves, mythes et mystères*, which would appear in 1961 and 1962. I did not succeed, however, in beginning the little book *Myth and Reality*, which I had promised to Ruth Nanda Anshen for her series, "World Perspectives."

The courses about Indian and Mediterranean religions were very interesting to me, but I was not entirely satisfied with the bibliography I was able to make available to my students. I recommended to them, of course, the most recent monographs, but I wasn't sure they'd have time to read them all. On the other hand, I wanted at all costs to have each student know at least a part of the original texts in the best translations available. I decided then to photocopy a number of Vedic hymns, fragments from the *Brahmanas*, and portions of the *Upanishads*. The selection of materials for the course on Mediterranean religions was, of course, more complicated. I chose excerpts from Homer, Hesiod, and Herodotus, a number of Orphic tablets, and various later texts. The total did not exceed fifty to sixty pages, and thus I was sure the texts really would be studied and pondered by all the students.

To be sure, several anthologies existed, but since I didn't repeat courses and therefore chose a new subject each quarter, I decided to build up, over a period of time, an anthology of my own in which the texts would be classified by theme: cosmogonies, types of divinities, species of sacrifice, initiation rites, and so on. Thus I began to collect and classify documents which, many years later, would be published in the volume *From Primitives to Zen*.

But suddenly, one night that winter, I was awakened by unusually severe pains in my shoulders and arms. Further sleep was impossible. The only position I could bear was to sit upright in an armchair with my arms elevated. The next day Dr. Le Roy came to see me. At first he thought it was a case of the gout, but soon he identified it as

13. The first issue, which appeared in January 1961, opened with my article, "The History of Religions and a New Humanism."

an acute attack of arthritis. From then on, I had to take six aspirin tablets a day. Sometimes the pain became bearable, and then, with great difficulty, I would work a few hours. Since that winter of 1960, my studies and books have been a long time in appearing.

On those nights when the arthritic pains were more severe, my favorite readings were biographies of Goethe and his *Conversations* with Eckermann. At the beginning of January, upon learning of the death of Pettazzoni, I was tempted to reread his books. Now and again I had surprises that lifted my spirits. A. Vasqués, director of the Institute of Philosophy at Mendonza and visiting scholar for six months, always attended my classes, and he told me about my "admirers" in Argentina. Vasquéz was preparing to write a book on my "philosophical thought." He kept telling me that basically I was a philosopher who was neglecting his vocation, that I was camouflaging my personal thought under the mask of erudition. But, he added, no one in Argentina was deceived by this camouflage. I defended myself as best I could: for the time being, I said, I *had* to complete my scholarly works. Their philosophical interest and originality would be seen later. Actually, I added, this "camouflage" is a part of the Western philosophical tradition (I reminded him of several medieval authors).

At the end of the winter I reread Nietzsche, engrossed. I alternated the reading with Part II of *Faust*. Students in my course on "Historical Man" seemed fascinated, especially because I kept referring to Greek examples.

I was surprised to receive that spring a copy of a master's thesis from Northwestern University. The young author, Richard Welbon, discussing *Mircea Eliade's Image of Man*, tried to present "an anthropogeny by a historian of religions." It was the first university thesis about my thought. In years to come, there were to be numerous doctoral dissertations, both in the United States and in Europe.

I had heard from time to time that some philosophers were not in accord with my method: I was dealing with too many areas and it was impossible for me to go into each one of them in sufficient depth. The argument sounded convincing, but it was based on a confusion. It was as if one were to reproach a biologist who studied insects for not knowing *all* the species of coleoptera, hymenoptea, lepidoptera, and hemiptera. (Such reservations continued to be repeated in subsequent years. I tried to justify my methodological position in a series of studies, but I'm not sure I always convinced my critics.) Nevertheless, I had the satisfaction of reading in a book by Professor George P. Grant, these words: "For what follows about archaic man, I must express my profound dependence on the work of Mircea Eliade. Professor Eliade seems to me unique among modern scholars of religion, not only in his grasp of the facts, but also in his philosophical and theological wisdom." [14]

Speaking one day to my students about the necessity for deciphering the *strata* and *morphology* of a religious phenomenon (for example, initiation), I began the lesson by asserting that it is not possible to conceive of Darwin before Linnaeus. In other words, the understanding of the *origin* and *evolution* of the species—that is, the "history" of biological creations—was not possible before the discovery of *morphology*. The morphological comparison of the two systems—the zoological (or vegetal) and the historico-religious—shows that there are fewer differences between an African myth and an Australian one than there are between two species of coleoptera or hymenoptera. And in spite of this, the naturalist *sees* that they belong to the same category: that of insects. Obviously, the biological context of a butterfly is different from that of a fly or an ant—precisely as, in the case of a myth, it is a matter of a different cultural context in Africa or Australia.

Toward the end of March Jean Gouillard informed me of the death of Gustave Payot. We both had been expecting it for several years. For a long time, Payot had been failing: his face was gaunt, he had become quite feeble, he could scarcely walk, and his body inclined slightly to the right, as though he were about to topple over. The previous summer, when I had looked for him at the press, I was told he came to the office only for an hour or two each morning.

One more contemporary of my Parisian beginnings was gone. He has remained in my memory as a character out of a Balzac novel. His stinginess, his business acumen, his aggressiveness (when he told you, upon meeting you, that he was deaf, you had the impression that he was going to give you a thrashing), his little manias (he suffered terribly when some of his colleagues, foreign editors, duped him out of a few hundred francs). But I shall never forget that it was

14. George P. Grant, *Philosophy in the Mass Age* (New York: Hill and Wang, 1960), p. 126.

thanks to his courage in publishing over a five-year period my three books *Traité, Le Chamanisme,* and *Le Yoga,* that I succeeded so quickly in making myself known as a historian of religions.

The arthritis attacks continued, in spite of the six or seven aspirin tablets I was taking each day. There were nights when, incapable of lifting my arms, I had to write on my lap. I was worried, realizing that I had not succeeded in finishing my lecture for Harvard or in beginning the little book *Myth and Reality.* In that terrible winter and spring of 1960, when I wondered if my health would allow me to finish what I had begun, I received several letters that encouraged me. A German psychoanalyst, G. R. Heyer, wrote that *Images et symboles* had helped him to understand, *finally,* the function of symbol. About *Naissances mystique* (*Birth and Rebirth*) the anthropologist Alfred Metram wrote me this testimony: "As before, I have not found anything I fail to admire: of the lucidity of your exposition or your astonishing erudition. How have you been able to keep up to date with so many publications and so many diverse religions? And with respect to South America, nothing of importance seems to have escaped you—and God knows how difficult that literature is to master." And the famous critic Northrop Frye, whom I had met recently at Harvard, wrote me enthusiastically about *Forgerons et alchimistes:* "I never expected to meet any writer who could fill me with the same sense of fresh discovery that Frazer did in my early student days, but I reckoned without Mircea Eliade. What is so amazing is not the breadth of your erudition, but its unity, the consistency with which you can make alchemy, yoga, primitive religious beliefs, and so many other things come together and form a pattern."

Between the 23rd and the 26th of April I was at Cambridge, Massachusetts, staying in the Continental Hotel. Northrop Frye opened the symposium, which was on "Myth Today," and the next day, Sunday, I delivered my lecture to a nearly full auditorium on "Myths of the Beginning and Myths of the End." I met then, at last, Northrop Frye, and I had long conversations with A. D. Nock, Roman Jakobson, and other scholars whom I would see again, also at Cambridge, the following year.

A few days later I was in South Bend, Indiana, for the colloquium on "Christian Culture." I had accepted the invitation especially to have the opportunity of meeting Charles Dawson, one of the organizers of the colloquium. I had heard that he had read with much interest *Traité* and *Le Mythe de l'éternel retour,* and I eagerly anticipated the conversation we would have. But I had no such luck. Dawson's seraphic silence reminded me of the silences of Lucian Blaga.

*   *   *

In the middle of June we spent several days at Elison Bay, as guests of Harriet Platt. And so I saw again, after two years, those towns and homes on the shore of the lake, but it seemed as though a much longer time had elapsed. I had begun to sense America in a different way. I knew that the immigration laws would allow me to stay until the following summer, 1961. After that, we would have to return to France for two years, and reenter the United States with a new, permanent-immigrant visa. We were both happy. We could call a halt to our summer peregrinations, and I should be able to make greater headway with my work. But destiny decided otherwise.[15]

15. Translator's note: The Eliades had come to America, by error, on visitors' exchange visas, which required that they leave in 1961 and reside outside the country for two years before returning again. Dean Jerald Brauer and other university personnel discovered that the Eliades could be kept in the country only if the Department of Defense would declare that Professor Eliade's presence in the country was "indispensable to the security and welfare of the United States" and would then convince the Immigration officials that they should be granted permanent residence. The university undertook to gain the cooperation of the Department of Defense. Dean Brauer, relating the story in 1985, reported a telephone call he had received from a woman in the department, who said that, out of all the hundreds of such cases she had handled, Mircea Eliade was, in her judgment, the first person who was truly needed for the security and welfare of the country. All the others were people involved with weaponry and such, but Eliade's work had to do with the kind of humanistic matters that the United States desperately needed for its security. The Eliades were granted immigrant status on May 1, 1961. (See Jerald C. Brauer, "Mircea Eliade and the Divinity School," *Criterion* 24, 3 [Autumn 1985]:25).

Postscriptum

(After Professor Eliade's death on April 22, 1986, the following note was found on his desk in his apartment, written on the morning after the fire that destroyed his office in the Meadville-Lombard School of Religion.)

19 December 1985.

Last night, at ten o'clock, I heard someone knocking at our door. Our neighbor, from the floor below, tells me: "Your office's on fire! . . . I telephoned the fire department. They've been working there for five minutes. Maybe you'd better come and see what's happened."

I dressed as fast as I could and went with him. I heard the firemen breaking the windows of my office. It was terribly cold, and the water flowing down the stairs of Meadville froze as soon as it reached the sidewalk.

They wouldn't let me go in. On the main stairs the water was pouring down like a mountain stream.

So it began. I had to go back home. Christinel gave me a double dose of sleeping tablets.

Index